DIFFICULT
TRANSITIONS

DIFFICULT TRANSITIONS

Foreign Policy Troubles at the Outset of Presidential Power

KURT M. CAMPBELL

JAMES B. STEINBERG

BROOKINGS INSTITUTION PRESS
Washington, D.C.

Copyright © 2008
THE BROOOKINGS INSTITUTION
1775 Massachusetts Avenue, N.W., Washington, D.C. 20036
www.brookings.edu

Library of Congress Cataloging-in-Publication data is available

ISBN: 978-0-8157-1340-1 (cloth)

9 8 7 6 5 4 3 2 1

The paper used in this publication meets minimum requirements of the American National Standard for Information Sciences—Permanence of Paper for Printed Library Materials: ANSI Z39.48-1992.

Typeset in Sabon

Composition by Cynthia Stock
Silver Spring, Maryland

Printed by R. R. Donnelley
Harrisonburg, Virginia

CONTENTS

TRANSITION MEMO

Hope, Hubris, Headaches,
and Cardboard Boxes

ALMOST EVERYONE WHO has served in Washington during a presidential transition—in any department or agency and at any level—has stories to tell of institutional disarray, personal aspirations, enormous optimism, and wrenching anxiety (often all in the course of the same day), and of the intensive planning, preparations, and wheel spinning that go on during the interregnum. We count ourselves among this legion.

In late November 1993, Kurt Campbell was a White House Fellow working at the Department of the Treasury. One Saturday he was asked to come in for a meeting with a few key players on the transition team who were just getting settled into the Old Executive Office Building. It was easy to tell the outgoing Bush staffers from the incoming Clinton ones. The former group wore frowns as they carried boxes out of the building. The folks from the latter group seemed to combine an almost frantic intensity with an air of optimistic expectation about the challenging work in service to the nation they would undertake in the months ahead. In the small waiting area of the ornate offices, as he sat waiting and hoping to make a good impression, Campbell could just glimpse the stars and stripes fluttering in the autumn breeze atop the White House across the way.

Having come straight from weekend duty with the U.S. Navy reserves, he waited in an anteroom in his dark uniform with the gold lieutenant's stripes on his sleeves. Somehow, an inexperienced young staffer from Little Rock mistook him for a senior military official from the Pentagon there to brief the senior transition team on the range of policy issues that confronted the country, and he was ushered into a large conference room filled with President-elect Clinton's most senior advisers. The mistake was quickly detected and Campbell was sent back to the Treasury Department, but the temporary confusion left a lasting impression of the transition process. (The young staffer who made the error was reputed to be the same person who later had a misunderstanding with a very senior military officer—a real one, unlike Campbell—in a subsequent visit to the White House, auguring an early and ill-fated relationship between the incoming Clinton team and the military.)

In June 1979, James Steinberg joined the Justice Department as a special assistant to the assistant attorney general for the Civil Division. Following the hostage-taking at the U.S. embassy in Tehran in November 1979, Steinberg was assigned to coordinate the U.S. position in all of the lawsuits seeking access to Iranian assets in the United States and Europe (which were frozen by President Carter to increase U.S. leverage in negotiating with Iran) and to assist in advising the State Department and White House on legal aspects of the hostage release negotiations. Steinberg and his colleagues were keenly aware that the failure to secure the hostages' release played a key role in President Carter's defeat in November 1980. Nonetheless, they all recognized that the hostage crisis might carry over into the next administration, and in any event, any resolution of the crisis would leave a messy legal and political aftermath.

So when the attorney general informed Steinberg and the Iran working group that the Reagan transition team had appointed transition officials to handle Iran-related matters, they dutifully set out to prepare detailed briefings on the status of the litigation and related legal issues. The team filled multiple binders with copies of important memos, court papers, and analyses of the strategies of all the key players. Dates were set for meetings with transition representatives, which were postponed again and again. After weeks of waiting, and of continuously updating the books, they finally received word from the transition team: no meeting would be held, because none was necessary—the Reagan team would develop its own strategy on all aspects of the hostage crisis. When Steinberg vacated his office at Justice in January 1981, one of his most poignant memories was looking at the untouched briefing books on the shelves—with carefully labeled tabs and a useful table of contents—as he made his way out of the building for the last time.

This book grew out of a series of conversations and contemplations we had while fly-fishing and during shared family outings over many years. Both of us have lived through the excitement and the disappointment of new administrations. Steinberg has served in two transitions "in" (Ford to Carter and Bush to Clinton) and two transitions "out" (Carter to Reagan and Clinton to Bush). Campbell has experienced transitions from inside both the Defense Department at the Joint Chiefs (Reagan to Bush) and the Treasury Department (Bush to Clinton). We were both struck by the repeated experience of troubled first months in office on the national security front. We were convinced that even seasoned professionals in the foreign policy arena had not systematically reflected on the opportunities and hazards inherent in the entire transition process. We wanted to write a book that would explore the history of previous transitions and the common challenges they confront, but perhaps more important, offer our own prescriptions for navigating these treacherous shoals. We hope to help candidates and their senior advisers think about how to implement a bold and creative foreign policy and national security agenda from the outset of a new administration without getting off on the wrong foot.

We found it easier to describe how and why things have gone wrong in the past than to advise on how to do better in the future. Nevertheless, we set about the task with an enthusiasm and optimism not too dissimilar from the attitudes of a new team of staffers working in a transition effort, so succinctly captured by the dean of transition advisers, Richard Neustadt:

Everywhere there is a sense of page turning, a new chapter in the country's history, a new chance too. And with it, irresistibly, there comes a sense, "they"' couldn't, wouldn't, didn't, but "we" will.

We just have done the hardest thing there is to do in politics. Governing has got to be a pleasure by comparison. We won, so we can! The psychology is partly that of having climbed one mountain so that the next one looks easy, partly that of having a run of luck that surely can't turn now![1]

Speaking from his own direct experience beginning with the Kennedy years, Neustadt described a presidential transition as something akin to a "mob scene" filled with frantic job seekers, generalized confusion, anxiety about the tasks ahead, and raw ambition all on full display—a description that could be fairly applied to all subsequent transitions. And Neustadt is certainly not alone in offering sage commentary and analysis on the intricacies of the transition process. Clark Clifford, a seasoned Washington observer who played an important role in the 1960 Kennedy transition, harshly criticized the elaborate process that has grown up over the years as "a seventy day monster that springs up overnight once every four years, has no purpose except its own existence, feuds with itself, and then suddenly disappears on January 20, leaving behind nothing except empty cardboard boxes . . . the transition has become The Transition."[2]

When we set out to write about this peculiarly American rite of political passage, we were inundated with advice and anecdotes. One friend likened the quadrennial transition process to the ritual return of the cicadas, the large burrowing insects that periodically descend upon the eastern and southern United States. "They come like clockwork. It's extremely noisy and messy and you think you'll never get through it. There are dead carcasses everywhere. Someone has to sweep up the mess and then suddenly it's over and life returns to normal." People's stories usually involved elements of chaos and disorganization or some form of political retribution and score settling. Transitions indeed offer particularly fertile ground for analogies and keen insights alike. David Rothkopf, the author of an acclaimed book on the National Security Council (NSC) and a transition veteran, noted: "An American political transition is a little like trying to change drivers of a car on a freeway at very high speed. Almost invariably there is a period in which no one has their hands firmly on the wheel when maximum peril is present." Indeed, one of Campbell's most vivid memories of the Bush-to-Clinton transition was of the nearly deserted third-floor offices of the senior staff at the Treasury Department during the days immediately before and after the inauguration, an image that inspired the cover art for this book.

It is, however, during this period of turmoil and uncertainty that the truly gifted policy entrepreneur can rise above the rest and exploit the lack of established structures. Another friend noted: "For guys like Kissinger and Brzezinski, very effective bureaucratic infighters and visionary policy players, transitions were a time to effectively establish dominance, deal with competitors, and begin to chart a course for the period of governance that would immediately follow. These guys could be ruthlessly brutal, but were also relentless and successful in helping to get through the transition and into the act of governing."

Participants in presidential transitions often resort to allusions to well-known films in order to make vivid the remarkable challenges involved with a presidential transition. Richard Falkenrath, a key player on the Bush transition team on the NSC, came to the White House almost immediately after the contested election of 2000 was decided by the Supreme Court. He told us: "For the first few days that I was there after many of the Clinton people had left, there was an eerie vacancy along some of the halls of power in the OEOB [Old Executive Office Building]. It was a bit reminiscent of that scene in "The Godfather" when Michael goes to visit his badly wounded father in the hospital only to find that he was alone and unguarded. The most important member of the family was left there unprotected and supremely vulnerable—a bit like the White House and the institution of presidential power during those early days of a transition."

To Richard Clarke, a key participant in and observer of several presidential transitions, the vacancies in crucial positions, the eager young staffers roaming the halls of the institutions of American power, and the occasional confusion around the handoff reminded him of another cinematic classic: "It's our presidential version of the movie "Home Alone," with the only thing standing in the way of the bad guys on the other side of the door a young kid who is left there at home on his own. In real life, this abrupt transition can be a little disconcerting, particularly for the professionals in the system assigned to help with the overall process."

As we canvassed experienced transition hands, we often found remarkably divergent perspectives on the same events. Veteran Republican insider Richard Armitage remembered the transition from Carter to Reagan as a relatively pain-free experience: "There were forty people on Carter's NSC staff and thirty-seven of them provided us with everything in terms of back channel briefings and internal papers after the election. The Carter guys could not take a poop without us knowing in advance. The professional staff just could not wait for us to come in. Only three guys refused to cooperate. Immediately after the inaugural we fired all thirty-seven and only kept on those three guys. But it was a smooth process overall, we were welcomed, and we got off to a very good start." But as so often is the case in Washington, where you stand is profoundly influenced by where you sit. Avis Bohlen, a respected career Foreign Service officer with a distinguished diplomatic pedigree, viewed the same transition very differently: "The Carter-Reagan transition was like the Assyrians marauding in over the plains, pillaging along the way. It was just very challenging for us career types."

Indeed, perspectives tend, not surprisingly, to be a function of whether one is with the incoming or outgoing team. Madeleine Albright, secretary of state under Clinton, remembered transitions "in" as times of great excitement and exhilaration: "In my career, I have transitioned into administrations and I have transitioned out; transitioning in is better. For all the chaos and uncertainty, an incoming transition team rides the rush of adrenalin that can only come from victory in a national election. Democrats, especially, have learned to cherish the feeling, for it does not come often. The job itself is simple enough: you have ten weeks to organize the new president's strategy for dealing with the world. This requires a transformation in mindset, from campaigning to governing; a transformation in workload, from heavy to crushing; and a transformation in relationships, as former colleagues compete for desired jobs. I found it exhausting, nerve-wracking, and about as much fun as it is legally possible to have."

For Sandy Berger, a key NSC figure from the Clinton years, the opening days of the transition in 1992 were heady and exciting: "It was a time of enormous promise, and we were part of a campaign that had survived a near-death experience to claw our way back to victory. We came into the transition to make a difference and we set to work with real determination to do just that from day one." Brent Scowcroft, the modern model of a national security adviser, had more melancholy memories of the transitions he had lived through: "I mostly remember being on the losing ends of elections in Ford and then Bush, and these were mostly sad occasions. There was the persistent sense of unfinished business and the need to pack up your offices. There were lots of very tired people, some of whom were not sure what they would do next. You almost always found stray résumés around the copy machine. A transition can be a very tough thing."

THIS BOOK OWES an enormous debt to the many people who helped make it possible. First and foremost, the intrepid George Mitchell provided essential research, early drafting, sage advice, and critical commentary on every chapter. Michael Horowitz helped us to conceptualize how transitions today are more difficult than in the past. Richard Weitz provided masterful research concerning the previous academic and intellectual work on the subject as well as vital context for how earlier postwar transitions fared. Whitney Parker was a constant source of inspiration and a model of organization who thought about everything, from book cover designs to publicity blurbs. Dedicated colleagues at the Center for a New American Security—Michèle Flournoy, Jim Miller, Derek Chollet, Nate Tibbits, Nirav Patel, Vikram Singh, Robert Kaplan, Tom Ricks, Sharon Burke, David Sanger—gave freely of their time and insights. From the Lyndon B. Johnson School of Public Affairs, Tanvi Madan provided invaluable support on the history of presidential transitions, and Brendan Lavy helped coordinate research and writing projects. We are also enormously grateful to the former administration officials who consented to be interviewed and quoted in the text: Madeleine Albright, Richard Armitage, Sandy Berger, Avis Bohlen, Richard Clarke, Richard Falkenrath, David Gergen, David Rothkopf, and Brent Scowcroft. Many friends provided insightful anecdotes about their personal experiences for us to use, and the reader will find these sprinkled throughout the text. Our families were an enormous source of inspiration, understanding, and support during the research and writing of this book. To our wonderful spouses, Lael

Brainard and Shere Abbott, this book would have been impossible without your partnership and patience. Campbell and Brainard have been blessed with three lovely daughters, Caelan, Ciara, and Chloe; and Steinberg and Abbott are proud parents of two magnificent girls, Jenna and Emma. It is to you that this book is dedicated. May all your transitions be smooth.

DIFFICULT
TRANSITIONS

1

DIFFICULT TRANSITIONS

Presidential Transitions and Foreign Policy Perils

PERHAPS THE MOST harrowing—yet simultaneously hope-ful—feature of the American system of government is the transfer of power from one president to the next, a period stretching from the quadrennial national election through the inaugural and into the first months of governance. For Washington insiders, this time is known simply as "the transition," and it is one of the most stud-ied yet least fully understood aspects of our democracy.

On a formal level, the transition has been a part of our national expe-rience since the election of George Washington, yet the reality has changed dramatically over the past two hundred and twenty years. The first inaugural was held on April 30, 1789, and the transition "team" consisted of President George Washington, Alexander Hamilton, Henry Knox, and Edmund Randolph—men who would go on to serve as the first treasury secretary, secretary of war, and attorney general, respec-tively. They all got together one afternoon for tea near the Federal Hall in New York City to coordinate their plans for the new administration. For the next one hundred and fifty years most presidents simply asked a few trusted advisers to spend several weeks assisting with the logistics and personnel matters associated with the move to the White House.

In 1938 the Twentieth Amendment to the Constitution changed the inauguration date to January 20. Particularly in the post–World War II era, the transition process preceding and following the inaugural became more elaborate with each passing president. While the Constitution stipulates a seamless flow of executive power from one president to the next, the process has become more turbulent than envisioned by the founding fathers. Indeed, the rituals and risks associated with modern transitions have grown exponentially over the past several decades.

The very idea of the transition is one of the features that distinguishes the United States from most other democracies and parliamentary systems around the world. During the recent handoff of the political baton from Tony Blair to Gordon Brown in the United Kingdom, for instance, the whole process was completed in a few days with the assistance of a couple of moving vans and a few personnel changes in some key jobs around the prime minister and in cabinet offices. Scarcely a beat was missed while Gordon Brown dealt calmly and effectively with a domestic terrorist attack against the Glasgow airport and a foiled plot in central London in the days immediately following the handover. Presidential transitions in the United States, by contrast, are increasingly prolonged and complicated affairs with thousands of people moving into new positions of responsibility over several months across dozens of agencies. The possibility that a comparable domestic terror threat might emerge in the first days of a new U.S. administration causes many government specialists, foreign policy practitioners, seasoned observers, and the candidates themselves to shudder.

While transitions present challenges for domestic policy, they can be deadly in the arena of foreign policy. There is an acute sense of vulnerability when power changes hands, accompanied by an extended period of uncertainty about how well the new team will handle the challenges of office. There may be a so-called honeymoon period on the domestic front as the new president sorts out the policies and candidates for senior government jobs, but there is rarely time for a honeymoon or learning curve in the international security realm. From the early era of the cold war, when new presidents and their advisers worried about being "tested" by their Soviet counterparts, to more recent concerns about whether a new crew fully grasps the myriad complexities of homeland security and intelligence provisions, and whether terrorists might seek to disrupt the period of power transfer, presidential transitions have been fraught with anxiety and uncertainty.

This is a book about how presidential transitions and foreign policy intersect every four years and why the process can pose such profound problems to an incoming team of officials seeking to serve and protect the nation. The very word "transition" typically evokes the period between the quadrennial first Tuesday in November, when the American people vote to elect a new president, and inauguration day the following January 20, when the new president formally takes office. But it has long been recognized by practitioners and scholars alike that the transition really begins during the campaign itself, when the candidates stake out their positions on foreign policy and begin to assemble a team of advisers, and continues for many months into the new administration. This book covers the entire process and offers recommendations for how best to traverse the full length of a transition.

We begin by presenting the perspectives of some who have participated firsthand in this unique process and then turn to an analysis of the factors that make transitions in today's environment riskier than in the past. We look in detail at four phases of the transition: the campaign, the initial staffing decisions after the election, the choices around structures and decisionmaking, and the early process of settling into government after the inauguration—devoting a chapter to each topic. On the basis of this analysis we provide recommendations for managing the transition in a way that achieves the newly elected president's national security objectives and avoids dangerous missteps in the crucial early days of a new administration. We conclude with some thoughts on how transitions are likely to unfold in the future amidst more contemporary challenges.

Difficult Transitions specifically describes how the early steps of a campaign can plague a transition during its formative days. We show how campaign pressures, particularly campaign promises made without full knowledge of the constraining facts, complicate the challenge of governing once elected. We also review the constraints on transition planning during the campaign itself, which make it difficult for a new president to get a running start on governing and, in some cases, create frictions within a campaign that carry over through the transition. The obvious point of departure for this book is the critical importance of candidates taking seriously the prospect that they might actually win and therefore have to govern. Policy switches once in office may be embarrassing for domestic policy, but they can be catastrophic for national security, conveying indecisiveness and vacillation in a world that needs steadiness in the sole superpower. At the same time, slavish devotion to rash campaign commitments poses a serious danger. Candidates therefore need to think carefully about making concrete proposals before they are in a position to fully understand the facts, including the perspective of international allies and partners.

This book also underscores the need for candidates and their advisers to think through the operations of government well before getting elected and to seek expert advice about how to organize and run the national security apparatus. New presidents should not outrun their capacity to act effectively in the first months in office. Their focus should remain on filling the top jobs and carefully getting up to speed before implementing new policies. And above all, new administrations should consult with Congress, with key allies, and with predecessors, who may have actually gotten some things right, even if they were from the opposite party.

We examine the problems associated with the formal transition itself—how and with whom to staff the national security team (including how to incorporate campaign staff); what managerial approach to employ to coordinate the vast range of policy issues and challenges of policy implementation; whether to heed or ignore the advice of the outgoing administration; and how to adapt to unpleasant surprises and constraints during the first months in office.

We look at the pressures associated with the first hundred days, including how to deal with career officials who may not share the objectives of the new administration, the challenge of governing with only a partial team in place, what kind of working relationship the president and his lieutenants should establish with Congress and the press, and how aggressively to jettison the policies of the past to implement a new agenda. This is the time of greatest peril, when the hubris of election and the desire to get off to a fast start collide with limits of capacity and the constraints of an unaccommodating real world, and when the effectiveness of the pre-inauguration transition planning is tested. We review some of the notable successes and failures of first months in office to illustrate both the perils and the opportunities facing new administrations.

We identify an extensive range of transition risks and perennial problems and conclude by providing a list of recommendations for how to successfully conduct a presidential transition with larger foreign policy and national security objectives clearly in mind. The record of modern transitions includes dodged bullets and direct hits, and this book shows how one particularly underestimated factor can make all the difference: luck.

The presidential transition of 2008–09 carries with it many great challenges, some as consequential as any in recent history. The next president will take office at an extraordinarily delicate and dangerous time in American history. He will face two ongoing conflicts in which U.S. troops are intensely engaged, our ground forces are overextended, and few good options seem available for stabilizing these situations to prevent wider conflict. There remain active nuclear programs in Iran and North Korea, which threaten to destabilize their regions and undermine the global nonproliferation regime. Our nation faces a continuous elevated terrorist threat, fueled by the conflicts in Iraq and Afghanistan, as well as social, cultural, and religious divisions from Europe to Southeast Asia. Instability in Pakistan remains a critical challenge, which contributes to the terrorist threat and risks an internal political breakdown in a nuclear-armed state. There is an urgent need to reconceptualize the "war on terror" framework that has guided American strategy since 9/11. Behind the immediate headlines are the longer-term challenges of an increasingly assertive Russia, an economically and militarily more powerful China, and transnational dangers including climate change, pandemic disease, and resource competition. National security challenges such as these always pose difficult tests, but they are especially acute during times of transition.

This review of the stakes on the global stage is important because foreign policy mistakes made at the outset of a new presidency are legion, and sometimes early wounds cause harm that lasts far beyond the initial debacle. Almost every modern president has grappled with these challenges, many of which were not even of their own making: Eisenhower and Nixon, who inherited wars in Korea and Vietnam; Kennedy and the Bay of Pigs fiasco; the drama of the Iran hostage crisis that played out like an arc at the end of the Carter presidency and into the beginning of Reagan's term; Clinton's struggle to manage the Somalia deployment, which began in the waning days of the George H. W. Bush administration; the EP-3 crisis that occurred at the outset of George W. Bush's first term when a U.S. plane strayed too close to Chinese territory and collided in mid-air with a Chinese fighter. President after president has been tested in the early days of his administration.

Over the years, there have been a number of important studies and analyses of presidential transitions, beginning with the landmark Brookings study *Presidential Transitions* by Henry Laurin, published in 1960, which was avidly consumed by the Kennedy transition team, and the now famous Heritage Foundation's *Mandate for Leadership* in 1980, which played such a crucial role in the early days of the Reagan administration. Several of these studies have focused on the specific challenges and problems of foreign policy during transition. Most were written by scholars who drew on a growing body of oral histories, including vital contributions by the Miller Center and the White House Project. These works have been complemented by the autobiographies of many key participants in foreign policy transitions, from Dean Acheson to Henry Kissinger, Zbigniew Brzezinski, and others. This work continues to be supplemented by a myriad of think tanks and study groups that hope to influence the course of the next transition.

There is a veritable cottage industry of transition and government affairs experts who form working groups and issue expert reports during every election cycle on how to perfect this unruly process, which is quintessentially about the hope for change and betterment in American politics. Thinkers and practitioners offer sage advice on think tank panels and cable news shows, in blog posts and newspaper opinion pages. Thoughtful and insightful recommendations are issued, usually in mid-November of the year of the quadrennial contest. Scholars and pundits rarely think about these matters in such depth at other times, but in the three- to six-month period before the election and into the first one hundred days of a new president's term, the Washington community is inundated with studies and opinion pieces for how to better manage this quadrennial process.

So why another book? In this volume, we bring the study of foreign policy transitions up to the present and seek to address the challenges in the contemporary international environment that make national security transitions today even more complex and perilous than those faced in the cold war years of superpower confrontation and hair-trigger nuclear alerts. As such, this book complements both the scholarly histories and the contemporary advice that bloom like desert flowers in the months just before and during the quadrennial transition. It is both something of a cautionary tale and a how-to self-help book in one. We undertook this study primarily for would-be and used-to-be practitioners, but it is equally appropriate reading for students, teachers and researchers, commentators, foreign policy and national security experts, journalists, foreign observers of the American political scene, and those among the interested public who simply want to acquire a sharper understanding of how our system of government works (and when and why it does not). We hope that *Difficult Transitions* will fill an important niche in the rich literature on American presidential transitions. We provide a concise survey of this body of work in the Appendix and highlight several important studies that inform our larger understanding of the process. In writing this book, we have attempted to blend the perspectives of these historians, practitioners, and political scientists with our own insights gleaned from over thirty years of experience in and around government, including service in four presidential transitions and on the campaign trail, reflections from academia, and staff work in Congress.

Difficult Transitions is a guide to what history tells us about transition train wrecks and offers advice to the next president and his foreign policy team for getting off on the right foot. And perhaps as important, this effort also offers prescriptions for avoiding the inevitable landmines and booby traps that will be encountered by even the most well-meaning and intrepid chief executive at the outset. The need for such a road map is particularly compelling today as the new administration seeks to restore American power and global prestige to face the challenges of the coming years.

2

FIRSTHAND PRACTITIONER ACCOUNTS

Present at the Transition

T HERE IS NO better way to begin a study of the opportunities and risks surrounding presidential transitions than to
listen to the participants themselves—the presidents and
their advisers who experienced firsthand the exhilaration and the dread
that come with a change of power. Their thoughtful reflections illustrate
one of the most important paradoxes of presidential transitions: on the
one hand, it is a well-established, regularly repeated, and largely
unchanging ritual; and at the same time, each new team has the sense
that, whatever happened in the past, "this transition will be different."

Looking back through American history, while most presidential
handoffs have arrived at the regularly scheduled intervals, some of the
most poignant have been the unplanned ones—those occasioned by the
death or resignation of a sitting president. Indeed, the first presidential
transition of the modern period—from Franklin D. Roosevelt to Harry
S. Truman—occurred because of Roosevelt's tragic death in office. The
import of this transition was well captured by Truman, who recalled
having been informed personally of the president's death by Roosevelt's
wife, Eleanor. Truman remembered asking her: "Is there anything I can
do for you?" Truman recalled: "I shall never forget her deeply understanding reply." She said: "Is there anything *we* can do for *you*? For you
are the one in trouble now."[1]

The awesome sense of loss and uncertainty readily spread over Washington—and the nation—as quickly as the news could travel. Dean Acheson was assistant secretary of state when he first heard of Roosevelt's death. He observed in his memoirs:

> During the next days a dazed sensation developed. No one at home, on the street, in the Department, had much to say. From our windows we watched the flag-covered coffin carried from the caisson into the White House, then out again to lie in state in the rotunda of the Capitol. Day and night the radio played dim, funeral music. "Large crowds," I wrote at the time, "came and stood in front of the White House. There was nothing to see and I am sure that they did not expect to see anything. They merely stood in a lost sort of way." One felt as though the city had vanished, leaving its inhabitants to wander about bewildered, looking for a familiar landmark. The dominant emotion was not sorrow so much as apprehension on discovering oneself alone and lost. Something which had filled all lives was gone. The familiar had given way to an ominous unknown.[2]

But all transitions pose difficult challenges, expected and unexpected. The sheer magnitude of the critical tasks involved was succinctly captured by Ted Sorensen, a key adviser to President-elect John Kennedy (Sorensen would later become the subject of his own transition drama in the Carter administration). Recalling the Eisenhower-Kennedy transition, he noted:

> There were seventy-two days to inauguration.
>   . . . Seventy-two days in which to form an administration, staff the White House, fill some seventy-five key Cabinet and policy posts, name six hundred other major nominees, decide which incumbents to carry over, distribute patronage to the faithful and fix personnel policies for the future. . . .
>   . . . Seventy-two days in which to work with Eisenhower on an orderly transfer of power, with Nixon on a restoration of national unity, with Democratic leaders on reshaping the National Committee, and with his own aides on handling all the administrative

problems of the transition period, including finances, transportation, accommodations, press relations and attention to the enormous number of letters pouring in from heads of state, well-wishers, job-seekers, old friends and myriad others. . . .

. . . Seventy-two days in which to make plans for the inaugural festivities, making certain nothing and no one was overlooked, arranging for the right successor to be appointed to his seat in the Senate, selling or transferring his financial holdings to avoid a conflict of interest, and writing an Inaugural Address. . . .

. . . Seventy-two days in which to make plans for the organization of Congress (which would convene before his inauguration), to prepare a legislative program that could be promptly incorporated into messages and bills, and to formulate concrete policies and plans for all the problems of the nation, foreign and domestic, for which he would soon be responsible as President.[3]

Henry Kissinger recalled his transition from campaign foreign policy adviser to national security adviser to the president as a radical jolt for which no appointee could expect to be fully prepared:

The period immediately after an electoral victory is a moment of charmed innocence. The President-elect is liberated from the harrowing uncertainty, the physical and psychological battering, of his struggle for the great prize. For the first time in months and perhaps in years, he can turn to issues of substance. He and his entourage share the exhilaration of imminent authority but are not yet buffeted by its ambiguities and pressures. His advisers are suddenly catapulted from obscurity into the limelight. Their every word and action are now analyzed by journalists, diplomats, and foreign intelligence services as a clue to future policy. Usually such scrutiny is vain; the entourage of a candidate has no time to address the problem of governance; nor have they been selected for their mastery of issues. And after the election is over they are soon consumed by the practical problems of organizing a new administration.[4]

In his memoir, Bill Clinton, reflected on his transition into the White House as the Bush administration left office during the 1992–93 transition:

On the day after the election, awash in congratulatory calls and messages, I went to work on what is called the transition. Is it ever! There was no time to celebrate, and we didn't take much time to rest, which was probably a mistake. In just eleven weeks, my family and I had to make the transition from our life in Arkansas into the White House. There was so much to do: select the cabinet, important sub-cabinet officials, and the White House staff; work with the Bush people on the mechanics of the move; begin briefings on national security and talk to foreign leaders; reach out to congressional leaders; finalize the economic proposals I would present to Congress; develop a plan to implement my other campaign commitments; deal with a large number of requests for meetings and the desire of many of our campaign workers and major supporters to know as soon as possible whether they would be part of the new administration; and respond to unfolding events. There would be a lot of them.[5]

"The transition period had been hectic and hard,"[6] Clinton remembered, recounting some of the difficulties he had encountered and some of the decisions he had later come to regret during the transition period:

I knew that the transition was only a foretaste of what the presidency would be like: everything happening at once. I would have to delegate more and have a better-organized decision-making process than I had as a governor. However, the fact that so many sub-cabinet positions had not been finalized had more to do with the fact that the Democrats had been out of power for twelve years. We had to replace a lot of people.[7]

By the time Clinton began making his transition into the White House, the process had already evolved into a dizzyingly complex array of challenges, all operating in punishing conjunction. "The required vetting process had gotten so complicated that it took too much time," Clinton remembered, especially in the midst of "political and press assaults."[8]

Of course, some of the challenge of a presidential transition is inherent in the nature of the office itself—the sobering realization that the nation has entrusted you with a position of unprecedented power and responsibility. Upon entering the Oval Office for the first time as president, for example, Dwight D. Eisenhower remembered: "There had been dramatic events in my life before—but none surpassed, emotionally, crossing the threshold to an office of such awesome responsibility. Remembering my beginnings, I had to smile."[9] President George H. W. Bush similarly noted: "The Oval Office itself is not that large, but it has a special atmosphere about it. Even as I left the presidency, I had the same feeling of awe and reverence for the room as when I first entered it in earlier administrations. It is a symbol of the institutions of the presidency itself, with an almost overwhelming aura of history."[10]

On Ronald Reagan's inauguration day, January 20, 1981, he recalled his first approach to the White House as president of the United States: "With its iron-grille fence and acres of green lawn, the big white mansion had had a mystical, almost religious aura for me since I was a child. I had first visited there when Harry Truman was president as part of a delegation of motion-picture labor leaders and then had come back when I was governor, when Lyndon Johnson and later Richard Nixon were president. But nothing had prepared me or Nancy for the emotion we felt the first time we entered the White House as its legal residents." He added, "Nancy and I couldn't escape a feeling of unreality as we went from room to room."[11]

For most incoming officials, the initial sense of awe and expectation soon turned to the proverbial question: "Now what?" Henry Kissinger aptly summarized the surreal quality of transition when he reflected that transitional periods are "enveloped in an aura of simultaneous expectation and uncertainty: expectation because they are a time of catharsis and renewal; uncertainty because they puncture continuity and occasionally uproot forests in order to ascertain whether the roots of the trees are still intact."[12]

Kissinger found himself at the center of this quadrennial confusion. He recalled his first substantive meeting with President-elect Nixon on November 25, 1968, as a rather bewildering encounter: "As I left the President-elect, I had no precise idea of what he expected of me. From the conversation it was unclear whether Nixon wanted advice or commitment and, if the latter, to what."[13] It wasn't until a subsequent meeting that Kissinger discovered, unbeknownst to him, that he had been asked to be Nixon's national security adviser:

> I found John Mitchell seated behind his desk puffing a pipe. Self-confident and taciturn, he exuded authority. He came straight to the point:
>
> "What have you decided about the National Security job?"
>
> "I didn't know I had been offered it."
>
> "Oh, Jesus Christ," said Mitchell, "he has screwed it up again."
>
> . . . This time it was clear what Nixon had in mind; I was offered the job of security advisor.[14]

Kissinger was not the only high-level national security official to encounter disarray in the appointment process. Jimmy Carter's national security adviser, Zbigniew Brzezinski, recounted a similar experience in his initial dealings with Carter about his role in a new administration. Carter contacted Brzezinski on December 15, 1976, to discuss his future role in the government. But when Carter began by saying, "I want you to do me a favor," Brzezinski recalled feeling some discomfort. He remembered it having been fairly clear at the time that he wanted to be the president's assistant for national security affairs, but since he and Carter had earlier discussed the role of under secretary of state, his first thought was that the "favor" Carter was asking for might put him that role instead. However, Carter did ask him to become his assistant for national security affairs, and the formal announcement was made the following day.[15]

Because many of the important decisions are made quickly after the new president is elected, the new team often is ill-prepared for its new responsibilities, even as consummate a professional as Kissinger. "When I was appointed," wrote Kissinger, "I did not have any organizational plan in mind."[16]

To some extent, how the transition is handled is a function of the individual and personal experiences of the person who joins the new administration. Carter brought two important figures into his administration, Zbigniew Brzezinski and Cyrus Vance. The very different experiences of Brzezinski and Vance during the Carter administration's transition into the White House would have implications for their later careers and, more important, for the conduct of American foreign policy. Even before their personal differences came into the spotlight, the manner in which these two men approached the Carter transition period had foreshadowed some of what was to come.

In the years after Carter declared his candidacy in 1974, Brzezinski and Carter corresponded with increasing frequency and grew well acquainted with each other. Brzezinski was impressed by Carter's character and actively worked with his campaign for a long period ahead of the election. Brzezinski had been in contact with numerous other campaigns and characterized his decision to join Carter's as partly a matter of timing:

> This was the time when putative Presidential candidates were beginning to sign up advisers as evidence of their seriousness. I had been invited to meetings by Senators Kennedy, Jackson, and Mondale, and also by Congressman Udall. Walter Mondale withdrew from the race; Edward Kennedy struck me as electorally very attractive but I had misgivings about the Camelot crowd returning to Washington; Morris Udall, I feared, might repeat in the foreign affairs area the disastrous McGovern phenomenon; while Henry Jackson, who appealed to me the most on substantive grounds, was vulnerable as a relatively colorless candidate. Jimmy Carter thus came along at the right moment.[17]

Brzezinski professed to have admired Carter's management style from the outset. He later wrote about Carter during this early period, observing that he "was on the whole struck by his coolness, deliberateness, and his obvious sense of systematic planning priorities." Brzezinski, for his part, was also a highly organized and detailed planner. "In general," he wrote, "I am quite struck by how systematic Carter is in his approach to decision making and by the degree to which he wishes to immerse himself in detail."[18]

Brzezinski approached the transitional period with detailed frameworks and proposals about how to staff and structure the National Security Council. He had reflected deeply on the challenges of the first months in office and had developed a sophisticated understanding of transition issues, which he unabashedly shared in his advice to Carter.

For instance, in his memoir he recalled counseling Carter that there were no fewer than "three alternative types of leadership":

> There was direct and dominant Presidential leadership, in which a strong president (like Nixon) is assisted by a dominant White House (Kissinger) overshadowing a weak Secretary of State; there was, secondly, the model of a predominant Secretary of State, as with Dulles under Eisenhower or Kissinger under Ford, with a relatively passive President and nonobtrusive White House; and, thirdly, there could be a more balanced "team" arrangement, combining a strong President (like Kennedy) with a relatively secure and strong Secretary of State (Rusk) and an equally confident and energetic White House (Bundy).[19]

In selecting his own top staff, Brzezinski performed an elaborate balancing act:

> I very deliberately sought to balance three different groups: professionals from within the Bureaucracy; forward-looking and more liberal foreign affairs experts from the non-Executive part of the Washington political community; and some strategic thinkers from academia whose views closely corresponded to my own.[20]

He also made it a point to establish productive operational procedures within his own operation, beginning with his first NSC staff meeting on January 24, 1977.[21] Brzezinski wanted to develop esprit by making his staff feel personally engaged with the president through him. Aware of the need to establish these relational dynamics as quickly as possible, Brzezinski effectively took the initiative and got a head start on putting in place informal structures and expectations among his trusted staff that would endure throughout his tenure.

These less formal paths of communication and influence usually take time to evolve, and the ultimate distribution and flow of power and influence that emerge are not always easy to predict. However, Brzezinski's demonstration of forethought and initiative shows that some degree of influence over these processes is possible.

Unlike Brzezinski, who was preoccupied with the overall national security decisionmaking process, Vance seems to have dedicated most of his energies during the transition period to the internal problems of the Department of State rather than building ties to the new president and his incoming team at the White House. Vance was trying desperately to reverse years of difficulties at the State Department: "The Foreign Service was suffering one of its perennial crises of morale when we took office," Vance noted.[22] Perhaps partly as a consequence of his focus on the career professionals at State, Vance failed to develop close relations with Carter's inner circle. Years later, Secretary of State Colin Powell followed a similar set of institutional priorities during the early course of the George W. Bush administration, and a similar gulf developed in his relations with the central players in the first term.

Although most of the firsthand accounts by the modern architects of American foreign policy and national security focus on the substantive and institutional issues inherent in transitions between presidents, they also reveal the daunting personal challenges they faced in taking on these unique roles. One of the most common experiences is coping with newfound fame and importance. Brzezinski described in acerbic terms the scene following Carter's electoral victory:

> Those of us who had supported Carter from quite early on, notably Richard Gardner and Henry Owen, as well as myself, now found ourselves engulfed by offers of "help" from various colleagues. It was both a surprise and a pleasure to discover how many of them had apparently always thought of Carter as the outstanding political figure on the American scene and the extent to which they were prepared to make a personal sacrifice by joining him in Washington! As in every post-electoral phase, this was also a time of quiet maneuvering and positioning.[23]

Thrust into the political limelight, Brzezinski commented at length about his encounters with Washington socialites and the "extraordinary hypocrisy" he experienced in discovering his new friends.[24] During transitions, suitors emerge from the woodwork and present themselves to new appointees with offers of assistance, while foreign and outgoing officials inundate appointees with requests for inside information about the new administration and its policies. Noted Kissinger: "Almost from the moment my job was announced, foreign diplomats sought appointments, driven by the necessity to write reports and in order to get a head start in dealing with the new Administration. The outgoing Administration sought to enlist the new appointees in support of its own preferences."[25]

Kissinger, too, commented on how the transition affected his personal life. After consulting with his academic friends and colleagues about whether he should accept a position in Nixon's administration, Kissinger reported that all advised him to make the move to Washington. He suspected that selfish motives occasionally came into play:

> Unanimously they urged me to accept. Their advice was, undoubtedly, tinged by the desire to know someone of influence in Washington who could provide the vicarious access to power that had become the addiction of so many academics in the aftermath of the Kennedy years. There and then were sown the seeds of future misunderstandings. Some friends and colleagues may have seen in our relationship not only a guarantee of access but also an assurance that their views would prevail. But this was impossible.[26]

Another element that makes up the "shock of the new" is the unprecedented personal toll that the new responsibilities take on key officials' lives. Brzezinski recalled his transition to the unfamiliar lifestyle of intense, nonstop work. "The beginning was hectic," he recalled, having written at the time:

> I was struck right away by "the fantastic pace of work. . . . Today I worked part of it literally standing up because there was practically no time to sit down; constant phone calls; papers crossing my desk; people to see; issues to respond to. And you wonder if it can be like this for four years, although the excitement and the challenge is probably more than enough to keep one going.[27]

Reflecting, he concluded, "It did stay that way."[28]

Scenes of confusion and disarray are commonplace in the early days of new administrations. Brzezinski noted in his memoir that he was nearly shot down in a helicopter during an ill-coordinated White House evacuation drill about a week into Carter's term.[29] James Baker recounted a similar, comically frightening episode when a large box from the Soviet Union mysteriously appeared at the White House just three days into George H. W. Bush's presidency. "There was no identifying information whatever on it, and a call to the Soviet embassy drew a complete blank," Baker recalled. "The Secret Service, exercising every precaution, mobilized its bomb disposal unit, removed the box to a safe place, and carefully opened it." Scowcroft put Robert Gates in charge of the case, who subsequently tasked Condoleezza Rice to look into the mystery. It turned out that a town in Russia had sent a 500-pound cake as a goodwill gesture. However, it took days to track down its origins, and by the time the mystery had been solved rats in the warehouse where it was being stored had already destroyed it. Noted Baker: "This first encounter demonstrated that our crisis-management system needed some improvement."[30]

Even old Washington hands come to recognize that despite their prior service, each new administration and each new transition is, to an important degree, a first time. When Alexander Haig resigned as secretary of state under President Reagan, his successor, George Shultz, noted his surprise at how much Washington culture had changed since he was last in government. "This was a different Washington from the one I had experienced a decade earlier as secretary of the treasury," Shultz noted. "The number of aides that surrounded the president and each of the top appointed officials had ballooned. Staffs of organizations, supposedly following the same administration policy, waged perpetual battle on behalf of—and often without the knowledge of—their principals."[31]

The combination of "déjà vu" and "first impression" is most dramatic among those who have served in multiple administrations. Colin Powell had such an experience when his appointment as chairman of the Joint Chiefs of Staff under George H. W. Bush extended through September 30, 1993, well into Bill Clinton's first year as president (his appointment was a nonpolitical one).[32] Powell recounted an early experience in his memoirs:

Soon after the inauguration, the Clinton national security team gathered in the Situation Room for the first time. The issue was Bosnia. Although I was a member of the team, I still felt a little like a skunk at the picnic. I had been up to my eyeballs in the Reagan and Bush national security policies that were held in some disrepute by my new bosses. They nevertheless welcomed me, aware that my institutional memory might prove useful.[33]

Powell was actually a holdover during both the Reagan-to-Bush and Bush-to-Clinton transitions and recalled that he had difficulty adapting to each new administration's style: "As President Reagan's National Security Advisor I had run structured meetings where the objectives were laid out, options were argued, and decisions were made. I had managed to adjust to the looser Bush-era approach, and I would somehow adapt to the Clinton style. But it was not going to be easy." He expressed some frustration about how meetings were run under Clinton. During meetings, he said, "the discussion continued to meander like graduate-student bull sessions or the think-tank seminars in which many of my new colleagues had spent the last twelve years while their party was out of power. Backbenchers sounded off with the authority of cabinet officers."[34]

The problem of holdovers is endemic to any transition, because any new team must come to grips with a permanent bureaucracy. James Baker found himself suddenly immersed in a surprisingly complex organizational culture complete with its own language when he inherited George Shultz's State Department during the Reagan-to-Bush transition. Baker noted:

> I quickly became aware of "the building" and its views on the matters at hand. I soon found out that different floors of "the building" had their own unique views on events: "the seventh floor won't want it that way." "The sixth floor wants to reclama on that." Indeed, letters of the alphabet seemed to have views, too: "S won't stand for it." "P bounced that." "EUR is out of control."[35]

Baker also recalled that "the building" put up considerable bureaucratic resistance and

relished dumping on the new team. They were aided and abetted in this exercise by some veteran State Department reporters whose sources were drying up as I centralized decision making, and were only too eager to publish the naysaying of some disgruntled careerists. It comes with the turf, but the only complaint that really ever got to me was the common charge that I was a foreign policy neophyte.[36]

Baker later reflected on his experience: "In retrospect, I might have been more attentive to the mores of the diplomatic culture. I could have done more to cultivate some of the younger and brighter FSOs," adding, "In truth, I was probably not as attentive to the protocol aspects of the job of Secretary of State as I should have been."[37]

Some of the greatest challenges of the transition occur because a partial vacuum emerges as the old team departs but the new one has yet to come fully on board. Powell recalled feeling somewhat disquieted in the Pentagon on January 20, 1981, as the Reagan administration took office following Carter's presidency: "I arrived at the office early as usual. The executive suites were empty. An unnatural quiet had settled over the Eisenhower Corridor. Passing the torch from one administration to another leaves a brief vacuum in the halls of power."[38]

But the apparent calm is quickly overtaken by the frenetic activity that accompanies all modern transitions. As the days wore on in the new Kennedy administration, for example, Sorensen noted that the so-called honeymoon period

> was not at all quiet. The exhilaration of securing the prize he had sought so long had not yet worn off. The adjustment from the days of constant campaigning was not complete. Politicians and reporters were constantly in and out of his office. The new President's first visitor had been former President Harry Truman, welcomed for the first time to his former home. Organizations, celebrities and award winners of every kind, from Baptists to beauty queens, were greeted daily in the oval office. Thirty thousand letters poured in every week. Twelve speeches were made in the first two months. Old friends were visited in their homes. Departmental meetings were visited in person. Press conferences and background briefings were held regularly. Legislative requests were contained in separate messages spaced for maximum publicity.[39]

Of course, transitions are not only about the incoming team; for some two and half months the outgoing team must man the ship of state as their power ebbs and attention turns to the incoming team. The flip side of the ebullience of the incoming policymakers is the forlorn resignation of orphaned bureaucrats and exiting officials. Those who have experienced transitions firsthand often recall a downbeat period accompanied by a bureaucratic lull. Kissinger remembered that the final days of the battered Johnson administration in the midst of a painful foreign war and domestic tumult were "a somber time":

> The surface appurtenances of power still exist; the bureaucracy continues to produce the paperwork for executive decision. But authority is slipping away. Decisions of which officials disapprove will be delayed in implementation; foreign governments go through the motions of diplomacy but reserve their best efforts and their real attention for the next team. And yet so familiar has the exercise of power become that its loss is sensed only dimly and intermittently. Days go by in which one carries out one's duties as if one's actions still matter.[40]

James Baker, secretary of state and White House chief of staff under George H. W. Bush, recalled his feelings when Bush lost the election to Clinton: "We were all sad and weary. The initial pain of seeing my friend lose the presidency—like being hit in the stomach with a baseball bat—had not dulled a bit." Baker, like many outgoing officials, remembered a sense of winding down combined with feelings of sadness and exhaustion: "For me, the excitement and responsibility of public service began to slip away shortly after the election. I still attended to my duties, but fatigue settled deep into my bones. I'm sure George went through the same experience on some levels. Truth be told, I also felt an enormous sense of relief. . . . I was simply worn out."[41]

These firsthand perspectives of practitioners offer unique insights into the complex process of transferring power. But as is often the case, the very fact of being part of the story may limit or distort their ability to see broader patterns or judge objectively the efficacies of their approaches. These personal accounts represent a veritable first draft of history, but scholarly and academic accounts are also important in providing objectivity and greater context for understanding modern transitions. We have therefore included a detailed treatment of the important scholarly and journalistic work on transitions in the Appendix in order to give the reader a larger sense of how our collective knowledge and assessments on the process have changed over time. Our book now pivots from these personal accounts to explore the larger factors at work in making each presidential transition more complex and challenging than the previous one.

3 | **TRANSITIONS TODAY**

*Enduring Challenges
and Accelerating Risks*

F ROM THE EARLY cold war era, when new presidents and
their advisers worried about being "tested" by their Soviet
counterparts, to more recent concerns about whether a new
national security team fully grasps the contemporary complexities of
homeland security, presidential transitions have been a perilous time for
new presidents and their administrations, as well as for the nation they
were chosen to lead. The specific problems unique to transitions are
especially acute in the international realm. As John F. Kennedy said,
"Domestic policy can only defeat us. Foreign policy can kill us."[1]

Transitions Are Inherently Dangerous

Many of the dangers of transition are inherent in the process of transferring power. When a new president is elected a new team must be
assembled, a process that under the best of circumstances takes months
to complete. The new team needs time to get up to speed on the policy
problems it inherits, as well as to formulate a strategy for implementing
(or otherwise adapting) the new president's campaign promises and
commitments. Transition briefings on imminent security challenges and
crucial national secrets cannot substitute for the experience gained from
working those issues on a daily basis, even for those who have served in

government before or have great knowledge of foreign affairs. Procedures need to be put in place to facilitate decisionmaking, and relationships need to be forged with the bureaucracy, Congress, and the media. Tensions between the outgoing and incoming teams complicate the smooth transfer of knowledge and experience, particularly when the outgoing administration is a defeated incumbent or from the opposite party.

For a period of months between the election and the inauguration a state of ambiguity prevails, with an outgoing president retaining the formal perquisites and authorities of power and an incoming president hovering in the shadows, awaiting the opportunity to begin the new regime. Neither friends nor foes have much incentive to deal with the departing incumbent, yet they are also uncertain about what to expect from the newcomer. As Frederick Mosher and his colleagues have written, "The period of transition is one of particular vulnerability for this country, because other nations, both foes and friends, may try to take advantage of our difficulties in making and implementing decisions when neither the incumbent president nor the president-elect is in firm control."[2]

The notion that one of America's enemies might try to challenge the United States even before the formal transition begins is far from idle speculation. In late 1980, following the presidential election that brought Ronald Reagan to power, the Soviet Union initiated a series of coercive measures against Poland that were designed to replace Premier Stanislaw Kania with the defense minister, Wojciech Jaruzelski. Former defense secretary Caspar Weinberger explicitly described these events as linked to the American presidential transition: "Apparently believing that the transition period in the United States between the end of one presidential term and the beginning of another provided a suitable opportunity for stamping out any freedom in one of their possibly unreliable neighbors, the Soviets had embarked on various intimidating actions toward the Polish people."[3]

During this period there is a risk that confusion over authority (especially the authority to bind the incoming administration) and uncertainty over intentions can develop, especially if the president-elect does not support the policy choices made by the outgoing president.

Although the Constitution is clear that the outgoing president still possesses all the powers of the presidency, the political authority of the incumbent wanes as key actors both in and outside the United States turn their attention to the incoming administration.

Unlike most, though not all, domestic issues, the option of postponing decisions until the new president takes office is often unavailable when it comes to unfolding national security problems. Virtually every modern transition offers dramatic examples: the balance of payments crisis at the end of Eisenhower's administration; the Paris peace talks at the end of the Johnson administration; the Iran hostage crisis at the end of Carter's term; the military deployment to Somalia under George H. W. Bush; the missile talks with North Korea at the end of the Clinton presidency; and the engagement in Iraq and Afghanistan at the end of George W. Bush's term. The simple and constitutionally correct position has always been, "we only have one President at a time."[4] Though the outgoing president's influence (as the so-called lame duck) is waning, the authority of office remains, and decisions made during the transition have, for better or worse, complicated and constrained the choices of successors, as was evident with the Carter hostage deal and Bush's Somalia deployment. On a number of occasions, the outgoing president has tried to enlist the support of the incoming one to buttress last-minute policy initiatives. For example, Truman consulted with Eisenhower on the repatriation of Korean prisoners of war; Eisenhower worked with Kennedy on the balance of payments crisis; and Johnson cooperated with Nixon on strategic arms negotiations (SALT), even inviting incoming officials to participate in formal negotiations like the Paris peace talks. All of these efforts demonstrate the outgoing presidents' recognition that for the world at large during the transition, the intentions of the incoming president are at least as important as those of the individual currently in office.

Despite the lack of formal authority, some incoming administrations have at least hinted at new policy initiatives after the election but before taking office. These have sometimes taken the form of foreign visits by the president-elect or his advisers, such as Eisenhower's visit to Korea, and Nixon's cultivating private contacts in Vietnam and dispatching Pennsylvania governor William Scranton to the Middle East. Sometimes these efforts even precede the election, such as President Carter's decision to send Averell Harriman to Moscow to discuss Carter's plans for SALT. Although most presidents-elect remain in the background, focusing on assembling their new administration and readying themselves for office, President-elect Clinton held a high-profile economic policy conference during the transition period and used a transition period press conference to announce his intention to change U.S. policy toward Haitian refugees.[5] There is a danger that such moves can send mixed messages, causing international confusion and providing avenues for exploitation by America's adversaries.

Although these transitional problems pose acute risks, it is in the early days after the president-elect actually becomes the president of the United States that the greatest dangers exist. At that moment the ability of the government to handle serious challenges is at its nadir—a risky situation characterized by a loss of institutional knowledge and a deficit of capacity that extends well into the first months of the new administration.

As Eisenhower noted, at this "dead center" moment in American foreign policy, "an emergency, arising at home or abroad during the first twenty-four hours after a new President takes his oath of office, would demand decisions and actions which, by reason of the unfamiliarity of new officials with their duties and authority, might result in bewilderment and lack of intelligent reaction, with resultant damage to the United States."[6]

An example of how all of these challenges can combine to create a foreign policy crisis can be found in the Bay of Pigs misadventure (the unsuccessful attempt by U.S.-backed Cuban exiles to overthrow Fidel Castro) during the early days of the Kennedy presidency. Having inherited the plans for the operation from the Eisenhower administration, the Kennedy administration was forced to make critical decisions before it had really settled into office. In the new administration's deliberations on the proposed plan, excessive deference to military and CIA experts, along with a lack of knowledge about the national security bureaucracy in general, contributed to insufficient scrutiny by Kennedy and his senior team of advisers. As he later explained, "If someone comes in to tell me this or that about the minimum wage bill I have no hesitation in overruling them. But you always assume that the military and intelligence people have some secret skill not available to ordinary mortals."[7]

The lack of experience among Kennedy's most senior and trusted advisers, both in the government and with each other, handicapped their ability to raise important questions about the operation and to make good decisions. At the time, Kennedy "did not have the time or opportunity to test the inherited instrumentalities of government. He could not know which of his advisers were competent and which were not. For their part, they did not know him or each other well enough to raise hard questions with force and candor."[8]

The result was a national security breakdown of the first order. Kennedy did implement some hastily designed changes to the planned attack, like shifting the landing location away from a concentration of preexisting anti-communist forces, a move he hoped would raise the prospect of deniability for the U.S. government but that instead severely undermined the chance of success. And once the attack was under way, a lack of coordination within the government caused the cancellation of air strikes necessary to ensure the safety of the landing party. The humiliating aftermath caused Kennedy to rethink his whole approach to national security decisionmaking and enshrined the Bay of Pigs incident in the American political lexicon as an exemplar of how not to execute foreign policy during a transition.

The National Security Risks during Transitions Are Increasing

The prospect of a confrontation between the United States and the Soviet Union or its allies during a presidential transition was the principal concern throughout the cold war and a sobering prospect that dominated the thinking of new administrations and outside commentators alike. As the cold war ended, some might have predicted that the risks associated with transitions would ease. But the range and complexity of national security challenges have actually grown significantly since then, and the risks posed by transitions have instead multiplied for current and future administrations.[9]

There are at least seven key factors that contribute to this new challenge: the increasing magnitude and immediacy of risks; the growing range and complexity of issues; expanding U.S. global interests; 24/7 news cycles; increasing politicization of foreign policy and security policy; the multitude of positions to fill; and the mismatch between old security institutions and processes and new security threats.

1. The magnitude and immediacy of risk

The end of the cold war eliminated the most prominent existential risk to the United States—a decapitating nuclear strike by the Soviet Union. But it also ushered in an era characterized by a new set of dangers and uncertainties that could confront an administration on day one with life-or-death choices.

These range from a terrorist attack to pandemic disease to the increasing likelihood of natural catastrophes like hurricanes and typhoons triggered by climate change. For terrorist groups in particular, targeting the early months of a new administration might be particularly appealing given their interest in the politics of disruption as well as destruction. Groups planning attacks against the United States know that there is no time of greater uncertainty in American politics than the days surrounding the inauguration of a new president.[10] The risk of an attack without warning is even more dangerous given the possibility that a terrorist strike could involve a weapon of mass destruction (WMD). While most attention has focused on the dangers associated with the detonation of a nuclear weapon, even a limited attack using chemical, biological, or radiological materials could trigger mass panic and uncertainty that would dwarf the number of direct casualties caused by the attack itself.[11] The first World Trade Center bombing in 1993 was an early precursor of the potential dangers that face a new president in the early days and months of a new presidency—as 9/11 later demonstrated and which a future attack may once again confirm.

What makes these risks so dangerous during the early stages of a new administration is that they can emerge with little or no warning at a time when the capacity of that administration is severely limited.[12] These scenarios would require rapid decisionmaking on the part of the White House to assess the situation, draw in the appropriate diplomatic and military advisers, and plan for an effective response, all before the people and procedures of the new team are fully tested.

2. Increasing range and complexity of national security issues

The dangers posed by transition are not only increasing in magnitude and immediacy, but also in number and complexity. This means that an ever wider number of policy actors must be drawn into the policy formulation and crisis management process early on. As a result, it becomes even more difficult for a new president to grasp all the necessary levers of power, come up to speed on the full range of issues, and prioritize which to tackle first, especially when multiple issues could unexpectedly become crises overnight. The contemporary security environment contrasts markedly with that of the cold war era, during which a president could focus on a smaller number of top advisers and agencies to handle more predictable (traditional) threats.

Some of these challenges could emerge from nation-states, such as a nuclear breakout by Iran, a confrontation on the Korean peninsula, or conflict with China across the Taiwan Strait. An example of this kind of post–cold war challenge was the EP-3 incident that arose early in George W. Bush's first term, which illustrated the difficulty and dangers in handling unexpected crises early in a new administration, even when the officials brought in by the new president have had a long history of prior service in high national security positions.

In early April 2001, a U.S. EP-3 signals reconnaissance plane collided with a Chinese J-8 fighter and was forced to land on Hainan Island. The Chinese government accused the U.S. government of illegally spying on the Chinese, triggering an international incident with serious potential for retaliation and escalation. After ten days of negotiations, the plane's crew was released by the Chinese and allowed to return to the United States. In the interim, the global media converged on Beijing and Washington and closely followed the movements of American and Chinese officials as they negotiated the release of the crew. The diplomacy was made more difficult by the perceived hostile attitude of the Bush administration toward China, which had its roots in campaign rhetoric that promised a tougher approach to a China that was characterized as a "strategic competitor." The administration had begun its term by reevaluating the U.S.-China relationship and shifting toward repudiating the Clinton policy of cooperation and strategic partnership. As the crisis unfolded, the new administration had to reconcile its desire to reconfigure American strategy toward China with its short-term need to secure the release of the American crew and avoid a major crisis in the first months in office. Quiet deliberations with the Chinese took place under harsh media lighting, which significantly raised the stakes and complexity of the interactions. After an initial, highly bellicose response that reflected the campaign posture toward China (and which had been preceded by comments from administration officials hinting at closer military ties to Taiwan), the administration opted for a more conciliatory response that led to a successful, face-saving solution for both sides.

Although the EP-3 incident has some similarities to the transition perils of the past because it involved a nation-state (as would a future conflict involving a nuclear North Korea or Iran), others have few historical parallels. In particular, even though the notion of a clear separation between domestic and foreign policy issues was always more myth than reality, in today's globalized and interdependent world the lines of separation have nearly dissolved. Just imagine the challenges a new administration would face in confronting a global bird flu pandemic in the early days in office, where agencies as diverse as Agriculture, Commerce, and Health and Human Services would need to be brought in, as well as the Departments of State, Defense, and Homeland Security and the CIA.

Similarly, the strong links between economics and national security—"geo-economics"—could pose acute challenges during the early days of a new administration, as the 2008 global financial crisis so devastatingly illustrates. The U.S. economy is closely tied to the global economy for trade and investment, which means that the health of the American economy depends on factors like the strength of the Chinese currency, the willingness of foreign governments and foreign investors to buy and hold U.S. debt, the price of oil from the Persian Gulf, and the demand for raw materials in places like Brazil and India. Thus economic issues (as well as health, environmental, and other issues) once relegated to "low politics" now affect the urgency and stakes of national security decisions and therefore must be integrated with national security personnel and processes.

This interconnectedness, and the challenges it poses for crisis management, was vividly illustrated by the Asian financial crisis of 1997–98, during which the full range of economic and national security teams was needed to coordinate efforts to manage a set of developments that not only threatened global prosperity, but also risked the stability of important U.S. allies and their perceptions of the United States as a trusted partner.[13] These challenges proved difficult enough for a seasoned team in its fifth year in office; imagine these events unfolding after only a few days or months in office.

Learning on the job takes time even for those with prior experience, and the loss of institutional knowledge during governmental transitions can reduce the ability of important parts of the executive branch to handle national security problems before they escalate.[14] The growing size and complexity of the federal government make rapid on-the-job learning especially difficult, particularly given the necessity of coordination between the Departments of State, Defense, Treasury, and Homeland Security, the Central Intelligence Agency, and others during a crisis. The ten to eleven weeks of transition is a very short period in which to get up to speed.

Shifts in the responsibilities of even long-standing departments like Defense and State can pose challenges even for those who join the new administration with substantial prior governmental experience. The shock of adjustment to the new complexities clearly had an impact on the George W. Bush administration, whose team came to office assuming the reins of a national security apparatus far different from the ones they had known in their previous executive branch incarnations. Perhaps the most dramatic example was Secretary of Defense Donald Rumsfeld, who faced a disorienting return in 2001 to a Pentagon very different from the one he had served in during the Ford years, with the military playing a much more significant role in decisionmaking.[15]

These challenges are intensified when the new team must assume control of new institutions and agencies. For example, since 2000, the last election in which party control of the White House changed hands, a whole new set of agencies and their associated leadership positions have been created, most notably the Department of Homeland Security, the Office of the Director of National Intelligence (and the reformed intelligence community bureaucracy), and the Homeland Security Council. If there is a change of party in 2009, the new president will need to staff those agencies with officials who in most cases will have no direct prior experience in them.

3. *Growing global interests*

The global nature of American interests and our increasing interconnectedness with the world means that the national security apparatus must be ready to handle even relatively obscure developments in remote places around the world. A cursory scan of contemporary U.S. diplomatic preoccupations—from Burma to Zimbabwe—shows that from the outset the new administration must have global reach. The long-term consequences of failure to do so were clear in the Clinton administration's management of events in Somalia and George W. Bush's lack of focus on Afghanistan in his first months in office.

It is instructive that as we look back on the past two transitions, the dominant challenges faced by new administrations have not originated from great-power politics, but from smaller and poorly understood conflicts in places such as Haiti, Somalia, and Darfur.

Clinton, for example, experienced an unexpected challenge from Haiti that was far out of proportion to the tiny island's conventional geopolitical significance to international security. The U.S. transition effort had included the preparation of a voluminous set of papers on the broadest possible range of topics—Russia's financial crisis; the status of the Balkan conflicts and the available options for the United States; how best to negotiate with Japan over trade tensions—only to find that the prospect of the Florida coasts being swamped by fleeing Haitian refugees suddenly elevated that matter to the top of the new administration's preoccupations. Unanticipated events forced the new administration to shift its earlier campaign stance toward Haiti and to devote considerable time and energy to dealing with the internal politics of a small Caribbean island.

Most poignantly, the September 11 attacks later brought home the fact that one of the remotest corners of the planet—the borderlands between Afghanistan and Pakistan—could harbor a dangerous threat to our security. Likewise, the possibility that a strain of vaccine-resistant bird flu, or the highly communicable Ebola virus, might develop in Southeast Asia or Africa means that the United States now has a profound interest in the public health capabilities of small and distant countries. And drug trafficking means that today a civil war in Colombia is a national security challenge that will test the capacities of a new president.

Increasingly, there are issues on every continent and in every ocean that pose concerns for a globally connected policy apparatus in the United States. There are new worries about political and religious radicalization spreading through new parts of the world; new oil producers in Africa are suddenly the focus of intense interest by outside consumer states; dwindling fishing stocks in the North Bering Sea are spurring sharp tensions among industrial fishing interests; and escalating grain prices are leading to global hoarding and tensions over agriculture policy. Many of these issues are interconnected, and all are the business of the United States. An incoming team will be expected not just to deal effectively with the obvious pots on the boil—Afghanistan, Iraq, and Iran—but also any of these other issues that could rise up overnight and threaten American interests as well as the prospects of a new and unsuspecting president.

4. The 24/7 news cycle and the emergence of new media

The contemporary international environment has not only created new challenges for the "what" and the "where" problems facing new administrations, but also the "when." The 24/7 news cycle and the revolution in communications technology have increased the speed and amount of information available to the president, raised the level of media scrutiny, and shortened the amount of time available for making decisions. Cable TV and political blogs only complicate matters. In the Information Age, American officials are bombarded with instantaneous and voluminous reports about developments around the globe. This information overload is particularly stressful for a new administration that is just beginning to establish its methods of operation.

The intensity of press scrutiny increases the pressure on a new administration to show results quickly and makes it difficult to escape glaring analysis of even minor missteps. This, of course, is not an entirely new phenomenon, but one that has become exponentially more challenging in the age of cable news, the Internet, and YouTube. During the Carter administration, for instance, Brzezinski noted that the growing media swarm surrounding the White House might make it difficult for the Carter administration to get credit for its policies.[16] The media expected Carter to "fix" American foreign policy in a matter of days, an unrealistic expectation that could not be met.[17] And the pressure to show movement on his campaign commitments led to an uncoordinated set of statements by mid-level officials that served to dissipate rather than highlight the intended new focus on human rights in U.S. foreign policy.

Clinton and his advisers took office with deep skepticism about the Washington press corps and developed a deliberate strategy to try to end-run the entrenched national press in favor of regional outlets. But the result was to further foreshorten a policy honeymoon that was already under pressure from disputes about issues ranging from Haiti to gays in the military.

During George W. Bush's transition into the White House, his press secretary, Scott McClellan, quickly found the administration engaged in a "permanent campaign" with the media and the public in which the tasks of governing and campaigning were "indistinguishable."[18] In the contemporary warlike media environment, government policymaking and dealing with the press go hand-in-hand. New policy initiatives must be carefully launched with complex media strategies in order to maintain effective relations with relevant stakeholders. Intense media attention and scrutiny require new administrations to be prepared to coordinate policy and communications continuously from day one.

The attacks on September 11, 2001, were the prototypical national security crisis of the new age—unfolding in real time through images of the burning twin towers and voice communications from the passengers of United Airlines flight 93. Today, when an incident occurs in Pakistan, such as former prime minister Benazir Bhutto's assassination, it instantly appears on the major twenty-four-hour networks—CNN, Fox News, Al Jazeera, and many others—most of which have a significant presence on the Internet as well. Moreover, anyone with a digital camera and an Internet connection can upload images and video to any number of popular websites within minutes. Offhand campaign statements in what are thought to be closed events can become fodder for policy debates when they are recorded and distributed by freelance web journalists. Thousands of blogs and small independent websites serve as outlets for everything from brave citizen journalism to enemy propaganda.

Responding effectively requires not only faster coordination between government agencies than ever before, but also faster analysis to coordinate responses. The great degree of scrutiny by the media made possible by real-time communications means that even initial missteps can be catalogued and replayed endlessly across television screens and over the Internet.

5. Increasing politicization of national security policy

Recent years have seen a dramatic politicization of foreign policy issues. Senator Arthur Vandenberg's adage that "politics stops at the water's edge" has certainly receded in the rearview mirror. The end of the cold war bipartisan consensus (already frayed from the Vietnam years and debates over Central America from the 1970s and 1980s) has altered the security environment that previously sustained bipartisanship around national security policy. Changes of administrations ever since have ushered in more significant oscillations in foreign policy. Even when there is general agreement about grand strategy today, there is still partisan disagreement about implementation.

Before the Vietnam War, while each party had relatively more internationalist and isolationist wings, the internationalists in both parties were in broad agreement about grand strategy and goals. This led to a relative stability in foreign affairs despite transitions between parties, partly because a group of elites with shared values and knowledge staffed each administration. This agreement began to crack over disagreements concerning the Vietnam War and intensified throughout the 1970s and 1980s as the differences between the two parties became more pronounced and the degree of consensus within each party increased. By the Reagan era, those with decades of experience in the national security arena had come to bemoan the rise of partisanship in foreign policy.[19]

In the post–cold war era, and especially since September 11, 2001, partisan bickering over foreign policy has escalated even further.[20] While there has been considerable focus on the George W. Bush administration's disdain for the policies of its predecessor, the transition from George H. W. Bush to Clinton foreshadowed this trend toward increasingly sharp repudiation of the policies of the past. This approach has heightened the risks of transition for two reasons. First, the haste to draw stark distinctions—which can happen even in a transition between presidents of the same party—can cause a president to "misunderstand the legacy" and throw out perfectly good policies just because his predecessor supported them. Second, the partisanship surrounding national security undermines the new administration's honeymoon period, which is a valuable time for settling in, coping with inevitable early mistakes, and adapting campaign policies to governing realities.

In repudiating the policies of the predecessor, new teams are under enormous pressure to implement quickly their preferred alternatives, even before they have had a chance to think through the complexities of implementation in the real world. The political element of foreign policy during a presidential transition is made worse by the heated rhetoric of presidential campaigns and the foreign policy promises that result.

The consequences of this trend became starkly apparent in the "Anything but Clinton" or "ABC" syndrome that influenced the George W. Bush team's approach when it took over from the two-term Clinton administration.[21] From dealing with the Israeli-Palestinian issue in the Middle East to handling the North Korean nuclear threat to AIDS policy in Africa, the new administration repudiated critical elements of the Clinton legacy, apparently rejecting many policies simply because of their association with Clinton.[22] Thus, in 2001, the newly arrived Bush team attempted to restructure nearly all American relationships in Asia, an effort cut short by the events of September 11. According to Asia scholar Kenneth Lieberthal, despite advances by the Clinton administration in Asia, and especially during his second term, "The Bush team felt that its predecessor had missed the boat in almost all key bilateral relationships."[23] Ironically, on almost every one of these issues, by its final year the Bush administration had come around to an approach not dissimilar to Clinton's—from the decision to engage directly with North Korea to reach an agreement on their nuclear weapons program to the Annapolis process that revived peace negotiations between Israel and the Palestinians. But in the meantime, both situations had badly deteriorated—with North Korea acquiring a more substantial nuclear arsenal and the rise of Hamas in Gaza, dangers that might have been avoided had there been greater willingness to consider the merits of the earlier approach.

The perils of "Anything but . . ." syndromes are endemic to both parties. Martin Indyk, a senior NSC official in the Clinton administration and a former ambassador to Israel, described Clinton's foreign policy in the Middle East as ABB ("Anything but Bush 41"). Indyk stated, "It's a natural response when the administration changes from party to party. . . . You tend to regard everything the previous administration did as wrong and stupid."[24]

As the politicization of foreign policy has increased in recent decades, it has also deepened the level of suspicion toward holdovers from the successor regimes This distrust can even extend to career government officials with valuable institutional knowledge, because of their association with the previous administration and its policies. This is particularly harmful during the transition period, when the political appointees of the previous administration have departed but the new team is only partially in place and slowly coming up to speed. Under these circumstances, the value of the holdovers is at its greatest, yet they are often kept at arm's length. Although many will eventually come to be accepted by the new team, valuable time is lost; and in the worst case, the failure to heed their institutional expertise leads to costly and avoidable mistakes.

6. A growing number and slowing pace of appointments
To respond to the expanding range of issues and the global scope of U.S. interests, the size of the national security establishment has grown dramatically. From the Kennedy administration to the Clinton administration, the number of high-level presidential appointees increased almost 400 percent.[25] The larger number of political appointees infuses more uncertainty into the foreign policy apparatus and leads to the loss of more institutional knowledge during transitions. Through a combination of bureaucratic sublayers and the displacement of career civil servants, political appointees are now responsible for a growing proportion of foreign policy decisions. So, although career civil servants in the Defense and State Departments are allowed to continue the routine daily work in foreign policy during a presidential transition, it is increasingly difficult to make substantive progress in any diplomatic or military areas without political appointees.[26] When the political appointees of

the previous administration leave, they take a great deal of knowledge with them, ranging from the best strategies for managing the bureaucratic and personal intricacies of their own offices to the details of ongoing negotiations with foreign powers. Yet the sheer number of positions to be filled means that the new administration is hobbled in picking up the slack. As Alexander Haig, secretary of state under Reagan, observed: "It is virtually impossible to find in the outside world eighty fervent partisans of any persuasion who possess the expertise to fill these posts and are at the same time willing to give up what they are doing in order to join the government at a loss in earnings."[27]

To put the political challenges involved in context, at the outset of the Reagan administration, Paul Wolfowitz was nearly eliminated from consideration for a job at the State Department simply because he had worked in the Carter administration. While in retrospect it seems obvious that Wolfowitz was far from a Democratic partisan, the politics involved in the decisionmaking process can complicate things even for a well-meaning administration intent on finding the most qualified people to fill positions.[28]

This broad-ranging turnover of personnel strips the institutions of knowledge about key issues and can lead to flawed assessments in crisis situations. In the Bay of Pigs example discussed earlier, the newness of the Kennedy administration clearly hampered decisionmaking.

The number of people employed by the federal government responsible for national security issues has increased dramatically since the 1947 National Security Act, and especially since the Reagan administration in the 1980s. For example, the National Security Council was originally created to help provide the president with national security advice and to coordinate the activities of the foreign affairs agencies. A handful of career civil servants originally staffed the NSC, but it now employs over two hundred people, split between substantive experts and administrators.[29]

The state of affairs is made worse by the slow pace of approvals for presidential appointees by Congress, with the average length of time from inauguration to confirmation for initial PAS appointees (positions subject to presidential appointment with Senate confirmation) taking just a few months at the outset of the Kennedy administration to more than eight months during the first term of Bill Clinton.[30] So in the first several months of a presidential administration, while many Cabinet and sub-Cabinet members are in place, the vast majority of political appointees are still queued up for congressional approval, creating authority voids inside important institutions like the Departments of State and Defense. Temporary appointments can help fill these voids, but some important matters and decisions will be placed on hold until the next "boss" arrives. For example, at the beginning of the first Reagan administration, only one of Reagan's eleven assistant secretaries of state took office before May 1981, and the assistant secretary of defense for international security planning was not confirmed until August 1981.[31] In 2001, according to Paul C. Light, an expert on the presidential appointments process, only about twenty to thirty nominees could be processed per week, even as the total number of appointments continued to rise with each new administration. Light noted that Kennedy had only 15 under secretaries to nominate, whereas George W. Bush had nearly 50; Kennedy had 87 assistant secretaries, Bush more than 220.[32] According to the Brookings Institution's Presidential Appointee Initiative, which surveyed former appointees, the percentage reporting that the process had taken more than six months doubled from 15 to 30 percent for those who served during the periods 1964–84 and 1984–99, respectively. And this troubling trend shows little sign of abating.

7. Mismatch between old institutions and new threats

A striking feature of the current architecture of American national security policymaking is just how many of its central institutions were established in the late 1940s—a substantive reality mirrored in the bricks and mortar landscape of Washington, D.C., and the monumental edifices of the Pentagon, State Department, and CIA. Their traditional capabilities mostly served the nation well during the nearly forty-year struggle with the Soviet Union and in other cold war–era policies, ranging from buttressing the war-torn states of Europe and Asia to promoting development in the third world to helping establish a global trading regime and regularizing international financial flows. A remarkable feature of the post–cold war world—a span now approaching twenty years—is the persistence of these old institutions and the limited scope of adaptation of the vast U.S. government bureaucracy in the face of the new mix of global challenges that face the nation today.

There are exceptions to be sure, including the creation of the Energy Department under Carter, the National Economic Council during the Clinton administration, the newly configured Office of the Director of National Intelligence, the Department of Homeland Security, and the Millennium Challenge Corporation during the term of George W. Bush. But the vast preponderance of institutions and processes that make up the national toolbox available for statecraft remain the ones that have been in use for generations.

Where these mismatches introduce significant obstacles, new administrations face a dilemma. The new president can undertake a radical overhaul of the national security machinery at a time when only a handful of new officials have been appointed and those who have been named are still struggling to get up to speed; but this approach runs the risk that the new procedures will be unfamiliar and untested if an early crisis breaks out. Alternatively, to minimize disruption and dislocation, the president could try to make do with outdated mechanisms at a time when the level of stress on the system is greatest, but with the sure knowledge that those processes are ill-suited to the substance of the challenges the administration faces.

Summing Up

All seven of these factors—the magnitude and immediacy of risks, the increasing range and complexity of issues, growing global interests, the 24/7 news cycle, the increasing politicization of foreign policy, the growing number of political appointments, and mismatches between old institutions and new threats—*in combination* make presidential transitions increasingly risky for foreign policy and national security. Although many of the challenges discussed in this chapter are inevitable, there is much both candidates and new administrations can do to minimize the dangers and maximize their ability to successfully launch a new presidency. In order to do so, however, it is important to understand in detail the specific challenges faced in each of the four phases of transition: campaigning; staffing the new administration; structuring the decisionmaking processes; and governing in the initial days in office—the subjects of the next four chapters.

4 | CAMPAIGN
TRIALS

O F ALL THE problems that have plagued the early months
of new presidencies, perhaps none are more persistent or
potentially more dangerous than those that arise from
commitments made or implied during the presidential campaign. From
Eisenhower's campaign pledge to roll back Soviet gains in Eastern
Europe through Clinton's promise to lift the ban on gays in the military
and George W. Bush's denunciation of nation building, campaign rhetoric regularly comes back to complicate the lives of new administrations. Often the consequence of ill-considered promises is limited
mainly to political embarrassment and loss of domestic political capital
for a new administration that must squirm uncomfortably to explain
why policy choices that seemed so compelling on the campaign trail
look so different in the cold light of governing. But on occasion these
commitments have caused serious harm to a new president's policy
agenda and have had a direct impact on important national security
interests.

In his memoir, Henry Kissinger eloquently summarized the fundamental problem, cautioning that even through the formal transition
period, "the pledges of each new Administration are like leaves on a turbulent sea. No President-elect or his advisers can possibly know upon
what shore they may finally be washed by that storm of deadlines,

ambiguous information, complex choices, and manifold pressures which descends upon all leaders of a great nation."[1]

Despite this and similar cautions, and a long history of promises and pronouncements gone awry, the problem remains endemic. As Mosher and his colleagues observed in their landmark 1987 study of presidential transitions and foreign affairs:

> In the enthusiasm of political campaigning, candidates for the presidency commonly promise things that are simply beyond the realm of possibility or would have unhappy effects or seem silly if honest efforts were exerted to carry them out. These situations often develop simply through lack of knowledge of the relevant facts, lack of understanding of the full ramifications of an issue, or partisan disparagement of the achievements of the predecessor administration.[2]

This should hardly be surprising. While all serious candidates are motivated to seek the presidency because they believe they can best govern the nation, they know that they will only have that opportunity if they can get elected. And all of them are confronted with a core dilemma: strategies conducive to getting elected may be inconsistent with wise policymaking once in office.

Dean Rusk, secretary of state under Kennedy and Johnson, once dismissed the significance of campaign promises. As he put it: "I've never heard anybody say, 'let's get out the party platform and see what it has to say about this.' These are quadrennial wonders and that's the end of it as far as policy is concerned."[3] It's questionable whether this cavalier dismissal of campaign rhetoric was justified even in Rusk's time. But today, when the 24/7 news cycle means every word spoken by a candidate is recorded for posterity and is often available in searchable form on the Internet, candidates are more inextricably tied to their promises than ever before. Moreover, as the American presidential election cycle gets longer, candidates are giving more speeches and making more promises. "Campaign promise creep" has become an increasingly important factor in the policymaking of new administrations. It is easier than ever to "catch" a politician who has not followed through on a campaign promise or a public pledge.[4]

The pressure to implement campaign pledges can introduce a harrowing set of constraints that confounds a new administration during its early days in office. The promises and slogans of the campaign can bind the hands of a new administration—its "thrust and tone" are based in many ways on the campaign.[5] A new president enters office fresh from the campaign trail, possessed by the sentiment, "We said this, so we have to do it." And his staff and advisers, often drawn from the campaign team, share this sense of personal commitment.

But however strong and central the campaign commitment, the incoming administration faces two, often inter-related problems. As experienced observer and practitioner David Gergen has observed, "Campaign promises often do not stand up well when they collide with reality." In addition, the new administration has to decide how much political capital it is prepared to expend to achieve its campaign promises—and at what cost to other, arguably equally important, campaign goals—in the face of resistance by the vanquished party. So what does a new president do in this circumstance? One option is to stand firm and push for the promised policy regardless. This can help a president look principled and resolute and can build support among the party's base, but could lead to early setbacks and trigger a costly political battle that hampers the ability of the president to succeed on higher-priority issues. The alternative is to defer or abandon the promise. This of course risks leaving the new administration looking irresolute, weak, and cynical, but avoids what might have been a substantive and political debacle in the crucial early months of governing.

Two of Carter's campaign promises illustrate this dilemma. Carter's campaign commitment to follow through on negotiations for a Panama Canal treaty turned into a top foreign policy priority once he took office, despite vehement congressional opposition and even some questions among his own advisers. Zbigniew Brzezinski, Carter's national security adviser, stated that the administration turned "immediately" to the canal treaty and that he thought the benefits of the treaty were worth the political cost.[6] Although the treaty, in which the United States agreed to give up control over the canal by the year 2000, ended up passing, Carter's devotion to this one piece of his campaign platform drained his administration of political capital with Congress early in his term. During the campaign he had also pledged to withdraw some U.S. combat troops from South Korea. But after much internal debate on the contours of American policy toward Korea, plans for withdrawing U.S. Army forces from the Korean peninsula were shelved—and Carter appeared vacillating and indecisive.

History vividly demonstrates the risks that highly specific campaign promises pose to subsequent conduct of national security policy, yet candidates continue to make them. At least eight factors explain why candidates systematically over-promise (and later under-deliver) on foreign policy commitments despite the best of intentions.

1. Sharpening differences

Political campaigns are often about "sharpening differences" that have the effect of eliminating nuance between the political candidates and their competing policies.[7] When presidential candidates run for office, they try to draw distinctions not only between each other, but also between themselves and the current administration. The challenger's strategy often comes down to an approach that denigrates everything that has come before, hypes the dangers of current policies, and offers appealing, often simplistic alternatives to the messy complexity and unsatisfactory compromises of real-world policy. These black-and-white contrasts can be effective in motivating supporters, but occasionally carry high costs.[8]

Sometimes these positions are drawn from ideological differences, like Reagan's opposition to détente, while at other times they are drawn from stark disagreements about the facts on the ground, like Eisenhower's criticism of Truman's China policy. Some differences are more heartfelt; others are more tactical.

A strategy of "contrast" is not always confined to the opposition party. Sometimes even candidates from the same party as the incumbent use their presidential campaigns to distinguish themselves from their predecessors, particularly when the policies of their predecessor have proved unpopular, as Vice President Bush did with respect to Iran-Contra in 1988 and as Senator McCain has done regarding President Bush's policy on climate change in the 2008 campaign. On the other hand, the incumbent administration or the incumbent party has powerful incentives to tout its achievements, downplay its mistakes, and focus on the dangers of change represented by the challenger. Thus the battle lines are sharply drawn.

This binary positioning immediately tests the newly elected president because, unlike campaigning, governing is about trade-offs and constraints—trade-offs between competing interests and objectives, and constraints imposed by resource limitations and other hard realities, even for the leader of the world's only superpower. In foreign affairs especially, presidents have to be flexible enough to adapt to complex and changing circumstances, which they often find they exercise less control over than they think.

While those involved in governing have to maneuver through these dynamic circumstances with nuanced and sometimes imperfect policy solutions, on the campaign trail silver-bullet solutions are particularly attractive. The latter are easy to explain; they resonate with voters hoping for a situation to be resolved quickly, and have the additional advantage that they cannot be proven wrong until they have actually been tried and found wanting. Examples of silver bullets are legion—Eisenhower's promise to "go to Korea," Nixon's secret plan to end the Vietnam War, and Clinton's commitment to stopping the killing in Bosnia, to name just a few. In practice, however, the range of options is often far more limited than it may appear to those on the outside.

But when incumbents challenge the "realism" of silver-bullet solutions, challengers can simply resort to criticizing the incumbent for lack of conviction, courage, or even imagination. Obstacles, such as the opposition of key allies to the proposed solution or the risks of unintended consequences, are often dismissed as mere excuses for inaction or incompetence.

2. Incomplete or inaccurate information

Campaign promises may be predicated on imperfect or even incorrect information and assumptions. Campaigns by definition do not have access to the full range of information available to the incumbent administration, a problem that is particularly acute in the national security realm, where considerations of classified information and sensitive diplomacy limit what can or will be shared with challengers. Even when campaigns are supported by seasoned national security experts (with significant previous experience), inevitably they are less up to date than those currently serving in government.

Whether the United States faced the prospect of a Soviet numerical advantage in strategic nuclear missiles, for example, became a campaign issue for Democrat John F. Kennedy in 1960. It turned out that the "missile gap" was a myth. Although some argue that Kennedy's use of this issue was simply a political play, there is strong evidence that it was based on a genuine, though inaccurate, assessment of the facts.

Despite the now long-standing practice of offering intelligence briefings to candidates, the disconnect between the knowledge of the challenger and that of the incumbent can be substantial. Such briefings tend to be limited to laying out intelligence rather than policy initiatives, and sensitive information is usually withheld, ostensibly to protect existing presidential prerogatives, delicate negotiations, or secret undertakings.

Challengers themselves have an incentive to limit the amount of information they receive, so as not to be hamstrung on the campaign trail out of fear of being accused of disclosing classified information. Candidate Reagan initially shunned intelligence briefings to maintain his freedom to criticize Carter.[9] Similarly, in 1988 Governor Michael Dukakis declined to be briefed on classified information related to Iran-Contra for fear that the knowledge would limit his ability to criticize the Reagan administration's efforts. Finally, in some cases, challengers' campaigns have feared that the incumbent would deliberately provide tilted or tainted information to undercut the challengers' claims.

3. Interest group politics

Campaigns seek to achieve an electoral majority by cobbling together coalitions of voters with diverse but highly specific interests. The candidates have powerful incentives to meet the demands of key interest groups and to support their very concrete priority agendas. Often these commitments get little attention during the campaign itself, because the issues pressed by these groups have only limited salience to the public at large. Party platforms, for example, which cater to the attentive and highly motivated few, are rarely read or taken seriously by the wider electorate. But once in office, the interest groups quickly move to collect on the commitments, and the public may become aware, for the first time, of just what was promised. Candidate Clinton's commitment to change policy on gays in the military is one example of a campaign pledge that was important to a small but highly motivated voting bloc, but got little attention from the wider electorate until after his election.

This problem is perhaps less acute in national security policy than for domestic issues, but the problems arise nonetheless, particularly where there are strong constituencies, such as the efforts of Americans of East European origin to promote "captive nations" resolutions during the cold war or advocates of legislation to condemn the actions of Turkey in the early 1900s as the "Armenian genocide." In these cases, only a few Americans have a strong stake in opposing the campaign pledge, yet implementing it can cause complications in sensitive foreign policy areas once a candidate becomes president.

Candidates are also seduced by the allure of campaign promises for which the benefits are highly concentrated and the costs are widely diffused. Trade policy offers the most prominent example of this pitfall. Because small, concentrated, and well-organized groups bear the brunt of the costs of liberal trade, while the benefits are spread imperceptibly across large numbers of Americans, candidates often succumb to industry and labor union pleas by promising to "protect American jobs" as a means of securing political and financial support.

But once in office, the president-elect has to worry not only about the effects on the American economy of promoting protectionist promises, but also about the impact on relations with key allies and trading partners. Other countries' views figure little during the campaign (since they don't vote), but take on much greater significance when the new administration turns to them for support on national security priorities. Candidate Clinton's stinging critique of President Bush's policies that encouraged overseas investment by American firms is only one in a long line of trade-related campaign pronouncements that had to be rethought after he entered the White House.

The impact of interest groups and focused constituencies is particularly powerful in the period leading up to the selection of the party nominees. The primary and caucus processes tend to give significant influence to well-organized constituencies who can mobilize voters at a stage when much of the American public has yet to "tune in" to the election. These constituencies are important in helping to mobilize volunteers and generate financial support at a crucial early stage. When there are multiple candidates, these constituencies can help foster a bidding war between rival candidates, throwing their support behind the candidate who offers the most unequivocal commitment to the group's agenda. Interest group "questionnaires" are a staple of the primary process, as each group seeks to elicit from the candidates specific policy commitments in return for endorsements. These constituencies often lose some of their influence in the general election because they have nowhere else to go, but the commitments they secured during the primaries can have long-lasting impact.

4. Tougher-than-thou syndrome

Fourth, there is a systemic bias in presidential campaigns for challengers to demonstrate that they are "tougher" than the incumbent or the other contender. This oft-repeated pattern is driven by two factors. First, the incumbent is burdened by a record that is replete with compromises and at best only partial successes in achieving the administration's stated objectives. The challenger, by contrast, can simply assert that by pursuing a clearer, principled line the United States can prevail without the need for messy compromises. Second, a challenger almost always has less foreign policy experience and fewer national security credentials than the incumbent and thus needs to establish the ability to stand up to adversaries, maneuver on the international stage, and defend the national interest.

This tendency for the challenger to seek to "out-tough" the incumbent can be seen in virtually every election since the end of World War II. In 1952 Eisenhower campaigned against the Truman administration's failures in China and Korea and its inability to roll back Soviet advances in Eastern Europe.[10] In 1960 Kennedy lambasted the Republican administration for the missile gap, the communist takeover in Cuba, and its weaknesses in the face of China's challenges to Taiwan over Quemoy and Matsu. Stanley Hoffman, a distinguished expert on American foreign policy, noted:

When the irresponsibility is, so to speak, marginal, ironically it matters more: where posturing in favor of "liberation" can obviously mean nothing but a choice between world war or stepped-up propaganda, the desire to be "tough" in a less impossibly risky way may commit a candidate far beyond his intentions. Candidate Kennedy's strong attacks on Castro and statements in favor of anti-Castro "fighters for freedom" made eventual disengagement from the incipient Bay of Pigs enterprise rather more difficult.[11]

Nixon criticized Johnson for failing to check Soviet nuclear modernization, a refrain echoed twelve years later in Reagan's taunt that Carter had created a "window of vulnerability" that fostered Soviet adventurism in Afghanistan and the Horn of Africa and put the United States at risk of a decapitating nuclear first strike. Reagan also attacked Carter for the Panama Canal "giveaway." Clinton challenged George H. W. Bush for weakness in the face of Serbian aggression in the Balkans and for the failure to defend democratic movements in Ukraine. George W. Bush returned the favor in 2000 by asserting that Clinton squandered American strength by cutting U.S. military forces and intelligence, needlessly involving the United States in "nation building," and taking a "holiday from history" by ignoring the national security challenges facing the United States from Iraq and other adversaries.

Of course, this strategy does not always succeed. In 1988 Governor Dukakis sought to counter Vice President George H. W. Bush's foreign policy experience by arguing that the Reagan administration's focus on nuclear weapons had led to cuts in conventional military forces such as the M-1 tank, but his effort to drive this message home, literally, through a campaign visual of him taking a spin in a tank (in which he was widely viewed as looking ridiculous) backfired catastrophically. And there have also been instances of a challenger taking the opposite tack. In 1976 when President Ford and Governor Carter faced off during campaign debates, Carter scored points by arguing that the incumbent was insufficiently willing to pursue arms control (although this critique sowed the seeds for a different kind of misstep in the early days of the Carter presidency).

5. Values

Closely related to attempts to appear "tough" are campaigns' foreign policy strategies based on "values" and "principles." There is clear campaign appeal in advocating for policy that mirrors the public's view of the United States as a "shining city upon a hill."[12] Similar rhetoric was used in candidate Eisenhower's call for a rollback of Soviet advances in Eastern Europe, Senator Kennedy's commitment to do a better job of defending freedom (encapsulated in his subsequent inaugural address promise to "pay any price, and bear any burden, to defend liberty"), Governor Carter's advocacy of "a government as good as its people" with a foreign policy based on human rights and democracy, and his critique of Ford's campaign statement that Poland was "free"—an important consideration in his electoral victory over President Ford and the "realist" foreign policy of the Kissinger era. Reagan, ironically, turned this against Carter with his own version of standing up to the "Evil Empire." Candidate Clinton's campaign in turn charged that President Bush coddled the "butchers of Beijing" and was timid in supporting the democratic aspirations of Ukraine.

These campaign narratives establish expectations that are difficult to live up to in practice and often end up weakening the credibility of the administration. This can be seen from the earliest days of the Carter administration, when zealous spokespeople began to stake out positions on the new approach to human rights before the new team even had the opportunity to coordinate policy or consult with the affected governments. It was also evident in Clinton's early efforts to address human rights abuses in Haiti and the genocide in Bosnia. President George W. Bush also overtly highlighted religious themes and language in his own campaign, and these sentiments became important ingredients in his worldview as well as in concrete policy strategies, such as his approaches to North Korea and the "global war on terrorism."

6. Shaking up the system

Since incumbents, or incumbent parties, typically have the advantage of "experience," which can be a powerful campaign asset with respect to national security, challengers often tout their outsider status to appeal to voters disaffected with the status quo. This inclination contributes to the "tougher-than-thou" and "values" pronouncements discussed above, and also leads to promises to change the way business is done in Washington. While this impulse may be less strong on the national security side, it has reared its head in a number of forms, such as promises to reform the military procurement system and end so-called gold-plated weapons systems (Democratic candidates routinely attacked President Reagan for a wasteful defense buildup featuring $435 claw hammers and $640 toilet seat covers). It has also tempted candidates into pledges about slimming down the bureaucracy.

One of the classic and oft-repeated examples of attractive but ultimately shortsighted campaign pledges is the vow to reduce the size of the White House staff, including the National Security Council. While these promises often make a splashy one-day news story and appeal to the public's view that the bureaucracy is bloated, the operational price paid by an administration once it has taken office is far out of proportion to the minuscule, if any, savings achieved. In practice, after taking office, administrations have either quietly shelved the commitment or resorted to accounting tricks to achieve the semblance without the substance. Closely related is the recurring campaign commitment to eliminate specialized foreign policy positions such as special emissaries and policy czars. Other problematic institutional commitments include those to restore Cabinet governance, diminish the role of the White House, and reestablish the primacy of the secretary of state—promises that most presidents, with the rare exception of Eisenhower, quickly abandon, and that some, such as Reagan, drop in the first days of the new presidency.

7. Hypothetical questions

The pressure to make concrete campaign commitments is reinforced by the media, which seek to pin down candidates on their positions in hopes of generating controversy and thus news. One of the most dangerous forms of this tactic for presidential contenders is the constant pressure to respond to hypothetical questions. Candidates are put on the spot and pressured into making improbable speculations based on artificial factual premises with virtually no time to prepare a thoughtful response, let alone time to consult experts and evaluate the costs and benefits of various options. This is most evident in foreign policy, when candidates are frequently challenged to make explicit exactly when they would authorize the use of force.

In 1988, for example, Governor Dukakis was regularly pressed to clarify his position on the use of nuclear weapons, leading to a short-lived firestorm when his language seemed to suggest he might be prepared to use nuclear weapons "preemptively" against the Soviet Union. In 1992, in response to a hypothetical question about the treatment of Haitian refugees, candidate Clinton appeared to imply that his administration would take a more open-minded view of granting widespread amnesty to the thousands fleeing the tragic economic circumstances and political repression by boat. These off-the-cuff responses to hypothetical questions set the stage for a foreign policy crisis early in the Clinton presidency.

8. Foreign policy think tanks

Finally, the proliferation of foreign policy–oriented think tanks has also contributed to the proliferation of campaign commitments. These institutions not only generate policy ideas that offer substantive advice for the campaign, but also employ former and future senior officials who provide ongoing advice on a nearly full-time basis for the campaigns. For better or worse, there is a deep mutual interdependence between the campaigns and the "idea factories." The candidates need fresh ideas to capture the attention of the press and distinguish themselves from their opponents, and the think-tankers need vehicles for promoting their cherished policy projects. The result is a proliferation of often highly detailed position papers that may receive little formal attention from the candidates themselves, but that become part of the baggage (or, on the flipside, part of the innovative policy proposals) that a successful candidate brings to office.

Managing Campaign Promises during and after the Campaign

As the foregoing discussion makes clear, the pressure to make campaign commitments is not likely to disappear. Indeed, in some respects that is the whole point of the campaign—to give the American people a sense of the candidate's goals and objectives and to illuminate the choice between the two candidates. Campaign promises also introduce an element of accountability into the political process: if candidates were free to promise and renege, then campaigns would be little more than a popularity contest.

Thus the challenge in the first place is for candidates to meet the public's legitimate need to understand the policy positions of a future administration without backing into commitments that cannot be honored and that may create a dangerous Hobson's choice: honor an unwise pledge with potential harm to national security or abandon it and damage trust in the new president, which would not only bring domestic political costs but could also affect the president's international credibility.

Over the past decades, we have seen candidates employ various strategies designed to gain the benefits of campaign promises without making the kinds of specific commitments that would unduly tie the hands of a new administration. Perhaps the classic case was candidate Eisenhower's approach to the Korean War. In a now famous speech on October 24, 1952, he promised to go on a fact-finding mission to the Korean peninsula to determine the best course of action.[13] As Eisenhower later wrote in his memoirs, "I announced my intention, if elected, to go to Korea before the following January and to determine for myself what the conditions were in that unhappy country."[14] However, he did not promise anything specific about ending the Korean War. It was unclear whether he intended to end the war by ratcheting up hostilities, drawing down, signing a deal, or pursuing another option. This approach allowed him to look robust to a Republican base worried about the spread of communism and wary of looking weak.[15] Yet when active hostilities concluded with an armistice in July 1953, Eisenhower got credit as a peacemaker rather than criticism for letting the communists off easy. His personal credibility on military issues likely played an important role in avoiding a campaign rhetoric trap that might have felled just about any other candidate.

Campaign commitments related to wars have often posed particularly great challenges for candidates. In 1968 candidate Nixon tried to square the same circle by pledging, if elected, to end the Vietnam War.

His refusal to specify the details of his proposal, ostensibly for fear of revealing his plan to the North Vietnamese, led some to call his pledge Nixon's "secret plan."[16] The 1968 Republican campaign platform included a promise to "sincerely and vigorously pursue peace negotiations."[17] The absence of details, however, allowed Nixon to appeal to war-weary Americans without alienating those who continued to believe that victory was vital to U.S. national security.

Henry Kissinger, national security adviser during Nixon's first term and an opponent of rapid troop withdrawals, later wrote about how Nixon altered his initial plan after taking office:

> The Nixon Administration entered office determined to end our involvement in Vietnam. But it soon came up against the reality that had also bedeviled its predecessor. For nearly a generation the security and progress of free peoples had depended on confidence in America. We could not simply walk away from an enterprise involving two administrations, five allied countries, and thirty-one thousand dead as if we were switching a television station.[18]

Hemmed in by his campaign promise, Nixon did increase the pace of troop withdrawals, but not at levels the public expected. Nixon's failure to specify exactly how he would end the war in the 1968 campaign probably saved him politically at the end of the day, since he had not committed himself to a specific course of action that he then had to reverse. Despite the fact that the war continued four years later, in violation of Nixon's most important foreign policy promise of the 1968 campaign, Nixon still managed to win reelection over Democratic candidate George McGovern. In the long run, however, Nixon's lack of candor about his handling of the war (including the secret war in Cambodia and the attempt to suppress the Pentagon's account of U.S. policy—the so-called Pentagon Papers) contributed directly to his political downfall.

Decisions about whether to implement campaign promises can play an important role in shaping public perception of a new president, and if mishandled, can impair a president's effectiveness from the outset. During the 1992 campaign, candidate Clinton promised to end ethnic cleansing in Bosnia by, inter alia, gaining UN approval for air strikes against the Serbs. But after taking office, Clinton found fierce opposition by NATO allies to that proposal, and U.S. policy sputtered for two years at considerable cost to both U.S. and NATO credibility until a more aggressive approach was finally implemented in 1995, leading to military action against Serb aggression and ultimately the Dayton Peace Accord.

Since campaign commitments are inevitable, one of the greatest challenges of a new administration is skillfully extricating itself from unwise commitments once the realities of office set in. Perhaps the most well known example is Kennedy's handling of the "missile gap." In 1957, after the Soviet Union launched *Sputnik,* the first manned spacecraft, a blue-ribbon committee first headed by H. Rowland Gaither released a report that claimed the United States faced a potential strategic threat over the next several years as the Soviet Union brought more strategic missiles online. An early advocate of the Gaither report, which became public despite the best efforts of the Eisenhower administration, was John F. Kennedy, who charged that the report showed the United States was losing the missile and space race with the Soviet Union, creating a "missile gap" that put American security at risk.[19]

President Eisenhower rejected the conclusions some had drawn from the report, which he claimed were based on faulty evidence and logic.[20] In a highly publicized speech on February 29, 1960, Kennedy made the missile gap a critical campaign issue, arguing that it would weaken American security in the coming decade and that the United States needed a "crash program" to fix the strategic imbalance the Eisenhower administration had allowed to develop.[21] While Eisenhower officials announced throughout 1959 and 1960 that they had new intelligence evidence demonstrating that a missile gap did not exist, Kennedy dismissed those reports as biased, claiming that unbiased private estimates and many military leaders sided with his interpretation.[22]

After the election, Kennedy then had to confront his missile gap commitments head-on. He asked Jerome Wiesner, his new science adviser, to examine the evidence. Wiesner reported to Kennedy in February 1961 that, in rather stark contrast to his campaign rhetoric, the missile gap did not exist. According to a 1982 interview with Wiesner, "[The] new president greeted the news with a single expletive 'delivered more in anger than in relief.'"[23] For a short period Kennedy appears to have prevented the news from becoming public. However, analysts across the government were coming to similar conclusions about the nonexistence of the gap, including Secretary of Defense Robert McNamara, who told a reporter in the same month, without consulting the president, "There is no missile gap." Later in the same week, Kennedy said that McNamara had misspoken and that the Defense Department was conducting an in-depth study of the matter.[24]

When completed in the summer of 1961, the new intelligence report showed that indeed the alleged missile gap did not exist. The United States had even maintained a substantial degree of nuclear superiority over the Soviet Union. This placed Kennedy in a political jam. The issue he had used repeatedly to bash the Eisenhower administration and bolster his credentials as a defense hawk was based on a faulty premise. So instead of implementing a major change in the nuclear modernization program foreshadowed in the campaign, the Kennedy administration simply increased funding to Eisenhower-era programs. The issue then faded somewhat from the public eye. As *New York Times* columnist Hanson Baldwin wrote at the time:

> The term "missile gap" was quietly, though unofficially interred last week. The latest intelligence estimates, compiled by all the services (the Strategic Air Command was the only holdout), agree. . . . by year's end the United States might well have more than Russia. Thus an "issue," which played a major part in the last Presidential campaign was finally declared—as many had long claimed—not to be an issue at all. What has changed in the past year is not finished hardware; there has been no miraculous speedup in our missile program or a slow down in the Russian build-up. Only opinions have changed. The Democrats now are in power and early studies of all available missile data by Secretary of Defense Robert S. McNamara and his assistants led last winter to the conclusion that there was no real "missile gap" impending. Mr. Kennedy has never repudiated his pre-election "missile gap" statements, but both he and his Administration have carefully refrained from restating them.[25]

Interestingly, as Kennedy began to think about his reelection in 1962, he worried that the missile gap issue would come back to haunt him and seemed genuinely concerned about why he had been wrong. He asked National Security Adviser McGeorge Bundy for a history of the issue so he could figure out why he had been incorrect and design an appropriate political response when the time came in the 1964 campaign.[26]

In another instance of a president skillfully extricating himself from a campaign pledge, Eisenhower was able to repudiate his campaign promises to reject the Yalta agreements and roll back Soviet gains in Eastern Europe. Eisenhower's promises emerged out of the fiercely contested 1952 Republican primary between Eisenhower and Senator Robert Taft, which reflected a deep divide between the more moderate wing of the Republican Party, represented by Eisenhower, and Taft's more isolationist, unilateral wing. Eisenhower triumphed, but at the cost of rhetorically accepting some of Taft's ideas. Both Eisenhower and Taft then turned to the secretary of state, John Foster Dulles, to write the new Republican foreign policy platform, which featured a promise to roll back the advances of communism.[27]

Once in office, Eisenhower soon came to recognize that implementing a policy of rollback would involve enormous costs and grave risks. Rather than abruptly announcing a rejection of the campaign promise, during his first months in office Eisenhower set up what became known as the Solarium Project, in which three competing national strategies, including rollback and a version of the Truman era containment strategy, were fleshed out and presented to the new president and his advisers. In the end, Eisenhower adopted NSC 162/2 as the national security policy, which did not differ in its core respects from the approach of his predecessor. Although critics from the right continued to assail Eisenhower for weakness, the skillful handling of the policy shift, combined with Eisenhower's own considerable credibility, allowed Eisenhower to escape with little damage at home or abroad.

A more troubled effort to deal with a campaign commitment involved President Clinton's experience with the gays-in-the-military issue. In the 1992 presidential campaign, Clinton promised to lift the restriction on homosexuals serving openly in the U.S. military. He first announced his promise not in a formal policy statement, but during an

October 28, 1991, speech at Harvard University in response to a question from a student about the issue. Clinton stated: "I think people who are gay should be expected to work, and should be given the opportunity to serve the country."[28] Clinton initially made the promise to gay activists during the Democratic primary campaign when he was trailing Paul Tsongas and Jerry Brown. Although Clinton would not support the top priority of gay and lesbian groups, the passage of a civil rights bill, he strongly supported military integration and received in return the strong support of gay and lesbian voters and interest groups.[29] However, the issue was not a particularly prominent one on the campaign trail.

After the election, Clinton told NBC correspondent Andrea Mitchell at a Veterans Day event that he intended to follow through on his campaign promise and lift the ban on gays in the military. Clinton's Veterans Day comments ignited a controversy over the issue, as veterans' groups and conservative commentators came out strongly against his proposal.[30]

Once in office, wrote political observer Elizabeth Drew, "Clinton and his aides were struggling to figure out how to act on his campaign promise to issue an executive order lifting the ban on gays serving in the military."[31] Military opposition quickly became public. William T. Corbett, a retired army colonel, criticized Clinton's proposal and described the political cost in *USA Today*:

> President Clinton's promise to legalize military service for gays could be a goof of "read-my-lips" magnitude. Military professionals say lifting the ban on homosexuals will severely impair discipline, morale and effectiveness, and 90% of all ranks who reacted to Army and Air Force Times editorials endorsing gays in the military expressed strong opposition.[32]

Colin Powell, the chairman of the Joint Chiefs of Staff, took a personal interest in the policy proposal. He resisted Clinton's attempt to compare the situation of gays in the military to that of blacks before Truman's executive order forcing military integration in 1948, and Powell directly warned Clinton in a meeting during the transition that the issue was very controversial.[33]

The issue dominated newspaper headlines and talk radio after Clinton's inauguration, while Senator Sam Nunn, who had warned Clinton away from the position during the campaign, held hearings and questioned the wisdom of revoking the ban.[34] This outcry placed Clinton in a precarious political position. In a speech on January 29, 1993, Clinton delayed resolving the issue, announcing that Secretary of Defense Les Aspin would study the best way to lift the ban on gays in the military and present him with a proposed executive order in July.

Clinton's dilemma was compounded by controversy over his decision to abandon his campaign promise on a middle-class tax cut. One Democratic senator said, "A lot of people can't understand why he's breaking his promise to the middle class and fulfilling one to gays."[35] In the interim between January and July, Clinton and his advisers attempted to come up with a compromise. Clinton's lack of experience dealing with military issues, combined with strong congressional opposition, overwhelmed his administration.

At the end of the day, Clinton announced a policy called "Don't Ask, Don't Tell" on July 20, 1993, which prohibited the military from asking service members about their sexual orientation but stated that openly gay or lesbian members of the military would be thrown out. He tried with little success to claim he had fulfilled his pledge at least in part, but the policy reality, especially after Senator Nunn and his allies legislatively tightened "Don't Ask, Don't Tell" in the following months, was very different.[36] Clinton thus achieved the worst of both worlds. He had not steadfastly followed through on his campaign promise, and he had failed to get the support of the military or conservative groups for his policy shift, both of which made him look weak. Over time, Clinton and his team worked hard to build stronger ties with the Pentagon and the military, but this process was much more difficult than it needed to be because of early missteps related to an ill-calculated campaign promise.

Some areas of national security policy seem to generate a chronic problem of mismatch between campaign pressures and governing realities. China policy stands out prominently in this regard. Ever since the communist takeover in 1949, candidates have found it difficult to resist the siren song of tough promises to reverse their predecessors' soft approach. Eisenhower attacked the Truman administration for "losing China" and promised to remove the Seventh Fleet from its spot between Taiwan and China, which many had argued "protected" mainland China from an invasion. Kennedy sharply criticized Eisenhower's weak response to the crises over mainland China's shelling of the Kuomintang-controlled islands of Quemoy and Matsu. Reagan called for closer, more formal security ties with Taiwan following Carter's normalization with China. Clinton attacked Bush senior for his handling of the 1989 killings in Beijing's Tiananmen Square and called for linking extension of China's most-favored nation (MFN) trade status to China's human rights record. George W. Bush rejected Clinton's aspirations for a strategic partnership with China and pledged to treat China as a "strategic competitor." Yet in every case, once taking office, the new president found himself adopting policies that bore a remarkable resemblance to those of his predecessor—a dramatic illustration of governing realities intruding on intended policies. While it is impossible to quantify the precise harm that these repeated reversals caused, there seems little doubt that, at least in U.S. dealings with Chinese leadership, the credibility of U.S. threats was seriously undermined.

Summing Up

No campaign is immune from the pressures to make risky or imprudent promises on the road to the White House. How well they are handled depends on a constellation of factors, including the candidate's own experience (which may lead to greater sensitivity to the danger of unrealistic or unachievable commitments and thus provide greater insulation from accusations of "weakness"), the salience of foreign policy issues during the campaign, the degree to which the press focuses attention on them, and the relative influences of foreign policy advisers and senior campaign staff (giving them a stronger or weaker voice when campaign tactics are being debated). Because the pressures are so great, new administrations will invariably face the need to adjust their positions once in office. The record of recent history suggests that early recognition of potential problems and quick action to right the course is the most effective way to handle the challenges.

It is worth reiterating that the pressure to make concrete commitments is not necessarily undesirable. Indeed, it is these promises and details about future policies that help convince the American public to vote for a candidate in the first place. And if elected, an empty national security platform would deprive the incoming president of any claim to a policy mandate. As presidency scholar Patricia Conley has remarked: "Mandate claims are statements that the public wants a major policy change. The president's capacity to achieve his policy goals is enhanced if the conventional wisdom attributes his victory to his policy positions."[37]

Indeed, some commentators have suggested that the problem of foreign policy and elections stems not from too many concrete commitments, but from too few. Harvard professor Stanley Hoffman described foreign policy rhetoric in presidential campaigns in 1968 in a way that still resonates today. He wrote: "Given America's world position and the nature of American aspirations, the candidates have a kind of rivalry in the promotion of lofty ambiguity; both will be for peace, and both will favor a patriotic posture, strength, and opposition to communism. . . . During the campaign, the danger for foreign policy does not lie in its being unattended but in its being attended in rather sorry fashion."[38]

THE RIGHT STAFF

I N MODERN TIMES, the preparatory period between the election and the inauguration has been dominated by three main challenges: *people, process,* and *policy.* During this time, the new president must begin choosing key personnel to staff the Cabinet agencies and the White House, decide how to organize the basic decisionmaking machinery of government, and choose which policies to pursue during the first months in office and how to prioritize them. Each of these challenges is formidable, and each has contributed to the difficulties that new presidents have encountered in their early days in office. This chapter examines how administrations from Truman to George W. Bush have staffed their top national security posts and seeks to distill lessons learned that could inform future transitions. The following two chapters examine process and policy, respectively.

One distinctive feature of the American presidential transition is the drama surrounding the selection of the president's Cabinet and key advisers. Unlike in many parliamentary systems, where the identity of the Cabinet is decided before the election by the identification of "shadow ministers," in the United States presidential candidates rarely tip their hand in advance. Thus almost from the moment a winner is declared, there is a frenzy of speculation about who the key officials will be. And in the hierarchy of personnel choices, identifying key national security officials has traditionally been one of the priority tasks of a president-elect. As the United States has taken on growing global responsibilities since World War II, the incoming president has typically felt considerable pressure to announce the administration's national security team early in the transition. This is seen as a way of demonstrating to allies that American leadership is reliable while cautioning foes that the nation is prepared to handle any challenge. There is a domestic political imperative to act quickly, as well as a desire to reassure the American public that they have elected someone decisive and up to the task of governing.[1]

Nonetheless, the process often takes time. Among post–World War II presidents, only three have announced a major national security appointment in the first month of the transition. Eisenhower announced his secretaries of state and defense on November 20, 1952; Richard Nixon named Henry Kissinger as national security adviser on December 2, 1968 (the only time a national security adviser was announced before the Cabinet appointments); and George H. W. Bush announced his selection of James Baker as secretary of state on November 10, 1988, a decision he communicated to Baker two days before the election.[2]

The rest took longer to make their announcements. Some have announced their selections as a largely complete team. As noted above, Eisenhower named his secretaries of defense and state together on November 20, 1952. Both Nixon and Reagan named their choices for state and defense in the sixth week, while Clinton made his choices known in the seventh week, after announcing his economic team in the sixth week.[3]

Those who made individual announcements typically led with the secretary of state. Kennedy named Dean Rusk as secretary of state on December 12, 1960; Robert S. McNamara as secretary of defense on December 13; and McGeorge Bundy as national security adviser on December 29.[4] Carter was early in naming his secretary of state, Cyrus Vance, on December 3, 1976, followed by Zbigniew Brzezinski as national security adviser on December 16, and Harold Brown as defense secretary on December 21, 1976.[5] George W. Bush announced General

Colin Powell as his choice for secretary of state on December 16, Condoleezza Rice as national security adviser a day later, and Donald Rumsfeld to head the Defense Department on December 29, 2000.[6]

As the national security establishment expanded during the cold war, the number of officials subject to "discretionary appointment" grew substantially, extending beyond the familiar Cabinet positions of secretaries of state and defense, director of the CIA (now director of national intelligence), and national security adviser, to their deputies, under secretaries, and scores of assistant secretaries.[7] With the growing complexity and interdependence of national security issues in the post–cold war world, the range of positions that arguably compose the national security universe has grown to include officials at Treasury, Office of Management and Budget, Justice, Commerce, Energy, and even Health and Human Services. Staffing these offices is a daunting task under the best of circumstances, and because many of these officials are subject to congressional confirmation, identifying candidates for these positions must be done quickly to allow time for formal vetting first by the executive and then by Congress to have a team in place by inauguration day.[8]

The impetus to move early on national security appointments will arguably be even stronger in the future, as the prospect of a terrorist threat or a sudden crisis early in a new administration puts a premium on having important personnel in place. The attack on the World Trade Center in February 1993 (a month after Clinton took office) may have been a harbinger of future crises that will confront a newly installed president. This imperative will add to the pressure to select even more national security personnel during the transition to staff the Department of Homeland Security, the intelligence agencies, and the White House. For this reason, some commentators have suggested an expedited vetting process (both within the executive branch and by Congress) for senior national security officials.[9]

The combined impact of the pressure to act early, the number of appointments that need to be made, and the growing complexity of the vetting process have led most candidates to begin a preliminary personnel vetting process even before the election. Indeed, in the case of Reagan and George H. W. Bush, the head of the transition was chosen precisely for his expertise in personnel matters. In rare instances, this has led to the selection of key officials even before the election, although they are often officially announced afterward.

For the most part, however, this process of preliminary, preelection vetting has played only a limited role for at least four reasons. First, the individuals who run these processes are rarely those with the greatest influence on the future president's decisionmaking. Some have had ties to the candidates, but most were chosen for their experience in personnel management, rather than in politics and governing. Thus during the 1980 campaign, the personnel operation was handled by Pendleton James, and in 1988 the same role was played by Chase Untermeyer, both of whom were professional experts on personnel issues.

In other cases, the transition managers have had stronger political ties to the candidate, but those ties created suspicion and mistrust between the transition team and the campaign organizations, with campaign officials eager to limit the influence of the transition team, lest the campaign team be shut out of the personnel decisionmaking after the election. The most prominent example of this approach was the decision by Governor Carter to appoint Jack Watson, a trusted adviser, to handle transition planning during the campaign, which led to intense conflicts with Hamilton Jordan (who subsequently became Carter's chief of staff) and the campaign staff. The conflicts carried over in a very visible way into the transition itself.[10] Similarly, in 1992 Governor Clinton tapped his campaign chairman, Mickey Kantor, to run transition planning while easing Kantor out of a day-to-day role in the campaign because of frictions with key campaign advisers such as James Carville and George Stephanopoulos. This move created deep tensions between the transition operation and the campaign.[11]

Second, candidates have a considerable interest in not prematurely narrowing the field of potential appointees. After all, they will want to maximize support from influential individuals who make up the pool of future senior officials. Keeping hope alive for the greatest number of aspirants to office is one important way to increase the number of individuals vigorously supporting the candidate. This is particularly important in the national security arena if the challenger lacks direct national security experience and is at pains to demonstrate credibility on security issues by pointing to the backing of prominent individuals with foreign policy or military expertise. One example of such a strategy was the endorsement of Governor Clinton by Admiral William Crowe, chairman of the Joint Chiefs of Staff under President Bush senior and a widely respected military leader and defense policy expert. The so-called Vulcans, a group of experienced foreign policy practitioners, played a similar role for Governor Bush in 2000.[12] These individuals can often prove effective surrogates for the candidate during the campaign, penning op-eds and articles in newspapers and influential journals, briefing reporters, and speaking to interested audiences such as World Affairs Councils.[13]

By attracting a wide range of supporters without settling on appointees, candidates hope to burnish their credentials without having to "own" any baggage associated with controversial positions taken by individual advisers. Conversely, if the candidate names key officials before the election, there is a risk that the putative nominees, not the candidate, will be become the focus of political attention, with the danger that the scrutiny will center on areas of controversy rather than strength.

Third, candidates may worry that voters will view early decisions on Cabinet appointments or other positions as taking the outcome for granted, with a possible blowback that could actually jeopardize electoral success. Ironically, this risk is greatest for a frontrunner, who might otherwise have the clearest incentive to accelerate the staffing process. Some have suggested that Governor Thomas Dewey, for instance, hurt his election prospects in 1948 by prematurely selecting appointees for his expected administration.[14] Although in principle this process could take place below the public radar, in practice the risk of leaks discourages action on this front. Some observers also suggest that some candidates are even "superstitious" about preelection transition thinking.[15]

Finally, early winnowing of high-ranking personnel usually takes a backseat to competing demands on the candidate's time. During the campaign every moment is precious, and candidates and their schedulers are deeply reluctant to budget any time for activities other than those directly connected to getting elected. Given all of these factors, although there are undoubtedly fleeting discussions around potential appointments during the campaign, the choices have rarely received sustained serious consideration from the candidate.

The net result is that in the immediate aftermath of the election the president-elect is likely to be presented with a rather lengthy list of lightly vetted possibilities for senior positions and therefore must turn quickly to sorting out these critical choices in the early postelection period.[16]

Who to Pick: Loyalists, All-Stars, Worthies, and Holdovers

Broadly speaking, four types of individuals will form the primary pool for staffing the national security establishment. The first type, "loyalists," consists of those who were actively involved in advising and supporting the candidate during the campaign, either as formal members of the campaign staff or as part of a broader network that includes members of advisory task forces. The second group consists of foreign policy "all-stars," who include former government officials and military officers and experts at think tanks and universities who may have had little or no contact with the campaign or candidate, but who are widely recognized as knowledgeable in their fields. The third group, "worthies," consists of influential leaders, especially current and former members of Congress, but also individuals from the private sector who may have had limited foreign policy or national security experience but are otherwise respected for their judgment or management skills. Finally, "holdovers" are senior officials from the outgoing administration (including career officials) who may or may not have strong personal ties to the candidate. Holdovers are more common in same-party transitions but played a role in at least in one post–World War transition (Eisenhower to Kennedy).

Each of these types of individuals offers distinctive advantages and disadvantages as the president-elect sets about choosing key officials. The loyalists are likely to have already established a good working relationship with the president-elect, to share the new president's views on significant foreign policy issues, and, by definition, to have demonstrated their loyalty. But these very virtues also have a downside in the danger of "groupthink" and a willingness to defer to, rather than challenge, the policy impulses of the president-elect. Because the advisers are to some extent volunteers, they are not necessarily the best suited or best qualified for government positions. At the same time, many potentially effective officeholders may have remained aloof from the campaign either because they initially supported other candidates or because of work or other competing commitments. Finally, because campaign advisers have been active in what are usually highly partisan campaigns nowadays, their ability to build bridges to the opposition party may be compromised.

The all-stars are the mirror image of loyalists. Appointing "national treasures" to senior positions signals a transition away from winning the election to governing in the public interest and may help facilitate bipartisan cooperation since these individuals are not tainted by the adversarial campaign. But there is a considerable corresponding downside. Although all-stars may be viewed as the most knowledgeable or best qualified for high government office, their lack of a previous working relationship with the candidate and an unknown level of commitment to the president-elect's programs means that the decision to appoint them is something of a gamble.

These problems may also afflict a decision to appoint worthies, with the further complication that a lack of substantive work in the field may make it even more difficult for them to perform effectively on the job, especially at the outset.[17] Like the all-stars, worthies instantly add an element of gravitas to the new administration. And if they have strong Washington ties and the accompanying political savvy, they may be able to facilitate bipartisan cooperation and work the system more effectively than the national security all-stars.

The appointment of holdovers offers an important opportunity to sustain continuity, which may appear attractive in times of crisis, but immediately raises questions about loyalty to the new administration and risks undercutting the honeymoon period for the president and his new team. In addition, it is often difficult to integrate the holdovers with the newcomers.

Team Dynamics

Closely related to the kind of men and women to choose for various jobs is what qualities or synergy the president should seek in national security appointments as a whole. Put another way, to what extent does the president-elect focus on selecting the right individual for a job versus focusing on the entire ensemble? Some presidents have presented their selections as a team (by announcing the appointments at the same time, for example), but whether the synergies and complementarities actually drove the initial selections is somewhat harder to discern. Nixon and Clinton announced their secretaries of state and defense at the same time, but Nixon tapped Kissinger to be national security adviser a week before the Cabinet announcements.[18] Thus, while Nixon's Cabinet was a team, the earlier selection of Kissinger seemed designed to signal that it was merely a "B" team.

By contrast, Carter announced Vance approximately two weeks before Brown and Brzezinski, while Reagan announced Defense Secretary Caspar Weinberger about a week before Secretary of State Alexander Haig and two weeks before National Security Adviser Richard Allen.[19] It is thus not surprising that both administrations were plagued by deep divisions among key advisers.

Over time, presidents have adopted various strategies to finding the right balance between the different types and backgrounds of their advisers. Most modern presidents have opted for a mix of the different types, although the composition of the mix has differed considerably from administration to administration.

HARRY S. TRUMAN

Upon assuming office, Truman initially decided to keep the Cabinet members he inherited from Roosevelt in their original posts. Because he had spent most of his life in Missouri and in the U.S. Senate, his circle of personal contacts from which to draw suitable appointees for high national security office was limited.[20] In the words of one of his biographers, the fact that "Truman himself seemed to many to have no political future beyond that of caretaker for the balance of FDR's fourth term" resulted in "a dearth of volunteers who were both eager and able to take over the field command posts in the new Truman army."[21]

But Truman ran into an immediate problem with this approach to presidential staffing: the dubious loyalty of the prior Cabinet. Some of its most important members thought they, rather than the inexperienced Truman, should have been president. Truman reciprocated some of these negative feelings, which may have reflected acute perceptiveness or petty jealousy. Less than three months after assuming the presidency, Truman had replaced a majority of his Cabinet officers.

Once Truman concluded that he could not effectively govern with holdovers, he turned to a group of worthies to fill key posts. Truman's own lack of experience and the desire to reassure the American people led him to seek out individuals with Washington credentials. In July 1945, Truman appointed the venerable politician James F. Byrnes as secretary of state.[22] Although Byrnes could hardly be characterized as a national security all-star, he did offer what appeared to be an important element of national security experience: Byrnes had attended the February 1945 Yalta Conference.[23]

As with many appointments of worthies, Byrnes's lack of obligation to, and close personal relationship with, the president created tensions as Byrnes increasingly acted on his own initiative and with limited coordination with the White House.[24] Not surprisingly, Truman's choice for his third secretary of state reflected a very different approach: the choice of a national security all-star, General George C. Marshall.[25]

It is perhaps no accident that the major national security achievements of the Truman administration were not secured until Truman finally found a group of individuals with whom he could work effectively and who were prepared to take on the challenges of the emerging cold war order. The tandem of Marshall and Truman, supported by key aides such as Dean Acheson and George Kennan, helped fashion the institutions that shaped America's long-term strategy—from the Marshall Plan to containment. Yet the delay in putting together an effective team not only opened the door to important Soviet advances in the early years after World War II, but also heightened the domestic political tensions that plagued Truman during the Korean War.

Dwight D. Eisenhower

Eisenhower's approach to the selection of his national security team was heavily influenced by his background as a military officer. Eisenhower was an unconventional candidate, with almost no prior political background and a campaign that was largely fueled by his war hero status and his own expertise in national security affairs. As a result, he became president without a coterie of campaign advisers with claims to office or a group of personal loyalists outside the military.[26] Instead, Eisenhower engaged his friends, General Lucius Clay, chairman of the board of the Continental Can Company, and New York attorney Herbert Brownwell, to help him find suitable candidates. He ultimately turned to an all-star, John Foster Dulles,[27] and a worthy, General Motors president Charles Wilson,[28] as his two primary national security Cabinet selections.

These selections illustrate both the strengths and the weaknesses of each type of appointment. In the case of Dulles, his stature and expertise gave him considerable clout but also considerable independence in the conduct of foreign policy, which often created frictions in the administration. Wilson's lack of foreign policy experience and expertise marginalized him within the councils of power. Although Eisenhower himself had clear ideas about the nature of the U.S. role in the world and the dangers and limits of military power, the fact that his principal advisers were not close confidants meant that there was often a disconnect between Eisenhower's own vision and the policies carried out by his administration.

Eisenhower complemented these high-profile national security appointments with staff appointments that drew more directly on close personal loyalties, in particular Chief of Staff Sherman Adams and military aide Andrew Goodpaster, as well as Robert Cutler, the first special assistant for national security affairs.[29]

JOHN F. KENNEDY

One of the most prominent examples of a decision to retain senior officials was made by the Kennedy administration—somewhat surprising given the sharp critique Kennedy offered of Eisenhower's national security policies. Kennedy retained Allen Dulles as director of the CIA and appointed Eisenhower's under secretary of state for economic affairs, C. Douglas Dillon, as Treasury secretary. It is instructive that both the greatest debacle and the greatest success of the Kennedy transition are associated with these two holdovers: Dulles for his role in the disastrous Bay of Pigs operation, and Dillon for the successful management of the balance of payments crisis.[30]

In carrying over Dulles, Kennedy was deprived of the fresh look that an incoming senior official would have given to the plans of his predecessor—someone who would have been as inclined to challenge as to accept the approach of his predecessor. In Dillon, Kennedy got credibility in implementing a shift of policy that he had already decided on before taking office and the cover associated with having that shift carried out by a senior official from the previous administration.[31]

Kennedy's administration is also notable for having ushered in the idea of appointing academics to key national security positions, a practice continued by most subsequent presidents. Kennedy's team was a blend of individuals with whom he had already developed personal relationships, such as McGeorge Bundy, and those who were highly regarded for their intellect, such as Dean Rusk and Robert McNamara.

In staffing his Cabinet, Kennedy benefited from his tactic of not committing to potential Cabinet appointees during his campaign. Theodore Sorensen, former special counsel to President Kennedy, wrote that this lack of political debt reflected Kennedy's choices for his Cabinet.[32] Kennedy felt free to bypass nationally known figures in favor of lesser-known ones. Although Kennedy reportedly considered several worthies for secretary of state, including former governor and presidential candidate Adlai Stevenson (who was ultimately made U.S. ambassador to the UN), Chairman of the Foreign Relations Committee William Fulbright, and former U.S. representative Chester Bowles, he ultimately chose the more academically inclined Dean Rusk, who also had substantial State Department experience in the Truman administration.[33]

After the Bay of Pigs fiasco, Kennedy supplemented his group of intellectuals with close political loyalists, most notably his brother, Attorney General Robert Kennedy, and White House aides Ted Sorensen and Kenny O'Donnell, both of whom played critical roles in resolving the Cuban Missile Crisis.[34] Ironically, and somewhat uncharacteristically, Kennedy chose to replace the holdover CIA Director Allen Dulles not with an intellectual or a crony, but with a quintessential worthy, John McCone, a Republican with prior service in the Truman and Eisenhower administrations.[35]

Kennedy's decision to place loyalists in key positions arguably facilitated the kind of candid dialogue and deep examination of alternative options that led to the creative resolution of the Cuban Missile Crisis, something that might have been more difficult if the level of trust had been lower (as it was, for example, with members of the Joint Chiefs). But the selection of the "best and the brightest" may have led to some overconfidence in what America could achieve in Southeast Asia and other remote outposts of the cold war, such as British Guyana, through rigorous analytic planning that ignored the messiness of the real world at home and abroad.

LYNDON B. JOHNSON

Unlike Truman, who quickly discarded the staff he inherited from his deceased predecessor after initial disappointments, Johnson kept many of Kennedy's appointees for years after his transition. He retained Kennedy's core national security team, including Dean Rusk, Robert McNamara, McGeorge Bundy, Assistant Secretary of State William Bundy, Deputy National Security Adviser Walt Rostow, and Under Secretary of State for Economic Affairs George Ball. Johnson also retained the White House staff that had worked for Kennedy, along with the staff that he had employed as vice president.

One reason for this embrace of continuity in staffing may have been that Johnson's lack of confidence in national security made him reluctant to overrule the presumed superior expertise of his senior staff.[36] At least during the transition period, Johnson felt less sure of himself on foreign policy matters than he did with respect to domestic affairs.[37] Johnson later concluded that he had made a mistake in not replacing the team he inherited from Kennedy with his own set of advisers. Over time, he increasingly relied on a group of loyalists.[38]

Johnson's heavy reliance on holdovers undoubtedly made it more difficult to give serious consideration to a radical departure in U.S. policy on Vietnam. Too many of his top officials had already settled in their own minds that the course embarked upon was a necessary one. And as the administration moved forward, the engagement in Vietnam deepened, the domestic conflict grew, and the tensions between the loyalists and the holdovers led to tensions over the policy as Johnson sought to find a way out through negotiations without appearing to show weakness.

RICHARD M. NIXON

President Nixon turned to Henry Kissinger (who was actually considered much closer to Nixon's political rival, Nelson Rockefeller), an all-star rather than a loyalist, to be his national security adviser. Kissinger, of course, followed in the line of Bundy and Rostow as an academic national security expert. In addition, Nixon appointed worthies in former attorney general William Rogers for State and U.S. Representative Melvin Laird for Defense. Laird's appointment was driven in part by a desire to neutralize congressional opponents to Nixon's policies. These two appointments signaled Nixon's clear intention to conduct foreign policy himself. Nixon implemented his approach of centralized control over national security policy and an abiding belief in the importance of secrecy and surprise to achieve his objectives through his reliance on his national security adviser, culminating in the unique arrangement in which Kissinger ultimately served as both national security adviser and secretary of state.

GERALD R. FORD

Like Truman and Johnson, Ford was faced with the challenge of reassuring both the nation and the world following the untimely departure of his predecessor. But unlike those two previous transitions, and in light of Nixon's political disgrace, Ford was faced with contradictory pressures both to preserve continuity and to break with the past—pressures that were accentuated by his decision to pardon Nixon. The most prominent element of continuity was the retention of Henry Kissinger as secretary of state and, for a time, as national security adviser. At the same time, Ford sought to establish his own identity by appointing staff members who were loyal to him. Integrating the two presidential staffs proved difficult. Ford also used a "kitchen cabinet," comprising friends and former congressional colleagues, to supplement the viewpoints provided by his senior staff. It included a former governor, representatives of business and industry, and officials from previous administrations.[39]

It was not until late October 1975 that Ford moved to shake up his foreign policy team. In a reorganization known as the "Halloween Massacre," Ford replaced three of the four top foreign policy officials. He fired James Schlesinger as secretary of defense and replaced him with Donald Rumsfeld, a former member of Congress who had become Ford's chief of staff. He fired William Colby as director of the CIA and replaced him with the U.S. envoy to China, George H. W. Bush. He also stripped Henry Kissinger of his dual role as national security adviser and secretary of state, transferring the former position to Kissinger's National Security Council deputy, Lieutenant General Brent Scowcroft. The Ford administration thus reflected a mix of loyalists, such as Rumsfeld, worthies, such as Bush, and all-stars, such as Scowcroft.

Ford's brief tenure makes it difficult to judge the impact of his personnel decisions. It was clear that, by the end of 1975, Ford hoped to establish a clear contrast with the politically discredited approach of his predecessor by pursuing a more collegial style of national security decisionmaking, drawing on his own congressional experiences and those of key aides. But he was outflanked on the change issue by Governor Carter in the 1976 campaign. One important legacy of the Ford years was the rise to prominence of many individuals who would become prominent all-stars in populating future administrations, such as Cheney, Rumsfeld, and Scowcroft.

Jimmy Carter

During the 1976 campaign, Governor Carter, running as the Washington outsider, seemed to promise a radically new approach to staffing his national security team. Carter's aide, Hamilton Jordan, was so convinced by Carter's rhetoric about getting new people into national security positions that he said in an interview: "If after the inauguration you find a Cy Vance as Secretary of State and Zbigniew Brzezinski as head of National Security, then I would say we failed. And I'd quit. But that's not going to happen. You're going to see new faces, new ideas. The government is going to be run by people you have never heard of."[40]

But the campaign rhetoric quickly gave way once the transition began and, ironically, Carter turned to the very people that Jordan had disdained. Like Kennedy, Johnson, and Nixon, Carter selected a university professor, Zbigniew Brzezinski, as national security adviser, but unlike Kissinger, Brzezinski carried additional cachet as a "loyalist," having served as an early foreign policy mentor to the governor and having played an active role in Carter's campaign.[41] Carter turned to a cast of worthies to fill the top jobs at the State Department, including prominent lawyers Cyrus Vance (who had served in the Pentagon under Kennedy and Johnson and thus could be considered an all-star) and Warren Christopher (deputy attorney general under Johnson). For defense, Carter chose another national security all-star, Harold Brown, who had served as secretary of the air force.

Carter relied heavily on Georgia lawyer Charles Kirbo, who was known to be Carter's "one-man kitchen cabinet," to help him select his senior national security staff.[42] Kirbo met with powerful Washington lawyers, heads of lobbying groups, and people in Congress to ask their opinions regarding who would be good candidates to become secretary of state, secretary of defense, and other key appointees. Kirbo and other senior advisers would then narrow down the list. Carter then proceeded to personally interview the top contenders, about three to six candidates per Cabinet post.

Carter and Kirbo's lack of Washington experience may have contributed to the most damaging personnel decision made during the Carter decision, the nomination of Ted Sorensen as director of the CIA, despite objections from conservative Democrats that Sorensen lacked relevant experience for the post. Rather than risking a bruising confirmation fight, Carter pulled the nomination and nominated a national security all-star, Admiral Stansfield Turner, to the job.[43]

The tensions between Vance and Brzezinski from the outset of the Carter administration can be attributed in part to the different relationship the two had with Carter before taking office, accentuated by the ongoing proximity of Brzezinski to the president by virtue of his position at the White House. The tensions infected almost every aspect of national security policy, from how to handle the Soviet Union and arms control to who was responsible for developing and implementing China policy to the most well known case, the conflict over whether to undertake the Iran hostage rescue, which Vance opposed. The infighting not only limited the Carter administration's ability to articulate and implement a clear and consistent foreign policy, but also accentuated Carter's own inclination to involve himself in the day-to-day details of policy.

The Carter administration was also the first administration in which the vice president played a significant and ongoing role in national security policy. The selection of Senator Walter Mondale as Carter's vice president served traditional political purposes (northerner to balance southerner, Washington insider to complement outsider), and also gave a measure of foreign policy expertise to the ticket. Once in office, Mondale played an active role in national security affairs, as did his own adviser, David Aaron, in the position of deputy national security adviser. Mondale played a central role in a variety of administration endeavors, including arms control and alliance management in Europe and Asia. He also was an invaluable sounding board for a relatively inexperienced incoming team on how institutional Washington might view a prospective policy proposal or initiative. Mondale also traveled widely for ceremonial purposes. His strong and deep ties to Capitol Hill and the Democratic Party establishment kept lines of communication open on difficult issues such as the Panama Canal treaty negotiations. Mondale created a modern precedent for an activist vice president and two subsequent vice presidents, Al Gore and Richard Cheney, who assumed central roles in the formulation and execution of American foreign policy.

RONALD REAGAN

Reagan's appointments were unique in the exceptionally strong role given to key campaign staff. Most notable was the decision to give his California confidant, Edwin Meese III, "counselor" to the president, the coordinating role for national security, despite his lack of any significant experience in that arena and the subsequent appointment of Caspar Weinberger at Defense. Similarly, the choice of California friend and campaign chairman William Casey to be director of the CIA was another example of the decision to prioritize personal connection over expertise and national security stature. (Casey had served as deputy to William Donovan in the Office of Strategic Services (OSS) during World War II but had little involvement in national security issues after the war.) Reagan did appoint two well-known national security all-stars to top positions, Richard Allen at the NSC and General Alexander Haig at State. Allen, like Brzezinski, had played an active role in the campaign, while Haig was a classic all-star, with no real prior relationship with the president. But both were quickly marginalized and replaced by individuals with strong California connections: Judge William Clark at the NSC and George Shultz at State.[44]

Reagan's selection of George H. W. Bush as his vice president can also be seen as part of his strategy in assembling a national security team. Like Carter and Mondale, he was heavily influenced by traditional ticket-balancing considerations, but one of those considerations was Bush's foreign policy expertise (China, United Nations, CIA). But unlike Mondale, Bush played a relatively minor role under Reagan on national security, a reflection of the dominance of campaign loyalists (after all, Bush was Reagan's rival for the nomination). Bush's outsider status was perhaps most vividly illustrated by his claim that he was "not in the loop" in connection with Iran-Contra.

Reagan's personnel selections illustrate both the benefits and the costs of heavy reliance on campaign insiders to dominate national security decisionmaking. The loyalists were highly focused on the campaign message. Indeed message, as embodied in the person of close aide Michael Deaver, was central to the Reagan approach. This produced strong discipline and great triumphs, both in Reagan's early budget victories and in cultivating the image of a strong and confident leader. But when it came to substance, the loyalists' lack of foreign policy expertise and strong ideology over time resulted in serious blunders and blinkered decisionmaking culminating in the Iran-Contra fiasco.

GEORGE H. W. BUSH

Bush's foreign policy appointees were friends from his campaign or long-time trusted associates who had served with him under Reagan or Ford. Part of the reason for this was Bush's near obsession with keeping loyal friends around him. He once said, "I would hate to be President without friendships . . . not just the loneliness of it, but the barrenness of it."[45] The result was a foreign policy team dominated by the moderate wing of the Republican Party.

Within twelve hours of his election, Bush had nominated James Baker to be his secretary of state.[46] In his memoir, Bush recalled that the decision "was what we call in golf a 'gimmie.'"[47] Baker was Bush's closest friend, having worked with Bush since 1970 when he ran Bush's campaign for Senate. Baker also served as campaign manager in the 1980 and 1988 presidential campaigns, and he had important experience as Reagan's chief of staff and secretary of the Treasury. Baker had domestic experience to be sure, but was not familiar with or fluent in foreign affairs. However, Bush did not view this as a problem, because Bush himself was so adept at foreign policy.[48] Furthermore, Baker was regarded as the "ultimate pragmatist" and was respected for his keen political sense and problem-solving skills.[49] Unlike some of the other advisers who served under Reagan, Baker was considered open to compromise. He also had extraordinary political skills and knew how to drive a foreign policy agenda through obstacles and difficulties.[50] The press and Congress worked well with him, and they appreciated his pragmatism. Baker managed to maintain bipartisan support in Congress through most of his tenure.[51]

Overall, the foreign policy team Bush chose during the transition proved to be competent and cohesive. More than any other president during the post–World War II period, Bush selected his senior advisers because of their ability to function collectively as a team. There were no internal schisms like those between Kissinger and Rogers, Vance and Brzezinski, or Weinberger and Shultz. However, some were concerned that the team was too homogeneous and tight-knit. There were no paralyzing divisions, but there was also very little argument or debate. Bush's appointment of a collection of largely like-minded thinkers made innovation in policymaking difficult at a time when many believed the new landscape of the postwar world demanded it.[52]

The Bush transition was a blend of continuity and change. Bush retained some members of President Reagan's Cabinet, including Richard Thornburgh at Justice and Nicholas Brady at Treasury, and others who had served in different capacities during the Reagan years. But even the holdovers were chosen more because of long personal association with the vice president and his team, and thus they could also be considered loyalists. Several (such as Scowcroft and his deputy, Colin Powell) fit into the category of all-stars, having served prominently in the national security establishment. In addition, the initial Bush selections did feature prominent worthies, including Senator John Tower (who, although he had served as a political mentor to the vice president, was not part of his inner circle) and his subsequent choice for defense secretary, Richard Cheney (who had been chief of staff to Ford and a member of Congress). Ironically, it was the failed confirmation bid of Tower, the classic Washington insider, that caused Bush his costly early defeat. Bush's decision not to retain more Reagan appointees caused considerable friction during the transition, as many of the Reagan team assumed that because the transition was an intraparty affair (with a sitting vice president taking office) it would be characterized by more continuity than change, an expectation that was quickly dashed.

Unlike his two predecessors, given his own national security background, Bush felt little need to take national security considerations into account in his choice of vice president, Dan Quayle, who was unfavorably compared with his two predecessors in this respect.

Bush's selections have important lessons for future presidents. On the one hand, his approach, which was to combine the strengths of loyalists and all-stars, created a cohesive team that shared the president's outlook and had the president's confidence. Bush had a strong enough sense of his own needs and inclinations to risk the tensions associated with ousting Reagan officials in order to get people with whom he could work well. On the other hand, the team's strengths—its personal and ideological cohesiveness—limited its ability to tackle unfamiliar issues that fell outside their shared national security experience.

BILL CLINTON

Clinton came into office acutely aware of his lack of foreign policy experience. As a result, he sought to appoint experienced foreign policy advisers to key posts. Clinton tapped old friends and associates from his 1992 campaign for a small number of key, but low-profile jobs and coupled them with high-visibility appointments of all-stars and worthies. The former group included Samuel "Sandy" Berger at the NSC and "Friend of Bill" Strobe Talbott at State. In the latter category were three all-stars/worthies: former deputy secretary of state Warren Christopher for secretary of state,[53] House Armed Services Committee Chairman Les Aspin for secretary of defense,[54] and James Woolsey as director of the

A massive throng of reporters crowds the Oval Office as Harry S. Truman holds his first press conference on April 17, 1945, after Franklin D. Roosevelt's death in office. (Corbis)

President-elect Dwight D. Eisenhower, with General Douglas MacArthur and John Foster Dulles behind him, emerges from Dulles's home after a strategy session, January 1, 1953. (Alfred Eisenstaedt, Time Life Pictures/ Getty Images)

During the presidential transition, President Dwight D. Eisenhower and President-elect John F. Kennedy meet with their cabinets, January 1, 1961. (Ed Clark, Time Life Pictures/ Getty Images)

Vice President Lyndon B. Johnson takes the oath of office on November 22, 1963, aboard *Air Force One* after the assassination of John F. Kennedy. Jacqueline Kennedy and Lady Bird Johnson are by his side. On the far left, seated in back, is Jack Valenti. (Corbis)

President-elect Richard M. Nixon and President Johnson meet reporters in front of the West Wing on November 11, 1968, after a two-hour policy briefing with Johnson's top advisers. Both men expressed their intent to cooperate with each other during the transition period. (Bettmann/Corbis)

President Richard Nixon meets with Henry Kissinger in the Oval Office on October 15, 1971. Kissinger held concurrent appointments under Nixon as both national security adviser and secretary of state. (Wally McNamee/Corbis)

Vice President Gerald Ford is sworn in as president on the day of Richard Nixon's resignation, August 9, 1974. (Wally McNamee/Corbis)

On November 5, 1976, President-elect Jimmy Carter, followed by his press secretary, Jody Powell, and chief of staff, Hamilton Jordan, carries transition books from his mother's summer retreat, following a meeting with thirty-four newspaper, television, and wire service reporters. (Bettmann/Corbis)

Heads of the Ford and Carter transition teams meet at the White House on November 5, 1976, to begin the task of turning over the reins of leadership from the Ford administration to that of President-elect Jimmy Carter. Left to right: John Marsh, counselor to President Ford and head of the Ford team; Richard Cheney, White House chief of staff for Ford; and Jack Watson, head of the Carter transition team. (Bettmann/Corbis)

President Carter holds an impromptu conference on November 8, 1979, with his top two foreign policy advisers, Secretary of State Cyrus Vance (left) and National Security Adviser Zbigniew Brzezinski. The latter remained close to Carter throughout his term, while the former was increasingly sidelined. Vance resigned in 1980, Carter's last year in office, after an aborted mission to rescue American hostages in Iran. (Bettmann/Corbis)

President Carter points out some of the sights on the White House grounds, November 20, 1980, to President-elect Ronald Reagan during Reagan's first visit to the executive mansion since defeating Carter. (Bettmann/Corbis)

President-elect Ronald Reagan meets with his top economic advisers at the Los Angeles Federal Building, November 16, 1980. Reagan is flanked by, beginning from the left, Walter Wriston, Milton Friedman, Daryl Trent, George Shultz, and Alan Greenspan (to Reagan's left). The group put the finishing touches on a new economic policy, which they presented to Reagan as in keeping with his campaign promises. (Bettmann/Corbis)

President Ronald Reagan stands to the right of George H. W. Bush, then vice president but soon to be president, and Dan Quayle, vice president-elect, outside the Oval Office on the day after the 1988 presidential election, November 9. (Wally McNamee/Corbis)

President George H. W. Bush greets President-elect Bill Clinton on November 18, 1992, as he arrives for his first postelection visit to the White House. Bush and Clinton conferred in the Oval Office, while three aides from each camp met to discuss the transition. (J. David Ake/AFP/Getty Images)

President-elect Bill Clinton sits with General Colin Powell in Washington, D.C., November 19, 1992. Powell's appointment under George H. W. Bush extended through the early months of Clinton's first term. At the meeting, Powell warned Clinton—unsuccessfully—against rapidly implementing his controversial campaign promise allowing gays to serve openly in the military. (Cynthia Johnson/Liaison, Getty)

A reporter for BBC-TV waits on November 27, 2000, in the Presidential Transition Team Welcome Center in Washington, D.C. During the controversial 2000 presidential election, the center sat vacant while a clear winner was determined. (Reuters/Corbis/William Philpott)

CIA.[55] In selecting his national security adviser, Clinton followed the model of most of his recent predecessors by turning to someone with strong academic credentials, Anthony Lake.[56] Lake had served as an important campaign adviser, but was a relative newcomer to the Clinton inner circle, having been brought into the campaign by Sandy Berger, who had been Lake's deputy during the Carter administration and a lifelong friend of the president and first lady. Clinton rounded out his team with the appointment of Madeleine Albright as the Cabinet-level ambassador to the United Nations. Albright's appointment combined many features that were appealing to Clinton, including a strong campaign association and thus was a "loyalist" (Albright had hosted a series of foreign policy dinners for Governor Clinton at her Georgetown home) and all-star national security experience and expertise (she had served on the Carter National Security Council and was a professor at Georgetown University); in addition, she helped Clinton make good on his commitment to diversity in his Cabinet selections.[57] Although Mickey Kantor and his team had done some preliminary work on appointments before the election, much of this work was discarded as Clinton personally engaged in extensive vetting of his Cabinet during the transition period.

Although the group was announced as a team, the mix proved an awkward concoction. The worthies were quickly marginalized, in part because the administration was dominated in the early days by political advisers in the White House, who were more focused on the president's domestic agenda, and because their more conservative views were out of step with the president's own instincts.[58] Aspin and Woolsey were the first to depart. Over time, the trusted loyalists with strong personal ties to the president and a shared outlook on national security, particularly Berger and Talbott, and later Albright, played increasingly influential roles.

Clinton, like Carter and Reagan, used his vice presidential selection to buttress the ticket's foreign policy credentials, and this choice had significant consequences for the operation of the national security team. Although Gore and Clinton did not have strong personal ties before his selection (and Gore thus could be considered an "all-star"), the close bond they developed during the campaign helped strengthen Gore's influence in the new administration, including the placement of Gore's close adviser Leon Fuerth as a member of the "principals" committee.

Clinton's personnel selections in some respects mirrored those of Reagan: many of the personnel occupying the principal national security positions had neither a strong personal connection to the president-elect nor a cohesive sense of what U.S. national security objectives should be. This lack of cohesive vision and weak connections to the president led to considerable turmoil in the first year, as policy options were constantly adopted and revised and setbacks ranging from Haiti to Somalia to the Balkans challenged the administration's ability to show strength and conviction in its approach to the world. Over time, two important developments took place. Clinton himself gained confidence as he gained experience, allowing for stronger leadership of the team from the top. A second wave of personnel with both foreign policy expertise and strong personal connections to the president assumed more influential roles in the administration. The result was a far more cohesive and effective policy in the second term.

George W. Bush

Like Clinton, George W. Bush followed a mixed pattern in choosing his key national security officials, appointing campaign confidant and former academic Condoleezza Rice as national security adviser, and all-stars Colin Powell (and as his deputy Richard Armitage) and Donald Rumsfeld (and as his deputy Paul Wolfowitz) to the jobs of secretary of state and secretary of defense. The Rumsfeld appointment was particularly interesting because it resulted from complex jockeying within the administration, with Vice President Dick Cheney prevailing in establishing his old boss at the Pentagon (in this sense, the Rumsfeld appointment had some of the elements of a campaign loyalist pick, although here the tie was to the vice president rather than the president).[59] It was also noteworthy that at least some influential campaign advisers were shunted aside, most notably Robert Zoellick, who had to be content with the consolation prize of U.S. trade representative.[60]

The Bush team included one surprising holdover in CIA Director George Tenet. The decision to keep him may be attributable in part to respect for the views of the elder Bush (a former CIA director) who had advocated depoliticizing the CIA (Tenet had served both as Clinton's CIA director and earlier as Democratic staff director on the Senate Intelligence Committee).[61] Although a clear outsider in a group with strong (if often conflicting) past connections, Tenet moved quickly to gain acceptance as a Bush loyalist, but ultimately paid the price for his outsider status by taking the blame for Iraq-related intelligence failures.

Like the three governors who preceded him, Governor Bush also turned to a foreign policy all-star to be his vice president. The selection of Cheney (Bush 41's secretary of defense) as well as Powell (chairman of the Joint Chiefs under Bush 41) was striking in view of indications during the campaign that the younger Bush would seek to distance himself from his father's administration. The choice of Cheney proved perhaps the most fateful of all the selections, particularly following 9/11, when Cheney's strong personal convictions, experience, bureaucratic skills, and ties to the "neo-con" wing of the Republican Party gave him influence with the president at a time when Bush's own lack of experience made him particularly dependent on others. At the same time, the closest Bush 41 loyalists (Scowcroft and Baker) were notably absent from the Bush 43 administration.

The George W. Bush experience may be the most dramatic illustration to date of the difficulty of trying to mix loyalists and all-stars. The frictions between Powell and his team at State on one side, and Rumsfeld and Cheney (supported by Rice) on the other, plagued the administration from its earliest days and led to early expectations that Rumsfeld might be forced from office.[62] But 9/11 changed the dynamic, and it was soon Powell and his team who were marginalized. Of course, there was a substantive dimension to the disagreements as well.

In many ways, the most surprising result of the George W. Bush selections was the failure of what was initially perceived as a highly experienced and professional team to appropriately handle one of the most dangerous and tumultuous periods in our nation's history. There are several lessons to be drawn. First, Bush's selections show the limited benefits that derive from the choice of an all-star who lacks strong ties to the president and who therefore is at a substantial disadvantage in influencing policy. Second, it demonstrates that prior government experience in earlier administrations (Rumsfeld, for example, had been out of office since the Ford administration) is of only limited value in tackling a rapidly changing national security landscape—a lesson provided by the Bush 41 example as well. Finally, it is an illustration of the value of strong bureaucratic and political skills even for national security officials, such as Rumsfeld, who like James Baker before him was successful in dominating a divided national security team.

Assessing the Historical Experience

The presidential personnel selections discussed here can be understood in terms of how much administrations relied on loyalists, all-stars, worthies, and holdovers in making their top staffing decisions. The task of managing continuity and change through presidential transitions is complicated by the need for effective interpersonal relationships and for facilitating presidents' own personal styles of management. The complex interplay of these issues manifests itself differently in each case, but there are still broad lessons that can be distilled from past presidents' experiences.

In a few instances, holdovers played an important role in staffing senior positions. The choice to turn to holdovers was, not surprisingly, most common in the three unanticipated transitions: from Roosevelt to Truman, from Kennedy to Johnson, and from Nixon to Ford. Holdovers also played significant but less central roles in the one other case of intraparty transition during this period, from Reagan to Bush.

For most transitions that involved a change of party, there was little interest in retaining the old guard. Instead, these transitions reflected competition between the loyalists, all-stars, and worthies. Although it is impossible to make all-embracing generalizations, it is notable that the new presidents with considerable foreign policy expertise, such as Eisenhower and Nixon, relied the least on campaign aides and personal loyalists. Kennedy falls on the same end of the spectrum—less experienced than Eisenhower and Nixon, but a sitting senator and veteran who had written and thought extensively about national security, and who also brought in many key officials, including Rusk and McNamara, who were not personal confidants. Presidents with much more limited experience, including Governors Carter, Reagan, Clinton, and George W.

Bush, by contrast, placed campaign loyalists in key positions. George H. W. Bush reflected a somewhat unusual approach: he brought considerable national security experience to the office, but nonetheless turned to his own inner circle for most of the top appointments.

An examination of how these national security teams functioned suggests some general conclusions about the do's and don'ts of the appointments process. On the whole, decisions to appoint all-stars or worthies without significant previous personal connection to the candidates has, with the important exception of Kissinger, proved problematic. At best, they have been marginalized or ignored in the decisionmaking process (Colin Powell, Les Aspin, James Woolsey, Cyrus Vance, William Rogers); at worst, they have caused significant disruption as a result of not being seen as team players (Alexander Haig, Donald Rumsfeld). By contrast, the George H. W. Bush team, with close personal ties to the president-elect and with each other, is widely seen as the most effective.[63]

This suggests that, as with a good basketball team, the synergies of the group are an important consideration, and that in selecting senior national security officials the president-elect needs to focus not only on the individual suitability of candidates for each position, but also on how well they are likely to work together. Thus in the Clinton administration, while both Anthony Lake and Warren Christopher played a role in the campaign (and had served together in the Carter administration), their personal chemistry, though not contentious, did not facilitate close working relations between the NSC and State. Ironically, President-elect Clinton stated an explicit desire to choose officials who could work well together as part of policy teams—something he achieved with his economic policy team of Robert Rubin, Lloyd Bentsen, Bo Cutter, and others, but less so on the foreign policy side.[64]

The history also demonstrates the importance of a strong personal chemistry between the president and his team, as well as a basic shared outlook. Despite the potential appeal of holdovers as a way to maintain continuity, in practice these individuals rarely have as much influence as campaign loyalists and are unlikely to have a strong commitment to the president's vision—a problem that burdened both Truman and Johnson. Similarly, a Cabinet of worthies that functions like a board of directors, chosen for diversity and stature but lacking in strong ties to the president, is also at risk of seeming rudderless, especially when the president himself lacks a strong foreign policy vision at the outset, such as Clinton. But even when the chief executive himself has strong experience and inclinations, those may be undercut by a national security team without similar convictions (Eisenhower).

The question of who to pick is, of course, intimately bound up with a president-elect's vision of the processes and procedures necessary for effective decisionmaking. The experiences of administrations past show that interpersonal dynamics can—and should—figure prominently in early decisions about personnel and processes. The following chapter turns to the important task of allocating roles and decisionmaking responsibilities among top staff.

6
STRUCTURAL
IMPERATIVES

THE IMPORTANCE OF selecting an effective team is closely connected to the second key challenge of the transition period, organizing the decisionmaking and policy implementation processes for national security issues. The central role played by a well-crafted structure has been evident since the early days of the cold war, when the National Security Act of 1947 was adopted to provide a mechanism—the National Security Council—for coordinating the newly launched elements of the national security establishment (the Department of Defense, the Joint Chiefs of Staff, and the Central Intelligence Agency), which joined the State Department as its main pillars.

During a transition, the president-elect faces a broad range of options on how to organize the processes of government, since little is mandated by legislation. The approach selected has a profound effect on the new team's ability to govern effectively, particularly in the early months of a presidency. The choices include what mix of formal and informal processes to put in place, whom to include, and the roles and responsibilities of the key players. The challenge of organizing decisionmaking has become vastly more complicated and important as the range of issues related to national security has grown from traditional military and diplomatic problems to include global financial stability, homeland security, energy, the environment, and public health.

There is a voluminous literature evaluating the merits of the approaches taken by chief executives, from Eisenhower's highly formal approach based on the military staff model to the informal approach favored by Presidents Kennedy and George H. W. Bush, who largely dispensed with formal NSC processes in favor of informal decision-making by a closed circle of close confidants.[1] Similarly, a recurring debate about the respective roles of the national security adviser and the secretary of state pits those who advocate placing the secretary of state at the apex of the foreign policy process against those who argue for the primacy of the National Security Council and the national security adviser. Each approach has its strengths and weaknesses. These can be seen dramatically in two cases, Henry Kissinger and Condoleezza Rice, where the same individual occupied each role successively and thus transitioned the government from being NSC-centric to being more dominated by the State Department. There is no single best way, and in different circumstances either approach may be more appropriate, but in any case the process must reflect the needs and style of the individual president. This chapter focuses on how post–World War II presidents have used their transitions to set up the mechanism of governance, and examines how the resulting structures affected the ability of the new administrations to carry out national security policy.

Harry S. Truman

After the death of Franklin D. Roosevelt, Truman inherited an executive staff he considered to be both inadequate and poorly managed.[2] Roosevelt was famous for his flexible and ad hoc approach to policymaking and policy implementation, as well as for promoting rivalries and friction among his senior staff in order to force decisions upward.[3] In contrast, Truman preferred an orderly decisionmaking process with clean lines of authority. He also discouraged rivalries between members of his administration, stressing instead the importance of loyalty to the Office of the Presidency among his Cabinet and staff members.[4]

The early years of the Truman administration were consumed with the struggle to develop a national security policymaking process suited to the United States' new status as a global superpower with significant peacetime national security responsibilities. In contrast with the prewar period during which day-to-day national security issues were dominated by diplomacy (and thus the State Department), there was growing appreciation of the need to better integrate military tools into the planning process. Moreover, the war effort had demonstrated inadequacies in the civilian-military structures on the defense side, with separate civilian authority over the army and navy and no permanent structures for managing intelligence since the disbandment of the Office of Strategic Services. Not until 1947 did Truman succeed in cobbling together a new structure for decisionmaking with the National Security Act of 1947.

Dwight D. Eisenhower

General Eisenhower was the first president to take office after the adoption of the National Security Act, and he proved to be the president most committed to the kinds of formal procedures the act seemed to prescribe for making and coordinating policy. In the 1952 presidential campaign, Eisenhower stated that the NSC would be the primary advisory body on military and international security affairs policy.[5] Once in office, Eisenhower publicly affirmed his use of the NSC as "his principal arm in formulating policy on military, international, and internal security affairs."[6] Eisenhower established the position of special assistant for national security affairs based on recommendations by Robert Cutler, who eventually became his first national security adviser.[7] Unlike in later administrations, the role was primarily administrative, focusing on facilitating the machinery of the NSC rather than serving as an independent source of policy advice.

Eisenhower's approach was heavily influenced by the military staff model to which he had become accustomed during his army service, with an emphasis on inclusive, formal processes backed by extensive staff work. He encouraged debate and wide-ranging assessments of options, but Eisenhower had little tolerance for dissent once a consensus was reached, especially the kind of open feuding he saw in the Roosevelt and Truman Cabinets.[8] Eisenhower had formalized his vision of White House organization before assuming the presidency.

The effectiveness of Eisenhower's approach has been the subject of much debate and controversy. It has been both praised for its rigor and completeness and derided for its excessive formality and lack of flexibility in dealing with fast-moving crises. In practice, the formal mechanism was complemented by informal mechanisms, including private conversations with Secretary of State Dulles, and his use of White House advisers such as General Andrew Goodpaster.[9] In general, the deliberative approach seemed best suited to long-term policy formulation, best illustrated by the Solarium Project, and most challenged in managing fast-developing crises.

John F. Kennedy

Kennedy and his advisers were deeply critical of what they viewed as the overly bureaucratic and formalized approach of the Eisenhower policy-making process.[10] But little was done to put a new mechanism into place during the transition, though Kennedy did swiftly get rid of Eisenhower's Operations Coordinating Board.[11] Their criticisms were reinforced by the Bay of Pigs experience, in which Kennedy believed that he had not been given an adequate range of policy choices, and which led him to adopt a far more informal and ad hoc decisionmaking process that relied on input from key confidants.[12] After the incident, Kennedy shifted his senior NSC staff's offices to the West Wing and also created what came to be known as the Situation Room in the White House to ensure that he would have better access to information and control of operations.[13] The strengths of Kennedy's approach seemed to have been borne out in the far more innovative and successful handling of the Cuban Missile Crisis.

Under Kennedy, Cabinet and NSC meetings were neither regular nor routine. In keeping with the advice of Kennedy family attorney and adviser Clark Clifford, Kennedy preferred to make major decisions with just the key principals present.[14] This philosophy of governance, combined with Kennedy's antipathy toward bureaucratic procedures and bureaucrats themselves, led him to enhance the role of his national security adviser, McGeorge Bundy, who quickly became a key player in developing the Kennedy administration's foreign policy. Under Bundy, the national security adviser's role changed from that of an impartial presenter of policy options to an independent policy adviser who offered his own recommendations: "In effect, Bundy shifted the focus of the NSC staff from being a group of career officials serving the presidency to a personal staff, serving the incumbent."[15]

Not surprisingly, the strengths and weaknesses of the Kennedy approach were the mirror image of the Eisenhower years. Kennedy's reliance on ad hoc mechanisms like the Executive Committee of the National Security Council (ExComm), and his dependence on trusted advisers whose role and importance were independent of the formal position they held in the administration, facilitated candid and confidential discussion and rapid adaptation. However, it also ran the risk of groupthink, as those with different perspectives were not guaranteed a place at the table.

Lyndon B. Johnson

Johnson's approach to national security decisionmaking was heavily influenced by his long career as a legislator. His was the opposite of the Cabinet approach, with a reliance on highly loyal White House staff and a hands-on decisionmaking style that reflected a deep reluctance to delegate. The tension between Cabinet and White House authority was magnified by the fact that the Cabinet was dominated by holdovers, while the White House harbored key Johnson loyalists. Johnson's approach proved highly effective in pursuing his domestic policy agenda, but much more troubled in the national security sphere, where the process tended to shield Johnson from dissenting views and involved him excessively in day-to-day operations. Johnson's preference for informal procedures could be seen in the central role played by the "Tuesday lunches," unstructured meetings with his primary national security staff that grew out of his desire to seek advice about the Vietnam War. Attending regularly were Director of the CIA Richard Helms, Secretary of Defense Robert McNamara, National Security Adviser Walt Rostow, Secretary of State Dean Rusk, and the chairman of the Joint Chiefs of Staff, General Earle Wheeler.[16]

Johnson's approach thus reflected many of the strengths and weaknesses of the Kennedy years, with important new initiatives such as the

Nuclear Non-Proliferation Treaty and the rapid decisionmaking around the Seven Day War in the Middle East, but continuing difficulty accommodating dissenting voices in connection with Vietnam.

Richard M. Nixon

Nixon's determination to run foreign policy from the Oval Office translated into very clear ideas about what kind of processes he did and did not want to employ in formulating national security policy, and over time resulted in a near complete abandonment of the formal decision-making processes contemplated in the National Security Act. Kissinger, along with Goodpaster, developed a formal process for interagency work. Their memorandum laid out the structure that was put in place, which involved eight interagency policy groups, as well as regionally focused interdepartmental groups.[17] Under the plan, approved by Nixon before he met with his proposed NSC principals, the national security adviser would chair most of these groups—a fact that reflected Nixon's desire to ensure that the State Department would not dominate or control the process.[18]

In foreign affairs, Nixon always envisaged himself as his own secretary of state.[19] To this end, he assigned extraordinary powers to White House staff, especially National Security Adviser Henry Kissinger, who codified this approach during the transition in a formal set of procedures for governing the national security process that were adopted at the outset of Nixon's presidency.[20] Although Nixon had indicated that he wanted to reinstitute the formal, regular meetings of the NSC, as a practical matter Kissinger dominated the process, and few real decisions were made through these formal processes.[21]

Nixon's approach was thus the clearest example to date of the benefits and costs of a highly personalized approach that devalued the formal processes of decisionmaking—an approach that fostered bold initiatives and clarity of strategic objectives at the price of excluding the perspectives of other Cabinet members (not to mention Congress and the public). This approach generated dramatic breakthroughs with the opening to China and détente with the Soviet Union, but carried the seeds of its own destruction as the lack of broad-based consensus for policy led to a backlash from the right (for example, on détente and China) and from the left (for example, on the secret war in Cambodia).

Gerald R. Ford

Ford's decisionmaking process was heavily influenced by the perceived flaws of the Nixon era, with its secretive, White House–dominated approach that excluded both key members of the executive branch and Congress. While Ford was committed in principle to returning to a more Cabinet-centric approach (which contributed to the decision in 1975 to remove Kissinger from his White House position), Ford, like Johnson, was also a creature of his legislative experience, which meant reliance on a small number of loyal aides. Ford's preference for low-visibility advisers was reflected in his choice of Brent Scowcroft to succeed Kissinger at the NSC.[22]

Ford's brief tenure makes it difficult to draw many conclusions about his approach to national security decisionmaking. His more open style was welcome in clearing the air after Nixon, but the combination of his lack of strong personal experience, lack of an electoral mandate, and a general degree of fatigue with national security affairs limited the ability of the Ford administration to achieve significant breakthroughs.

Jimmy Carter

Like Ford's, Carter's initial approach to organizing the policymaking process reflected a deep disdain for the secretive, White House–centric model of the Nixon era. As if to drive the point home about strengthening the Cabinet at the expense of the White House, Carter first announced his picks for secretary of state and secretary of defense and waited two weeks before announcing the appointment of Brzezinski as national security adviser.[23] The formal rules for decisionmaking were drawn up by Brzezinski and issued in the first days of the Carter presidency. But continued conflicts among the national security team, coupled with Carter's own tendency to micromanage policy and operations, soon led to a recentralization of authority in the White House and the increasing marginalization of State.[24]

Carter devised his national security decisionmaking structure in collaboration with Brzezinski during the transition, after initially rejecting Brzezinski's first proposal, which had suggested a process with seven committees, three of which (on arms control, crisis management, and sensitive intelligence matters) would report to the national security adviser. But Carter wanted a "simple, cleaner structure," with fewer committees. Carter's desired structure, formalized through a Presidential Directive, involved a Policy Review Committee that would consider issues related to foreign, defense, and international economy policy, and a Special Coordination Committee that covered arms control, sensitive intelligence policy, and crisis management. The fact that Carter and Brzezinski together formulated this plan and only then discussed it with Vance generated tension between Carter's key foreign policy advisers, which would only increase over time.[25]

Ronald Reagan

President Reagan's choice for a decisionmaking process was the flipside of his heavy reliance on long-time friends and advisers at the expense of the national security all-stars and Washington worthies who nominally held key foreign policy positions. Alone among the modern presidents, Reagan did not issue formal rules to govern national security decisionmaking during the first days of his presidency. Indeed, Counselor Ed Meese deliberately shelved the draft plans drawn up by Secretary of State–designate Al Haig during the transition.[26] Decisions on all issues, including national security, were tightly controlled by the triumvirate of Ed Meese, James Baker, and Michael Deaver.[27] National Security Adviser Richard Allen did not even have Cabinet rank or direct access to the president, but reported instead through Meese. Allen himself equated his role with that of the national security adviser under Eisenhower, rather than his more immediate predecessors.[28]

The lack of formal processes, coupled with the limited national security experience of Reagan's top advisers, created havoc in the first year of the Reagan administration. Reagan was isolated from any serious policy debates, and members of the national security team had little clue how or why decisions were made.[29] Although the process began to perform somewhat more smoothly when Judge William Clark replaced Richard Allen in January 1982 and Haig resigned six months later, the process continued to impede effective policymaking through the Reagan administration, leading to notorious conflicts between Secretaries Shultz and Weinberger, surprise policy initiatives like the Star Wars missile defense proposal, and the calamity of the Iran-Contra scandal.[30] Not until the installation of long-time Washington worthy Frank Carlucci as national security adviser did the process finally find its footing.

George H. W. Bush

The organization of policymaking under President Bush benefited considerably from the close personal relations among all the key national security principals. Not surprisingly, given his military background, National Security Adviser Brent Scowcroft moved quickly to put in place a set of formal national security processes based on three levels of decisionmaking: principals (at the Cabinet level), deputies, and assistant secretaries (at the working level).[31] While this process functioned relatively smoothly, in practice it was the informal procedures, set up during the early days and involving Wednesday-morning breakfasts, that became important.[32] The combination of formal and informal procedures, undergirded by the strong personal ties among the principals, made for relatively smooth-functioning decisionmaking machinery. But as noted in chapter 5, some have argued that the flipside was the lack of meaningful debate or consideration of alternatives, which led to a degree of groupthink during a time when the rapidly changing international landscape demanded new thinking.[33]

Although Bush is remembered for being somewhat remote from political considerations in his governing style (which some believe cost him reelection), the foreign policy decisionmaking processes explicitly contemplated involvement with the political side of the house—with Chief of Staff John Sununu and Press Secretary Marlin Fitzwater sitting in on NSC meetings and Deputy Chief of Staff Andrew Card attending deputies' meetings.[34]

Bill Clinton

Despite the very different personal styles and backgrounds of Bush and Clinton, President Clinton adopted, at least on the formal level, a policymaking process that was strikingly similar to that promulgated by President Bush, perhaps reflecting recognition that the processes under his predecessor had worked more smoothly and predictably than those of previous administrations.[35] The Clinton structure was set forth in Presidential Decision Directive 2 (PDD-2), which, like Bush's, provided for a three-layer process.[36] One important difference, however, was the growing centrality of economic issues in the Clinton international strategy, and the concomitant adaptation of the decisionmaking processes to reflect that priority. In particular, Clinton created the National Economic Council (NEC) and designated a national economic adviser, Robert Rubin, with equal status to the national security adviser. To provide better coordination of economic and national security policies and to ensure that economic issues received appropriate consideration in national security decisions, Clinton established a new directorate in the White House, the International Economic Directorate, which reported jointly to the national security and national economic advisers.

Like the Bush administration, the Clinton team supplemented the formal processes with a weekly national security breakfast, involving the national security adviser, the secretaries of state and defense, the chairman of the Joint Chiefs of Staff, and the CIA director (as well as the UN ambassador when in town).

The most important lessons from the Clinton adaptation of the Bush approach was the value added from broadening the national security community to include a wider range of actors and perspectives. Although the effort was a work in progress, Clinton's approach allowed for the flexibility and inclusiveness required to meet changing challenges and devise effective solutions. This adaptation included, in addition to the NEC, the creation of the position of national coordinator for counterterrorism strategy, in 1998, which was first filled by Richard Clarke, and the creation of "dual hatted" directorates for the environment (reporting to the national security adviser and the chairman of the Council on Environmental Quality) and for science and technology (reporting to the national security adviser and the president's science adviser.[37] That more open approach sometimes led to unpredictability and conflict as the number of voices and perspectives around the table grew (for example, during the Asian financial crisis), but it also offered a better way to mobilize all the levers of power available to a U.S. president. These considerations will prove increasingly important in the years to come.

George W. Bush

On paper, the George W. Bush administration adopted procedures that mirrored those of his two predecessors. This might seem surprising given the Bush team's obvious desire to separate itself from both Clinton and George H. W. Bush.[38] But the procedures that had proved a relatively reliable platform for decisionmaking in the two proceeding administrations became little more than a framework for contention under George W. Bush.

There are at least two explanations why this apparently tried-and-true approach broke down. One concerns the deep policy divisions and personal animosities between the principals. Whereas the procedures adopted by Clinton and George H. W. Bush were used by key officials to help narrow differences and foster consensus, under George W. Bush they served only to harden disputes and force every issue to the president for decision. A second is a function of the unique role played by the vice president and his staff in national security policy: a parallel staff process allowed bureaucratic contenders to sidestep the National Security Council process in favor of a decisionmaking route that took the vice president's more hard-line approach.[39]

Another important organizational departure from the Clinton administration was National Security Adviser Condoleezza Rice's decision to downgrade her formal status from the Cabinet rank held by her predecessors and to pare NSC staff by eliminating the public affairs and congressional relations functions. These moves were justified as a way to restore the NSC to its role as coordinator and facilitator of policymaking, rather than acting as an independent source of advice, but the unintended net result may have been to weaken the ability of the NSC to broker disputes among the agencies.

During the transition, the Bush administration adopted its own approach to integrating international economic and national security policy by creating the new position of deputy national security adviser for international economic affairs. Like the Clinton administration's senior director for international economic affairs, this official wore two hats, also acting as a deputy to the national economic adviser. This move presaged other innovations at the White House in the early years of the Bush administration, including the appointment of a deputy national security adviser for counterterrorism, who also served as a deputy to the newly created Homeland Security Council, which was created in the wake of 9/11, and later deputy national security advisers for Iraq and for strategic planning. Thus, after an initial impulse to lower the profile of the NSC in favor the national security Cabinet agencies, the ongoing challenges of counterterrorism and Iraq drove the White House to strengthen the centralized tools of policy formulation and implementation.

Assessing the Historical Experience

Perhaps the most important, and obvious, lesson learned is the need, at a minimum, to decide clearly and early in the transition what the process for decisionmaking will be. Lack of agreement around process has been a critical Achilles' heel in the early days of new administrations. Perhaps the most well known example, the process failures around the Bay of Pigs invasion, led the Kennedy administration to adapt its process in ways that produced a far more successful outcome during the Cuban Missile Crisis. The prolonged failure of the Reagan administration to institutionalize its own procedures led to constant bickering and ultimately to the Iran-Contra scandal. And the shadow, parallel policy processes around Vice President Cheney undercut orderly decisionmaking and perpetuated divisions within the George W. Bush administration, contributing to serious lapses of both policy formulation and implementation. As with Kennedy and the Bay of Pigs, this took a particularly serious toll on the ability of the system to effectively analyze and employ intelligence.

In recent years the basic structures have remained relatively constant, although each administration has taken some pains to develop new processes as a way of demonstrating that there has been a change in leadership.[40] In recent years there has been growing interest in reform to address the dramatic changes in the global security environment.[41]

Given the dangers of the contemporary age, it is difficult to overstate how important it is to establish clear procedures for policymaking and crisis management at the outset of an administration. A new administration could confront a life-or-death crisis on day one. This need had a precursor in the "continuity of government" planning in the days of the U.S.-Soviet nuclear confrontation, when the danger that a new president might face a nuclear exchange in the early days seemed a real (although in hindsight remote) possibility. It is, however, a much more worrisome prospect in the current context, with terrorist threats to the homeland that could conceivably be aimed at government operations. These would be all the more threatening during a period of presidential transition.

The federal government has undergone a dramatic transformation in its organization and capabilities to deal with the terrorist threat. Although the effectiveness of reforms such as the creation of the Department of Homeland Security, the Office of the Director of National Intelligence, and the National Counterterrorism Center has been hotly debated, it is fair to say they are still works in progress. The new administration thus will face a key choice: make immediate changes to this evolving infrastructure, or take some time to become familiar with the new institutions and processes before implementing change.

The second lesson learned is that it is difficult to choose the right process without taking into account the decisionmaking style of the president and the working relationships among key players. For this reason, finalizing key process decisions must wait until the top officials have been chosen. While the president-elect's views on the most suitable process should inform the initial selection of personnel, it is vital that once the players are chosen they are consulted and agree on an approach that each believes will be fair, thoughtful, and practical and reflect their own operating styles, rather than being presented as a fait accompli. If there is not a meeting of the minds and a degree of comfort about process, then substantive disagreements, which will inevitably arise, become that much more difficult to resolve. Since national security problems often require time-sensitive, highly consequential decisions, the participants' confidence in the process is particularly important. The Bay of Pigs crisis is the most obvious example, but the early years of Carter and Reagan show how conflicts over process can hamper the development of clear and consistent national security strategies.

Third, whatever formal processes are adopted, an administration must recognize from the outset—and plan ahead for—the vital role played by complementary informal processes. Experience shows that these will inevitably emerge, for several compelling reasons, including the need to find a forum for candid exchange of views, to handle highly sensitive information and policies while minimizing the dangers of leaks, to avoid the institutional posturing that frequently afflicts formal processes, and to respond rapidly to fast-paced events.

Closely related is the need for flexibility to address the range and diversity of national security challenges. Unlike in the cold war era, it is simply impossible today to "hard-wire" the national security processes. The appropriate cast of officials and advisers needed to address the problem of climate change, for instance, is very different from those needed to handle a global financial crisis or a terrorist incident. Yet it is also important to avoid either an excessively ad hoc approach that risks excluding important facts or perspectives, or a bureaucracy that becomes so large as to be unwieldy. These requirements put a premium on the ability of the White House and the NSC to develop mechanisms that provide both order and flexibility—a blend of Eisenhower and Kennedy that was probably best achieved in the later years of the Clinton administration.

Finally, the decisions regarding process must come to terms with the relationship between the national security establishment and the more "political" side of the White House. It is tempting but unrealistic to suggest that national security decisionmaking should take place in a political vacuum. Decisions should be made through a conscientious effort to ascertain the public interest independent of the president's or the party's electoral future; but without popular and congressional support no policy, however sound, can be sustained. During the George W. Bush transition, National Security Adviser–designate Rice decided to abolish the public and congressional affairs positions at the NSC; yet experience soon demonstrated that without that input into policymaking and implementation, the president's agenda was severely hampered and the decision was later reversed. Conversely, the strong political and public affairs input in the Reagan years contributed to early successes.

The early Reagan years illustrate the benefit of developing a political strategy to support the transition process, beginning with Reagan's own outreach to key Democratic members of Congress, as well as the central role of message formulation in gaining support for national security strategy. These insights were carried over by Secretary Baker, a veteran of the Reagan years, into the Bush transition, where his successful efforts to defuse the partisan controversies over Central America allowed the Bush administration to concentrate on its own priorities.

During the second Clinton term, there was an effort to increase congressional and public outreach through the selection of a member of the Senate (and member of the opposition party), William Cohen, as secretary of defense and the institution of regular consultations with key congressional leaders (the so-called Gang of Eight). Although these efforts had only limited success given Clinton's deteriorating relations with Congress in connection with the impeachment proceedings, they might have been more effective if they had been put in place at an earlier stage.

The need to bring the "political" and the "policy" together during the transition will be particularly important in the 2009 transition, as partisan differences over national security that characterized the George W. Bush years could severely hamper the ability of the next president to move forward on his main national security objectives.

Today there is near universal agreement that existing national security processes are inadequate and in need of substantial reform to meet the emerging challenges of the twenty-first century.[42] But this poses a conundrum for transitions. On the one hand, the beginning of a new administration seems an appropriate time to introduce procedural and organizational innovations. On the other hand, substantial reform can be highly disruptive, with a steep learning curve as the innovations, which look appealing on paper, meet the realities of day-to-day governance. At a time when the system is most under stress, with new people and new policy initiatives, adding untested processes to the mix could fatally hinder the new team's ability to handle early crises. For process, as well as for substance, the temptation to act swiftly and decisively to implement change must be balanced against the limited capacity of the system to absorb change in the early stages of a new presidency. The next chapter explores these and other trade-offs and challenges associated with a new administration's first hundred days in office.

7 | GOVERNING REALITIES

As IF THE challenges of choosing people and process were not enough for the crucial ten-to-eleven-week interim, the newly elected president must also make key decisions about the policy agenda for the new administration. There is considerable pressure to act quickly while the incoming president enjoys the tailwind of an electoral mandate.

When the afterglow of the inaugural balls fades in the dawn of the first day in office, the real test of an effective transition begins. There is no more perilous time for a new administration than the much ballyhooed "first one hundred days." Many of the legendary clichés of transition lore stem from this period: the need to "hit the ground running" to take advantage of a "window of opportunity" created by the political "honeymoon" that accompanies a new presidency. Yet even a cursory glance at the historical record suggests that missteps of omission and commission during the early months bedevil most incoming presidents, wreaking havoc with their attempt to gain control of the powers of the presidency, implement their campaign agenda, and, most important, sustain the nation's security.

At the core, the problem of the hundred days stems from a deep dichotomy. A president's standing on the first day of office is often at its highest at the moment when the capacity of the administration is at its weakest. As scholar Paul Light has noted, the course of a presidency is characterized by a declining curve of influence as the wear and tear of office dulls the shine of the election, and an increasing curve of effectiveness as experience deepens over time.[1] Presidents who act too quickly are prone to errors that can damage their presidencies over the long run, while presidents who are slow to get on track may see their presidencies hijacked by events not of their own making.

Getting the first hundred days right requires a judicious blend of boldness and caution that exploits the political opportunity of the honeymoon while minimizing the risks of ill-considered action. The early days of an administration are especially challenging because it hasn't yet reached full strength. Its new starting lineup is untested, the coach is new, the playbook is new, the second team has not been recruited, and the holdovers are suspect. The new administration is expected to go on offense and defense simultaneously without a complete team.

This chapter addresses six important issues that face new administrations during their first hundred days in office: filling second- and third-tier positions, congressional relations, dealing with the policy legacy of the predecessor administration, starting new initiatives, managing potential crises, and dealing with the press. We conclude with perspectives on how the new administration can plan for both expected and unexpected challenges as the team members settle in to their new posts and begin the tasks of governing.

Filling the Second- and Third-Tier Positions

During the early months of a new administration, the top officials are consumed with trying to grip the reins of power, manage holdovers, address emerging crises, and implement new initiatives. Even for senior officials with prior government experience, this is a daunting challenge. But their task is further complicated by the fact that second- and third-tier officials at the working level have not yet been appointed. The challenge is almost unique to the United States, where so many working-level officials are political appointees, in contrast to most other democracies where all but the members of the Cabinet and the chief executive's inner circle are career officials.

Populating the second- and third-tier positions poses a number of problems that differ from those faced by an administration making its initial Cabinet appointments. First, the process is slow because the sheer number of appointees tends to overwhelm both the political and security vetting processes. Second, Congress is less likely to give a new administration the benefit of the doubt on these appointees (in contrast to the Cabinet), and as time moves on, the honeymoon fades and problems in executive-legislative relations mount. When this happens, second-tier appointees may be held hostage to substantive policy disputes.

Third, these appointments can get caught up in a test of wills between Cabinet members who want subordinates who are loyal to them and a White House that wants to ensure loyalty to the president's agenda. Over the past sixty years this has led to a seesaw battle in which some administrations have granted Cabinet officials significant leeway in choosing subordinates (Carter, George H. W. Bush, Clinton, George W. Bush), some have asserted strong White House control (Nixon in his second term, Reagan), and others have taken a mixed approach. When Cabinet members exert strong control and staff loyalty is to the agency and its head, not to the administration as a whole, disagreements between agencies tend to be amplified. The fierce fighting that characterized the George W. Bush interagency process is a dramatic illustration of this problem. Yet by pursuing a mixed approach, Bush seems to have suffered the worst consequences of both: sharp divisions between agencies, but also divisions within agencies, especially at State, where the White House insisted that some neo-conservatives, such as John Bolton, who was under secretary of state for arms control and international security (before serving as ambassador to the UN), be hired over the opposition of Secretary Powell. Taken together, these three factors have substantially lengthened the time it takes for an administration to reach full strength.

Meanwhile, the key day-to-day jobs are filled on an acting basis by career officials who have spent the previous four, eight, or even twelve years working for a different president, in some cases from a different party. Although each new administration pays lip service to the desire to make better use of career talent, in practice the holdovers are almost invariably treated with suspicion. A "guilty until proven innocent" approach can develop, which makes the incoming administration reluctant to share confidences with the career officials or to empower them to act on their own judgment. The result is that either the principals try to do too much themselves (because they don't have deputies they trust) or they neglect all but the most immediate and urgent problems.

There is also a natural amount of apprehension and uncertainty on the part of career civil servants faced with a new political appointee as boss, especially when that appointee is younger, less experienced, and less knowledgeable.[2] Although many political appointees are very qualified for the jobs they receive or can quickly learn on the job, others receive jobs for reasons that have more to do with patronage than subject-matter expertise.[3] Ambassadorships, in particular, have been a frequent source of contention between Foreign Service officers (FSOs) in the State Department and presidential transition teams, as FSOs lobby for ambassadorial posts to go to career Foreign Service officers rather than to political appointees.

The dangers posed by this problem were highly apparent in the George W. Bush administration's approach to counterterrorism. It is clear from both the 2000 campaign and the emerging historical record that counterterrorism was not at the top of the Bush national security agenda in January 2001. For many Bush advisers, issues such as Iraq, the need to develop missile defenses and move beyond the Anti-Ballistic Missile Treaty, taking a tougher line on North Korea, and developing a more forthcoming one toward Taiwan took pride of place. Moreover, unanticipated crises, particularly the EP-3 incident, consumed important time of the principals.[4]

Counterterrorism, in the early months, was largely left to career officials, such as Richard Clarke, and holdovers, such as George Tenet, who tried to move the issue up on the principals' agenda. But they did not have the confidence of the new Bush appointees and were largely pushed aside. As a result, the principals held only one full meeting on counterterrorism in the period leading up to the 9/11 terrorist attacks.

The staffing-related vacuum in the early days also inhibits effective policy planning by a new administration. Because the urgent often crowds out the important, the shorthanded new administration has few resources to devote to developing long-term strategies. It is no accident, for example, that despite the congressional requirement (in the Goldwater-Nichols Act) that the administration prepare and submit to Congress a "national security strategy report" six months after taking office, no president since the law was enacted has submitted a report during his first year. And the failure to conduct effective long-term planning early can cripple an administration's ability to set and pursue its affirmative agenda.

Congressional Relations

In many ways, one of the most important challenges of an incoming administration in the national security arena is getting its relations right with Congress. Although the powers of the executive are greatest in the area of national security, no president can effectively conduct foreign affairs and defense policy without substantial support from Congress. Congressional relations present a core dilemma during the early months of a new presidency: on the one hand, new presidents need to set a firm direction to show that they are in charge (particularly when one or both branches of Congress are controlled by the opposition party); on the other hand, too confrontational an approach can sour important relationships at the outset and make the conduct of national security even more difficult.

For most administrations, the first brush with congressional relations comes in connection with securing Senate approval of Cabinet appointments. Generally speaking, the Senate is deferential to the president's Cabinet selections because of the election mandate a president brings to office. This is especially true with respect to national security officials, who Congress recognizes need to be in place on day one. Nonetheless, nomination disputes regularly plague new administrations, and the national security realm is not exempt. Two of the most notable controversies in recent years involved President Carter's nomination of Theodore Sorensen to head the CIA and President George H. W. Bush's nomination of Senator John Tower as secretary of defense. In the case of Sorensen, Wendell Rawls Jr. noted in the *New York Times* that Republicans, "still smarting from the residue of Watergate," saw a nomination battle as a way to embarrass the administration.

For Tower, even after the Senate Armed Services Committee voted to reject his nomination on the grounds of revelations about his alleged "drinking habit" and "conflict of interest," the White House persisted with the nomination. After a rancorous debate, the Senate, too, voted against him, resulting in the first rejection in thirty years of a nomination to a Cabinet position by a newly elected president. Accused by the Republicans of indulging in "partisan politics," the Democrats argued that instead their rejection was "an exercise of constitutional responsibilities, a reluctant use of the 'advise and consent' power against a man tainted by allegations of excessive drinking and conflict of interest." The way the nomination battle played out led Senator Strom Thurmond to ponder the implications of it for the president: "What effect is this having all over the world? . . . What are heads of nations thinking all over the world—that this man has no influence in Congress?"[5]

In both cases, there seems to have been an inexplicable failure by the transition team to anticipate the likely congressional attitude toward the nominations: in Senator Tower's case, perhaps because of an assumption that the Senate would not reject one of its own. Undoubtedly, a conviction that the selection of a nominee should remain closely held until a formal public announcement is made contributes to such errors of judgment.

What is particularly noteworthy about these two nomination fights are the different approaches taken by President Carter and President Bush once the nominations were challenged. President Carter relatively quickly jettisoned the Sorensen nomination once his suitability was questioned. President Bush, by contrast (and perhaps explicitly because of the Sorensen experience), stood by Tower and suffered a drawn-out and costly defeat.[6] Although it is dangerous to generalize too broadly, it would seem that the greater danger to the transition comes from sticking too long with a controversial nominee. In effect, it represents a lose-lose proposition: either the nomination is defeated, with an early blow to presidential prestige, or if confirmed, the newly installed official (and the president) faces an uphill climb in repairing testy relations with Congress.

The challenge of getting congressional relations right at the outset is complicated by the growing tendency of campaigns to stress candidates' "outside-the-beltway" credentials. Although this has proven to be a sustained vote-getter over the years, it has led candidates and presidents-elect to shy away from appointing seasoned Washington hands to high-visibility administration positions, especially because many of those with the greatest experience in dealing with Congress are tainted by prior associations. Many have served as lobbyists—the ultimate political stigma.

Both the Carter and Clinton administrations vividly demonstrate the pitfalls of this approach. The Carter administration came to Washington explicitly scornful of the role of Washington insiders, and went to considerable lengths to prove the point, for example, by appointing Frank Moore as its chief congressional liaison, a man whose entire career had been based in Georgia. More symbolically, but with equally pernicious effect, was a snub of Speaker Tip O'Neill in connection with an inaugural concert at the Kennedy Center, an act that poisoned White House congressional relations for years, even though the Speaker and the president were from the same party.

Clinton, too, challenged the Washington establishment in large and small ways. He did so first by disparaging the Washington press corps and the Georgetown social scene, and second by following in Carter's footsteps in choosing a chief of staff with limited Washington experience.[7] This lack of sensitivity to congressional prerogatives proved especially damaging in connection with the gays-in-the-military problem.

By contrast, President Reagan demonstrated that judicious congressional management could dramatically bolster a new president's chances for early success. Although Reagan used his outsider status effectively during the campaign, he quickly pivoted once elected. During the transition Reagan's team deliberately enlisted members of Congress with national security expertise from both parties as advisers.[8] On the symbolic level (and as an explicit rebuke to the practice of his predecessor), Reagan extended a welcoming hand to Speaker O'Neill and other leading congressional Democrats. These gestures brought the Reagan administration considerable goodwill even as it was pushing through a budget package that challenged many of the Democrats' favorite domestic spending programs and provided a dramatic increase in defense spending.

President George H. W. Bush, who himself was a consummate insider, used James Baker effectively to build ties with Congress. Baker emphasized the importance of building consensus before seeking to push through new initiatives—a strategy of listening, then acting.[9] But Bush's own personality created a certain distance from members of Congress, and he developed few strong ties with congressional leaders.

George W. Bush's approach resembled that of his Democratic predecessors, with little focus on congressional relations, perhaps because there was a Republican congressional majority and Bush had a relatively low regard for Congress in the overall scheme of governance. The downgrading of congressional relations was apparent early in the Bush administration, as evidenced by Secretary of Defense Rumsfeld's prickly relationships with some national security committees and National Security Adviser Rice's decision to dismantle the congressional affairs office at the National Security Council.[10] The antipathy deepened following the 9/11 attacks as the administration's sweeping assertions of executive prerogative in the field of national security (the so-called unitary presidency) and executive privilege began to antagonize even members of the Republican party (these included the Cheney energy task force; an unwillingness to disclose information to Congress on detentions and warrantless surveillance; and others). Bush's relations with Congress were further troubled by a highly partisan approach to governing, derived from the approach of his principal strategist, Karl Rove, who emphasized achieving success by relying exclusively on Republican votes in Congress rather than seeking broad-based solutions.[11] This was apparent in the handling of the runup to the Iraq war, when the Bush administration pointedly excluded Democratic congressional supporters of the administration, such as Majority Leader Richard Gephardt, from sharing the White House stage with the president and Republican backers of the war.

Even President Reagan had an early misstep in congressional affairs, in his case involving the decision to sell Airborne Warning and Control Systems (AWACS) to Saudi Arabia.[12] Although Carter had offered to propose the arms sales to Congress during the lame duck period, the incoming Reagan team declined, believing they had a better chance with Congress than Carter did. The intention to proceed with the sale was proposed even before the completion of a policy review on arms sales that Reagan himself had commissioned.[13] Taken aback when this announcement met with opposition in Congress, he put it on hold but then announced the sale of an upgraded package including AWACS and tankers a few months later. Once again, there was opposition from Congress, which was not notified until the fall and, smarting from the lack of consultation, barely approved the sale (52–48 in the Senate).[14]

The importance of congressional relations in the early months of a new administration has been magnified in recent years by increasing partisanship in the conduct of foreign affairs and the breakdown of the broadly accepted cold war paradigm governing U.S. national security strategy. Whatever the outcome of the 2008 election, deep party differences over Iraq and counterterrorism will pose major challenges to the new president's ability to start off on the right foot.

Dealing with the Legacy

The natural inclination of a new administration is to get on quickly with the agenda that propelled it to victory. There is understandable impatience with having to deal with the messy inherited policies of the predecessor, especially when the transition is from a president of the opposite party. Yet failure to deal effectively with the old legacy may make it impossible—for political and substantive reasons—to move forward with the new agenda.

Past administrations have fallen prey to two very different perils: making a decision to continue a policy of the predecessor without fully examining its wisdom or, in contrast, jettisoning old policies in their zeal to show that "everything has changed." The most notorious example of the first danger, of course, is the Bay of Pigs operation in which President Kennedy assumed that the Eisenhower national security officials involved in the planning had done their homework. Furthermore, Kennedy was unwilling to risk a backlash if he tried to delay or cancel the effort at the outset of his administration, fearing that he would be seen as "weak on Castro" after campaigning on a hard-line platform critical of Eisenhower's inaction on national security issues. Some would argue that the same problem led to the Johnson administration's incremental deepening of U.S. engagement in Vietnam in 1964, and to the mission creep that afflicted the U.S. role in Somalia during President Clinton's first year.

In the second category fall decisions such as President George W. Bush's determination to abandon the U.S. role in fostering an agreement between Israel and the Palestinians as a way of distancing himself from the activist approach pursued by his predecessor, reflected in the cavalier assertions by President Bush's press spokesman that Clinton's peace efforts at Camp David had contributed to the violence.[15] His decision to do so, without any real consultation with the parties in the region or those involved in the American effort, contributed to a steady deterioration of security in the region, with grave consequences for America's friends in the Middle East and for the United States itself. The Bush administration ultimately abandoned that decision and threw itself back into an activist role with the Annapolis process, but the long interregnum contributed to a dramatic worsening of the prospects for achieving an agreement. The Bush administration also precipitously rejected the Clinton administration's approach to managing the North Korean nuclear challenge, including its support of South Korea's "sunshine policy" toward the North, causing significant damage to relations with allies in East Asia, most notably South Korea. Other notable early reversals, including the abandoning (and disparagement) of the Kyoto climate change treaty and the termination of the Anti-Ballistic Missile Treaty with little or no consultation with key allies, caused serious and long-lasting damage to critical alliance relations.

But President George W. Bush was not the only president who in his zeal to distance himself from the past failed to fully consider the consequences. In 1992 candidate Clinton sharply criticized the George H. W. Bush administration's policy toward intercepted Haitian refugees who were being held at the American naval base in Guantanamo, Cuba. The Bush policy called for the refugees' immediate repatriation, even though many had already been screened to apply for asylum in the United States. After more carefully considering the potential ramifications of his position, Clinton was forced to backtrack even before taking office.

Similarly, candidate Clinton challenged the hands-off approach of the George H. W. Bush administration toward the violence in the former

Republic of Yugoslavia and vowed to seek UN authority for air strikes against the Serbs. Yet once in office, the Clinton administration soon discovered that its proposed policy course had little support among European allies, who had peacekeepers on the ground in Bosnia. Clinton was again forced to backtrack in order to avoid a major crisis in transatlantic relations.

One might have expected the Johnson-to-Nixon transition to be characterized by sharp frictions between the outgoing and incoming teams given candidate Nixon's critique of the Johnson administration's handling of Vietnam. But the record was quite mixed. Indeed, in his first public statement on Vietnam after the election, following a meeting with Johnson, Nixon pledged continuity on Vietnam and on several other prominent policy issues. But behind the scenes, Nixon and Kissinger were laying the groundwork for major new initiatives to be undertaken immediately upon taking office, both on the diplomatic front (implementing a strategy linking progress in U.S.-Soviet relations to Russian help on Vietnam) and on the military front (initiating the secret bombing campaign of Cambodia). One visible measure of the change in approach was the abrupt replacement of Averell Harriman with Henry Cabot Lodge Jr. at the Paris peace talks immediately upon Nixon's taking office.[16]

A sharp course correction does not in every case lead to disaster. The Kennedy administration's swift initiation of a new approach to the balance of payments crisis that erupted in the waning months of the Eisenhower administration was a well-considered and -executed policy departure that reaped positive results.

An instructive example of managing inherited legacies concerned U.S. policy toward Central America at the outset of the George H. W. Bush administration. Throughout the Reagan era, Central America policy was a deep source of conflict between the White House and congressional Democrats. Reagan and his foreign policy team had a deep ideological commitment to challenging what they viewed as communist encroachment into this hemisphere—a conviction that culminated in the notorious Iran-Contra episode. In contrast, the efforts of Democrats in Congress to tie the administration's hands resulted in the Boland amendment, which prohibited "the CIA or Defense Department to use funds of the bill to furnish military equipment, military training or advice, or other support for military activities, to any group or individual, not part of a country's armed forces, for the purpose of overthrowing the government of Nicaragua or provoking a military exchange between Nicaragua and Honduras."[17]

The issue of Central America was an important feature of the foreign policy debate in the 1988 presidential campaign, with Governor Michael Dukakis echoing the congressional Democrats' critique of the Reagan administration. Candidate George H. W. Bush sought to distance himself from Iran-Contra, but was careful not to challenge directly his own administration's approach to Central America.[18]

Once in office and free from the need not to embarrass his own administration, Bush moved quickly to take the Central America issue off the table. He dispatched Secretary of State–designate James Baker to Capitol Hill to craft a compromise by which Congress agreed to aid the Contras and the White House agreed to seriously support peace efforts in Central America.[19] In short order one of the most contentious issues in American foreign policy receded from view.[20]

The Reagan presidency also offers an important example of how an administration can successfully defuse the problem of legacy policy issues, freeing itself to concentrate on its own affirmative agenda. During the 1980 campaign, candidate Reagan was deeply critical of the Carter administration's inability to resolve the hostage crisis, blaming it on the administration's weakness in the face of foreign threats. Once the Carter administration successfully negotiated the hostages' release in the final moments of the Carter presidency, there were some among President Reagan's advisers who advocated repudiating the agreement as one that unduly rewarded Iran's illegal behavior.[21] After a short review, however, Reagan and his team quietly decided to honor the agreement, thus relegating the Iran issue to the back burner.[22]

The legacy problem is a particular challenge on budget-related issues, because the congressional budget process requires a new administration to offer any changes to an outgoing president's budget within the first few months of taking office. Yet experience shows that outgoing administrations have often laced their final budgets with unrealistic assumptions about spending, revenues, and economic growth that make the outgoing administration look good and force the incoming administration to incur the political fallout when the rosy scenario fails to materialize.

The task of quickly mastering the mind-boggling detail embedded in the federal budget is illustrative of the broader challenge facing the new administration—simply becoming sufficiently knowledgeable about the governing reality in order to make an informed policy decision. This challenge is particularly acute in the national security arena because so much of what is relevant is sensitive (and often classified) so not available to the candidate and advisers until after the election. However, getting up to speed on the issues is not just a matter of taking a crash course in global politics and people becoming familiar with one another. Once officials take office, digesting and interpreting that new information and intelligence takes time and effort. During the transition, insufficient information can lead a new administration to launch an initiative prematurely or respond inappropriately to a crisis.

The depth of the legacy problem has varied from transition to transition and is deeply affected by the level of cooperation offered by the outgoing administration. In general, the legacy problems tend to be least severe in the case of a "friendly takeover," such as when an incumbent vice president becomes president.[23] But even incumbent vice presidents may not possess a full understanding of the inherited challenges, as the case of President Johnson and Vietnam so vividly showed. There were also important elements of friction between the Reagan and George H. W. Bush teams, particularly as it became clearer that not all of Reagan's appointees would be retained in office. Transitions in which the outgoing president was not defeated (Truman, Johnson, Clinton) were somewhat more cooperative than when the campaign rival took office (Ford to Carter and Carter to Reagan). As Mosher and his colleagues observed:

> Regardless of other factors, the very nature of the contest militates against friendly and constructive relationships between the two sides. . . . Each party represents some general, even if vague, principles, ideologies, slogans, and policies at least in part opposed to those of the other. . . . The differences between the parties and

between the candidates—seldom their agreements—are the foci of political campaigns. The party out of power is usually the more aggressive, attacking the policies, the alleged inefficiencies, at times even the character, of those currently in power. . . . When to these factors are added perhaps long-standing personal dislikes between the candidates or their followers, the problems of transitions are further aggravated. Even when president and president-elect have had a prior mutually respectful acquaintance, as Truman and Eisenhower did, the stresses of the campaign can result in abiding hostility that impedes cooperation.[24]

No matter how conscientious the outgoing administration, there are inherent limitations to the completeness of the handoff. Critical information may not be shared, simply because of the volume of material or the fact that its relevance may not be readily apparent until later. Those assuming positions of authority in a new administration have to be brought up to speed quickly, but the accumulated experience of four or eight years is difficult to reduce to a briefing book. Relying on the different components of agencies to provide the necessary background also runs the danger of "stove-piping" as each component transmits its worm's eye view of the problem while the integrating perspective disappears with the departed political appointees. A new regional assistant secretary at the State Department (such as the assistant secretary for East Asia) might be well briefed by the staff of that component, but miss out on the knowledge of the economics bureau—knowledge that can be gained only by participating in intradepartmental and interagency meetings over time. Similarly, stove-piping might prevent a new appointee in a regional post in the Department of Defense, for example, from learning what other departments know about the same area.

Even when the outgoing administration expresses a desire to share candidly with the incoming administration, an incoming team that is skeptical about its predecessors' motives or policies might be inclined to disregard information that is offered (as Reagan did on the Iran hostages, and as George W. Bush did on Osama bin Laden). Quoting both Democratic and Republican former officials, Charles O. Jones, an expert on transitions, has pointed out the perceived asymmetry between the willingness to help on the part of the outgoing team and the willingness to receive or accept advice on the part of the incoming team.[25] Others have characterized the attitudes of incoming officials as an "unsavory mix of exuberance and conceit, of arrogance and suspicion," or in the words of Richard Cheney, "If you're so smart, how come we beat you?"[26] Similar skepticism is often shown toward career officials as well.

Transition teams typically try to supplement their dependence on briefings by the outgoing administration through more or less elaborate efforts to send "teams" into the agencies to ferret out key information and develop briefing materials for incoming officials. But these efforts face some important limitations. They depend in the first instance on the team members knowing where to look and what to look for—a daunting challenge even for former officials, regardless of how well they have tried to remain well informed during their period of exile. And the effort faces an inherent trade-off: if the material is too detailed and voluminous, it will be hard for new officials to digest; if too cursory, it will omit key facts and perspectives. The problem is further compounded if the initial teams include individuals from the campaign who may not have the trust or confidence of the incoming official, who is typically selected after the initial briefing materials are prepared. Thus many transition books prepared by these teams suffer the same fate as those prepared by the outgoing administration: relegation to the dustbin.

Yet another dimension of the challenge of understanding the legacy is the poor or nonexistent documentation of commitments made or alleged to have been made by the outgoing administration. Eisenhower, for example, remembered: "About three weeks after inauguration, we discovered that we had a situation wherein our government had promised to grant Brazil a loan to help settle its debts."[27] Lending to Brazil was a controversial issue, and there were some heated arguments between State and Treasury over the amount of the loan until "Finally State uncovered a note which showed that prior understandings made the government morally obligated to make the entire loan."[28] The powerful secretary of the Treasury at the time, George Humphrey, who had initially opposed making the whole loan, eventually had to tell Eisenhower: "Mr. President, we're hooked."[29] Eisenhower signed the relevant papers and the loan was made for the full amount promised.

The challenges of implicit agreements were illustrated more strikingly in 1970 when the Soviet Union began building a submarine base in Cienfuegos, Cuba. National Security Adviser Henry Kissinger became suspicious when he was visited by a Soviet chargé d'affaires wishing to "reaffirm the Kennedy-Khrushchev understanding of 1962 with respect to Cuba." Kissinger immediately reviewed the official correspondence from the Cuban Missile Crisis in an attempt to discover some sort of explicit agreement by the Soviet Union to remove its missiles in exchange for an American commitment to not invade Cuba. "It emerged that there was no formal understanding in the sense of an agreement," noted Kissinger, "either oral or in writing."[30] What he did find was that although implicit understandings clearly pointed to an agreement, it was never made formal. Given that the submarine crisis occurred in an administration with someone as well trained in the subtleties of international politics as Kissinger, one can only imagine the possibilities for officials in a new administration with less experience and preparation.

When the people who negotiated agreements leave office, sometimes important knowledge goes with them. This may happen because there are no records (for example, on Eisenhower's military commitments to Jordan). Or the facts may be disputed (Eisenhower's advice to Kennedy on Vietnam, or Russian president Mikhail Gorbachev's assertion that Secretary Baker had promised not to expand NATO to the countries of the former Warsaw Pact). Sometimes complications associated with the Presidential Records Act have made it difficult for incoming officials to gain access to the records of their predecessors.[31]

Taken together, these factors show that an incoming administration faces extraordinary hurdles to understanding its inherited legacy—a critical prerequisite to successfully launching new initiatives or handling crises.

New Initiatives

The chance to put a new and distinctive stamp on policy is, of course, what drives candidates to seek office, and it sustains them and their supporters through the arduous campaign process. Not surprisingly then, there is enormous enthusiasm for moving quickly to implement the campaign agenda, as well as pressure to do so. In some cases this means reversing the policies of predecessors, with all the challenges discussed above. In others it means pressing forward on a new idea that was a signature campaign issue or that emerged during the interim between the election and assuming office. Here, too, the problem is finding the right balance between seizing the window of opportunity and reassuring supporters on the one hand, and carefully preparing the ground for a successful result on the other.

One dramatic illustration of the problem of new initiatives can be seen in President Carter's approach to arms control negotiations with the USSR. During the 1976 campaign, Carter had largely focused his discussion of arms control on the need to move swiftly on the Vladivostok agenda.[32] But during the transition, and in the early days of the new administration, President Carter grew to favor a more radical approach featuring deeper cuts in both sides' nuclear arsenals. The administration's senior officials were divided over the wisdom of the proposal, with some arguing that such an abrupt change of course without adequate preparatory work would be unsettling to Moscow and could have long-lasting repercussions for U.S.-Soviet relations. President Carter dispatched Secretary of State Cyrus Vance to Moscow with a proposal for deep cuts, which was dismissed out of hand by Communist Party General Secretary Leonid Brezhnev. As a result, U.S.-Soviet relations under Carter got off to a rocky start, and only deteriorated further as the administration wore on.[33]

The Carter administration's approach to national security also embraced the mirror-image problem of excessive delay in rolling out new initiatives. At the same time that Vance was advancing the hastily developed arms control proposal in Moscow, the administration embarked on a more comprehensive policy review. In PRM 10 (for Presidential Review Memorandum 10), the Carter team set for itself the daunting task of reviewing all of the elements of national security.[34] Not surprisingly, this ambitious effort resulted in a cumbersome, all-consuming process that created deep tensions within the administration but produced little in the way of effective new policy initiatives.[35] A similar effort by the George H. W. Bush administration to undertake a comprehensive national security review in the first months went nowhere and was ultimately abandoned.[36]

Carter's first months were plagued by several rocky starts on new initiatives. One signature feature of Carter's 1976 campaign was its emphasis on human rights as an element of foreign policy.[37] But behind the broad and electorally attractive appeal to values in American foreign policy, there had been relatively little thinking about how to integrate human rights considerations into day-to-day policy decisions. Thus, in the first weeks of the Carter presidency, the administration was plagued by off-the-cuff assertions concerning human rights policy before it had conducted the necessary detailed policy review that culminated in a formal policy pronouncement in April 1977.[38]

Here again, the Reagan administration offers an important contrast. During the transition, Reagan officials decided to pursue a highly focused agenda for the first months of his presidency, concentrating almost exclusively on budget issues, including cuts in domestic spending and substantial increases for national defense. No major foreign policy initiatives were unveiled despite the sharp critique of Carter's foreign policy during the 1980 campaign. The strategy paid substantial dividends in keeping the public debate focused on Reagan's priorities and allowed Reagan to capitalize on the electoral mandate that had swept him and a new Republican Senate majority into office.

More generally, a new president's first budget offers both opportunities and pitfalls that can have a lasting impact on the success of an administration. It represents an attractive early opportunity for a new administration to put its mark on policy, but the compressed timetable imposed by the congressional budget calendar creates substantial difficulties. Under the current budget law, any changes to the outgoing administration's budget request need to be sent to Congress by February 15.[39] This gives the new team at the Office of Management and Budget and the executive agencies only a few weeks to review and digest the outgoing budget requests and develop alternative proposals. Although in principle some of the intellectual work precedes the election of a new president, in practice it is only after the incoming team has a chance to fully understand and absorb the assumptions underlying the budget that it can meaningfully decide what to change and how.

This process can be particularly difficult during a hostile takeover, when the outgoing administration will be tempted to propose a politically attractive budget (often undergirded by rosy assumptions) to make itself look good, knowing that it won't have to live with the consequences of unrealistic assumptions and unkeepable promises.[40] And the challenge is further complicated when the outgoing team does not feel motivated to facilitate the policies of an incoming administration that the incumbents oppose.

One dramatic illustration of this challenge involved President Reagan's first defense budget. During the 1980 campaign, challenger Reagan criticized Carter for hollowing out the U.S. military and vowed to increase defense spending by 2 percent in real terms over the Carter administration's level.[41] During the campaign, Carter sought to emphasize his own commitment to increased defense spending, particularly following the Soviet invasion of Afghanistan. As if to burnish his own legacy (and contradict the charge of neglecting defense spending), Carter's final budget for defense, which he sent to Congress in January 1980, provided for a 5 percent increase. Rather than reexamine the budget in detail in order to assess whether the new Carter administration increases met U.S. national security needs, Reagan and his team chose to stick with their promise to spend 2 percent more than Carter, resulting in a massive 7 percent real increase, which proved difficult for the military to digest effectively and almost certainly contributed to some of the legendary cost overruns and gold-plating of that era.[42]

During a press conference about six months into his administration, President Eisenhower aptly observed that his administration "had not done all the things [it] wanted to do" but that "You cannot take a railroad and have a right-angle turn in it . . . ; you have to build a curve."[43]

Overreach during the first hundred days is fairly common and can lead to profound regrets as dashed hopes and unrealized ambitions come to taint the formative months of new administrations—even in spite of important accomplishments in other domains. Commenting on the constant vicissitudes of his early presidency, Bill Clinton wrote that his first year in office "involved an amazing combination of major legislative achievements, frustrations and successes in foreign policy, unforeseen events, personal tragedy, honest errors, and clumsy violations of the

Washington culture."[44] Reflecting more deeply on his first hundred days, he regretted he hadn't been more tempered in his ambitions:

> Clearly, I had overestimated how much I could do in a hurry. The country had been going in one direction for more than a decade, living with wedge politics, reassuring bromides about how great we were, and the illusory, though fleeting, comforts of spending more and taxing less today and ignoring the consequences for tomorrow. It was going to take more than a hundred days to turn things around.[45]

Instructively, he added: "In addition to the pace of change, I may have overestimated the amount of change I could achieve, as well as how much of it the American people could digest."[46]

This contemporary record illustrates both the pressures new administrations feel to undertake bold diplomacy at the outset, as well the risks associated with such an approach. This is not to say that a new administration should simply defer making major changes in foreign policy early on, particularly if foreign policy arguments were a central element of the preceding campaign. On the contrary, it is precisely in order to achieve success on key policy initiatives that a new president should choose carefully which efforts can be prudently undertaken early in the new administration, taking into account all of the risks (staffing shortages, knowledge shortfalls of the government itself, and many others) that are endemic in the early going

Managing Crises

Most studies of the perils of transitions take as their cautionary point of departure the Kennedy administration's handling of the Bay of Pigs, and for good reason. The calamity that befell Kennedy demonstrated vividly many of the risks identified here: the danger of campaign rhetoric, the failure to understand the legacy, the difficulties of acting with inexperienced personnel before effective policymaking structures have been put in place, and so forth. But it is important to remember the positive side of the story as well. Most veterans of the Kennedy administration credit the learning experience following the Bay of Pigs incident for the far more successful management of the Cuban Missile Crisis a year and a half later. And it must also be remembered that the Bay of Pigs debacle did not damage President Kennedy's political standing; on the contrary, his popularity actually rose in the days following the failed invasion.

Although the Kennedy administration has become legendary for its flawed handling of one major crisis during the early months of the presidency, it has received less attention for another, more successful effort in dealing with the balance of payments crisis. In contrast to the Bay of Pigs situation, where the new administration rather slavishly followed the policies of its predecessor, in the balance of payments crisis the new team successfully adopted a new approach that defused the crisis and sustained important U.S.-European security ties.

At the end of the Eisenhower administration the United States faced an acute balance of payments crisis brought on by high defense expenditures and declining U.S. exports, particularly to Europe. The Eisenhower administration adopted a policy that focused on reducing U.S. dollar expenditures overseas by cutting back on dependents of military personnel abroad and attempting to negotiate new burden-sharing agreements with European allies. During the transition, the Eisenhower administration sought unsuccessfully to get President-elect Kennedy to back the policy strategy in order to calm jittery currency markets troubled by uncertainties over how the new administration would approach the crisis. But Kennedy demurred, using the transition period to craft an alternative approach, which proved successful in shoring up the dollar.[47]

Kennedy's ability to engineer an effective alternative solution to a complex problem in the early days of his new administration can be attributed to two factors: an intense focus during the transition by key personnel on the specifics of the policy problem, and the decision to appoint to a key policy position a high-level individual—Under Secretary of State Douglas Dillon—from the outgoing administration who was intimately familiar with the facts surrounding the crisis and with the important players inside and outside the United States.

The Clinton administration was plagued by crises in the early months of the presidency. In Haiti, as noted earlier, the administration was forced to reverse its campaign commitment to protect Haitian refugees who had taken to sea even before Clinton was inaugurated. Once in office, the crisis deepened as the generals who had seized power continued their brutal crackdown on the opposition and perpetrated severe human rights abuses. The new team was caught, on the one hand, between important constituencies in Congress and those among the public who had supported candidate Clinton's position on Haiti, and on the other by the new president's desire to focus on the U.S. economy, the issue that had helped propel him into office. Divisions surfaced within the administration between those, particularly in the White House, with strong ties to the human rights community and exiled Haitian president Jean-Bertrand Aristide and the defense and intelligence communities, who had deep reservations about Aristide's reliability and who were reluctant to commit U.S. prestige (not to mention U.S. forces) to what they viewed as a secondary national security concern. The State Department found itself in the middle, with differing views among career foreign service officers and a secretary of state who wished to support the president in keeping the focus on domestic priorities while also honoring his campaign commitments on Haiti. Policy floundered for months until the dramatic confrontation between the coup-makers and a UN peacekeeping force demonstrated to the new team that a more coherent and broadly accepted approach was needed, which culminated some eighteen months later in the show of force that led to the restoration of the elected Aristide government with no U.S. casualties.[48]

Not all of the early Clinton administration crisis management efforts were plagued by serious difficulties. On Iraq, for example, the Clinton team moved quickly to respond to an assassination plot against former president Bush, and deployed forces quickly to the Persian Gulf region in response to threatening troop movements by Saddam Hussein. In both cases, prompt action in the face of an early test may well have helped to induce new caution in the Iraqi leader.

More recently, the role of holdovers versus new personnel played an important role in the George W. Bush administration's handling of its first foreign policy crisis, the downing of a U.S. EP-3 aircraft after a collision with a Chinese fighter jet (discussed in chapter 3). In the initial reaction to the collision, President Bush took a hard-line, uncompromising stand that seemed in accord with his campaign rhetoric about U.S. strength and skepticism about China's intentions, as well as with statements early in his presidency that appeared to take a less qualified approach to U.S. support for Taiwan. However, as the crisis wore on, the handling of policy devolved to mid-level, primarily career officials who pursued a less confrontational line. This ultimately led to a face-saving statement by the United States and subsequently the release of the navy personnel aboard the EP-3. Commentators on this incident have suggested that had more of Bush's own appointees been in place at the State and Defense departments the crisis might have played out differently.[49]

Dealing with the Press

One of the most difficult challenges facing a new administration involves dealing with the media. A new president and his senior staff must adjust to a whole new set of demands and pressures associated with public relations. During a campaign, a candidate and his crew have a variety of tools they can employ to try to control the message and enforce message discipline, including what issues to address and what to avoid. But upon taking power that becomes almost impossible. A new president becomes accountable for vastly more issue areas in full view of an enormous media infrastructure that scrutinizes the new administration's every move. Incoming team members often want to enforce secrecy on matters of internal deliberation, but maintaining confidentiality in a government not dominated by loyalists is much more difficult. A new administration also faces immediate choices about how often and under what conditions the president should be exposed to the press. One of the most important early decisions of a presidency is how frequently to hold press conferences. Reagan gave press conferences only sparingly, even from the beginning, while George H. W. Bush held conferences about once a week, on average, during his first hundred days,[50] and Clinton met regularly with the White House press corps and held forth from the beginning on the widest possible array of government initiatives and activities.

Almost from the outset, a new administration must also learn to deal with leaks and the unauthorized release of sensitive materials. Leaks fall into several categories, including revelations about the details of internal deliberations at the highest levels and the public disclosure of sensitive intelligence that bears on a national security threat or delicate diplomatic proceedings. Each can be exceptionally harmful to the forward momentum of a new administration. Seasoned Washington hands appreciate the inevitability of leaks and often plan accordingly, but campaign insiders and newcomers find these unauthorized disclosures deeply disconcerting. When this leads to a veritable "witch hunt" in search of the leakers in their midst, the resulting angry recriminations can undermine the trust and coherence that are so necessary for the early success of a new administration.

Perhaps the most important thing for a new team to acknowledge is the difficulty of completely controlling the message and the "spin" on the foreign policy and national security stories that will arise. A new administration should strive for a balance between absolute discipline and unwieldy openness in making the case for both early accomplishments and new directions in foreign policy. There will always be unwelcome surprises and difficult news accounts to deal with, but understanding the inevitability of this from the beginning can help ease some of the early stings.

Assessing the Historical Experience

These historical experiences with shepherding second- and third-tier appointees, supervising congressional relations, legacy issues, starting new initiatives, managing potential crises, and dealing with the press point to several important lessons that can help smooth future transitions.

Unlike personnel and process challenges, new administrations benefit from the considerable policy head start that comes out of the campaign itself. After all, the candidate has been sketching out, in greater or lesser detail, plans for governing throughout the campaign process. For the transition team the challenge is not so much to come up with new ideas, but to make the transition from campaign rhetoric and position papers to real budgets, executive orders, and legislation. Thus the first lesson is the need to set clear priorities for the first months in office and adapt the campaign rhetoric to the unexpected realities of governing. The first one hundred days is a time in which key choices must be made, such as whether to prioritize a campaign initiative, reaffirm but defer its implementation, or adjust the policy. A sure route to a foreshortened honeymoon is to overload the political and legislative agenda by seeking to accomplish too much of the campaign agenda at the outset. For example, during the Carter administration, the transition team identified more than one hundred initiatives (domestic and international) to put forward in the early months of the presidency.[51] According to Brzezinski, "we were overly ambitious and . . . we failed in our efforts to project effectively to the public the degree to which we were motivated by a coherent and well-thought-out viewpoint."[52] Clinton too developed a laundry list of presidential initiatives during the transition, but without a clear sense of presidential priority, nearly all sank beneath waves of opposition.[53] By contrast, the Reagan administration's laser-like focus on a small number of high-profile initiatives—notably, increasing the defense budget and cutting domestic spending—met with remarkable success.

The second lesson is the need to do the political homework. The honeymoon period is a double-edged sword. It is a unique opportunity to make swift progress on some of the incoming president's agenda, but if it is carried out in a way that creates a political backlash with Congress and the public, the effort could produce a Pyrrhic victory. The Reagan administration's failure to do the homework to gain support for the sale of AWACS to Saudi Arabia in 1981, discussed earlier, was a classic case of overconfidence by a new administration. President Clinton's experience with his campaign pledge on gays in the military was another; although the policy would have proved controversial under any circumstances, the failure to do the groundwork with Congress and the uniformed military fatally doomed the initiative and, more important, seriously undermined the honeymoon period and cast a shadow on the president's future interactions with the military. By contrast, Reagan actually appointed a bipartisan group of sitting members of Congress to act as a foreign policy advisory team.[54]

Third, it is crucial to take the time to understand the legacy of the outgoing administration—especially when the new administration intends to radically change the course pursued by its predecessor. Failure to confirm that the campaign assumptions accord with the reality is the surest path to early problems. But even where the intention is to carry forward the outgoing administration's plans, a fresh scrub is warranted. The Bay of Pigs incident is a powerful cautionary tale: because the inherited legacy is so rich in detail and nuance, prioritizing the issues and focusing on getting up to speed on those at the top of the list is likely to prove more successful than trying to swallow the entire legacy in one gulp.

Fourth, as with decisionmaking processes, it is vital, when possible, to make the key personnel decisions before developing elaborate policy documents and plans.[55] At best, ignoring this tenet results in wasteful efforts. Past transitions are rife with examples of outgoing officials working heroically to produce briefing books that their replacements subsequently discarded. More perniciously, these transition operations can generate conflicts between the transition teams and the new appointees, giving the impression of an administration in disarray even before it takes office. A transition veteran noted that when Caspar Weinberger took the reins at the Defense Department in the Reagan administration he dismissed the staff who performed policy work: "Cap's first day on the job, he fired them all, ran them all off and started fresh."[56] Experience suggests that agency-centric transition teams (and their work products) offer limited value before the new top officials are selected, a point stressed by Clark Clifford in his memoirs:

> In recent transitions . . . large temporary bureaucracies have set up shop in Washington, with advance teams from the new Administration moving into each of the departments and agencies. In 1980 for example, the Reagan administration . . . headquarters was a "blizzard of task forces, committees and teams." This is not merely a waste of money, it is also a diversion for the President-elect and his senior advisors when they should be concentrating only on the most critical matters—especially the all-important task of selecting the right people for the top job.[57]

8

TWENTY RECOMMENDATIONS

Getting Off to a Successful Start and Avoiding Transition Traps and Trip-ups

THE HISTORY OF presidential transitions is a highly cautionary tale replete with dangers and missteps that have bedeviled not just the novice, but even the wisest and most experienced of practitioners. Yet it is important to recall that transitions are also times of opportunity. The lessons of the past are reason for caution and prudence, but not paralysis. Indeed, by carefully avoiding some of the common mistakes of past transitions, a new president will be even better positioned to achieve the enormous hopes and grand designs that motivated the decision to run for the highest office in the first place. This book has examined four aspects of the transition process: campaigning, selecting the people, organizing the government, and implementing policy in the early days of office. The following recommendations roughly follow this framework.

Campaigning

It can appear presumptuous or politically naive for a presidential campaign trudging through the snows of Iowa or New Hampshire to worry about how early statements or positions might one day constrain their options or even compromise U.S. security, but history shows that nothing can induce greater "buyer's remorse" in a freshly minted president than ill-considered campaign commitments made in the heat of the political battle. History also demonstrates that campaigns offer a crucial opportunity to either get a fast start in the formal transition process or seriously complicate the crucial weeks between the election and inauguration. From the experience of the past sixty years we distill six recommendations for how best to wage the short-term political fight while keeping one eye on the prize (and the difficult job) that lies in the distance.

1. Be judicious when making promises.

Campaigns are meant to give voters a clear indication of what a president will do if entrusted with the highest office in the land, and to allow them to understand the differences between the candidates and what their presidencies would mean for important areas of policy. To some extent, this caution to think carefully about campaign promises applies to both domestic and foreign policy. Lightly considered commitments designed to appeal to specific constituencies or to make a news splash are staples of all aspects of the electoral process. But promises in the area of national security pose particularly acute challenges and risks for at least three reasons.

First, the president has considerably more leeway in the conduct of foreign affairs than on domestic policy (although even in foreign policy Congress has important levers of control through the confirmation process, in making appropriations, and in providing advice and consent to treaties). This tempts candidates to make sweeping assertions about how they will swiftly use this authority upon taking office. Moreover, because the United States is the most powerful country on earth, there is a tendency for candidates to believe, and for voters to expect, that presidents can and should achieve their goals in the foreign policy sphere. But promises that are beyond the power of the president to deliver can lead to disappointments and a loss of credibility early on in a new presidency.

Second, new presidents always learn facts and details that they didn't know or appreciate during the campaign, which can complicate the fulfillment of promises. But the problem is particularly acute in national security, where considerations of classified information and sensitive negotiations prevent the candidate and advisers from being fully informed about the state of the problems and the barriers they face. And there can be a considerable lag time before a quorum of key advisers gets up to speed on a specific issue once coming to power.

Third, the "credibility trap" that arises from ill-considered promises is particularly dangerous in foreign policy. An abandoned campaign promise on domestic policy may cause embarrassment and political damage, but failure to carry through campaign commitments in the area of foreign policy can damage the new president's international credibility, dismaying allies and emboldening foes, who might then be tempted to doubt the determination and reliability of the new chief executive. On the other hand, carrying through on a poorly conceived commitment can literally mean the difference between war and peace. Very few transition veterans looking back at their roles in the campaign period express any remorse about not having made more campaign promises, while many more wish they had been more careful in what they had promised. In general, when it comes to national security promises, less is often more.

2. Avoid answering hypothetical questions about situations that have not yet—and may never—emerge.

It is hard enough for a candidate to give a thoughtful policy response to an ongoing crisis or policy debate, much less to effectively speculate on how to handle some dilemma in the future. "Hypotheticals" (as these speculative questions are often called in policy circles) by their nature oversimplify highly complex situations with many unknown variables and unpredictable contingencies. Yet by venturing an answer to a hypothetical question, the candidate appears to commit to a policy course for a future administration that may reduce the flexibility to respond effectively to an actual crisis. This does not mean that candidates can and should simply dodge all questions about future policy. Instead, it is better to describe the principles that would guide future decisions rather outline the specific policy option that would be chosen once a decision became necessary.

3. Read before you sign.

Washington is full of interest groups and influential actors seeking to commit candidates to policy positions because they know that, once committed, a candidate who reneges on a commitment faces political costs. The growth of grassroots activism and the Internet have fueled the demands for candidates to pledge their fealty to a bewildering array of causes dear to the hearts of small numbers of highly motivated voters. Faced with a vast array of checklists with highly detailed, highly constraining demands, campaigns may be tempted to sign on to positions without fully considering their implications. This is particularly tempting when the candidate largely agrees with the positions advocated and doesn't wish to antagonize the group or hand a primary opponent a campaign advantage. Whenever possible, candidates should respond to these requests to "sign on" by offering their own interpretation or statement of policy rather than by simply accepting the formulation or language of the advocate.

4. Keep policy development integrated with the campaign.

Precisely because some campaign promises and policy guidance are inherent in campaigning, it is important that the candidate's development of policies for governing be firmly integrated with the campaign and not shunted off to a separate track or side room during the campaign, to be unveiled only after the candidate is elected. While it is tempting to set up elaborate policy "task forces" to get the transition off to a faster start, in practice there are great risks associated with such a massive policy mobilization. Most of these efforts are an enormous waste of energy that is abandoned once the candidate is elected and the key officials are chosen. Many such efforts are intended to keep important constituents and volunteers busy and involved in the campaign, but these attempts are often derisively referred to as "the illusion of inclusion" or "make-work groups."

At its worst, this approach can create tensions between policy people working on the campaign and those working on the transition, which can thoroughly complicate the post-election transition itself (as the Carter experience amply shows). Unlike the campaign policy staff, which has regular interaction with the candidate, the policy groups tend to get disconnected from the candidate's own thinking in the period before the election and become creatures of their members rather than providing direct support to the candidate and the future administration.

Although some campaigns have sought to limit this risk by having the transition teams develop "option papers" rather than policy documents, these efforts tend to be so generic as to be of limited value and so voluminous as to be virtually undigestible in the hectic weeks of the transition itself.

5. Use the campaign to reflect on and to develop the future president's specific style of decisionmaking.

Campaign decisionmaking has much in common with many aspects of national security decisionmaking, particularly in the arena of crisis management, where the pressures of time, the urgent demands of news cycles, and the presence of imperfect information all conspire to complicate deliberative processes. The campaign therefore provides a good opportunity to reflect on how the candidate functions and makes decisions most effectively under duress. For example, does the candidate like to delegate, to encourage advisers to find consensus, or to encourage dissent and debate to maximize his or her own role and flexibility in decisionmaking? Understanding these preferences and building an organization that reflects them is one of the most important internal tasks of a campaign, and transferring compatible procedures into governance structures is one of the most important challenges of the transition period.

6. Get a head start on selecting the key officials.

The most successful modern transitions (notably Reagan's and George H. W. Bush's) have made the best use of the preelection period not by establishing elaborate policy teams and task forces, but by establishing a focused effort to identify personnel to assume key positions immediately or soon after inauguration. Precisely because there is a heavy premium on early announcements of crucial staff in the national security sphere—early action helps provide reassurance to the country and to the world and maximizes the time for new appointees to get up to speed on the crucial issues of national security—the preelection period is critical for getting this process under way. Although demands on a candidate's time are enormous, particularly as the election approaches in a close contest, taking the requisite time to meet with and get to know the policy orientation and styles of potential senior officials (particularly those who are not part of the campaign apparatus) is time well spent.

As our historical review of the post–World War II era of initial national security appointments suggests, there has been a troubling pattern of presidents making selections either hurriedly or based on insufficient information or inadequate personal acquaintance. Indeed, there is a strong record of executive disenchantment with early appointments in the foreign policy and national security realms, and at least part of this is based on inconsistent styles or lack of early understandings about governing approaches. Greater early attention to the senior appointments process might well alleviate such misunderstandings and failed expectations and help to identify critical gaps in perceptions, procedures, and priorities earlier rather than later.

The Formal Transition: Selecting the Team and Setting Up Processes

This book has examined making personnel appointments and establishing the processes for governing in two separate chapters. However, in practice these two aspects of the transition go hand-in-hand, so the following six recommendations treat the two together. History shows the repeated folly of efforts to make appointments without a general sense of the preferred decisionmaking and governing style of a new president. Conversely, new presidents frequently stumble when they try to make broad pronouncements about their preferred organization without at least some sense of the kind of people they will choose to advise them. The key to success therefore is to capture the synergies of a well-integrated approach to decisions about personnel and organization in order to diminish the potential areas of discord.

7. *Think about the president's governing and decisionmaking style before establishing processes and making critical appointments.*

It is imperative to select people who will buy into, and work well with, the style that a president prefers, whether this is a highly consensual approach among agencies or one that is driven from the White

House. The classic case of mismatch in expectations in this category is the short-lived tenure of Al Haig as secretary of state in the Reagan administration. Even before Haig's famously incorrect comments on the constitutional line of succession following the assassination attempt on President Reagan, some in the White House were worried about Haig's decisionmaking style and assertions about his preeminence in the national security process. It is also important for a new president (or president-elect, as it is best to have these conversations before taking office) to clearly convey his or her expectations about decisionmaking and staff process before offering jobs. Presidents-elect who know what they want from process and people are more likely to achieve their goals than those who focus primarily on the initial political response to their appointments and hope that things will turn out for the best.

8. Establish priorities for personnel decisions.

Given the number and diverse range of national security appointments, it is impossible for the president to make all the decisions personally and to make them all before the end of the formal transition. Candidates should plan out far in advance and develop, with the most trusted of advisers, a system for prioritizing appointments, emphasizing those positions that would be essential to handling a crisis on day one. Given the profound risks associated with the early days of a new administration, a president-elect should carefully consider the value of holdover appointments in areas where understanding both the legacy and the levers of government power are critical to effective early actions. Richard Clarke, the counterterrorism czar in the NSC who was kept on by the Bush team from his position in the Clinton White House, is a good example. Given the urgency surrounding homeland security since 9/11, an incoming president would be wise to consider a similar approach in the intelligence and counterterrorism areas.

In making appointments at the key agencies, presidents and White House staff should give considerable authority and leeway to Cabinet officials to select their own subordinates, both to speed the staffing process and to help establish the authority and accountability of principals. A process heavily dominated by White House personnel where campaign loyalists or representatives from important constituencies are placed in influential positions over the objections of Cabinet officials can create a difficult working and decisionmaking environment from the outset. It may also discourage talented potential Cabinet officials from accepting a job that is offered. The danger that individuals selected by the new Cabinet officials won't work well as a team on an interagency basis is outweighed by the inability of a principal to operate effectively without trusted subordinates. Of course, the new president cannot and should not ignore the hard efforts of devoted campaign workers, but there are many ways to accommodate this legitimate interest without crippling the ability of new Cabinet secretaries and other principals to do their jobs. A recent example of this counterproductive instinct to place campaign loyalists "behind enemy lines" (as a member of Vice President Cheney's staff described it) was John Bolton's appointment to a senior position in Secretary Colin Powell's State Department.

9. Think about teams and synergies, not just individuals.

Too often, a president considers a whole range of appointments without carefully balancing loyalty with expertise, familiarity with competence, star power with team player, and individuality with complementarity. It is tempting for a new president, particularly one who comes to power with some question marks about previous foreign policy or national security experience, to pick people who offer instant credibility or star power. But presidents must then live with these choices long after the initial public acclaim over their appointments. Candidates also are strongly tempted to take valued campaign advisers on to the top jobs in a new administration. Although the candidate may have grown to trust and respect those advisers, it is important to think about how and in what roles campaign advisers can best serve a president-elect. It was an enlightened political operative in the Clinton years who once remarked that "sometimes the guerrilla fighters in the bush do not make the best public officials in the capital." Further, a new administration needs people who complement each other in style, substance, and expertise. An effective appointments process would begin by mapping out the characteristics officials should have for particular posts and then work backward, rather than simply starting with a list of names.

10. Avoid groupthink, but recognize the strains that too much policy divergence can place on decisionmaking.

Striking the delicate balance between consensus and vigorous policy debate is one of the most difficult challenges facing a new president. While groupthink is a major cause of foreign policy mistakes, there is little value in including individuals in an administration who don't share the basic outlook and orientation of the president. History suggests that they either become marginalized or paralyze the process and force the president to make all the decisions. This is particularly important in thinking about cross-party appointments. Across-the-aisle personnel selections can have great value in building congressional and public support, but there still needs to be a core element of philosophical and political commonality among the key members of the team and with the president if that benefit is to be truly and effectively reaped. Kennedy's appointment of Republican C. Douglas Dillon as secretary of the Treasury, for instance, shows it can be done; but the specific individual must be able to establish a productive working relationship with other key colleagues if this is not to be a one-day story that comes back to haunt an administration for weeks, months, or even years.

11. Accept the emergence of informal practices and procedures early on and integrate them into established mechanisms over time.

All administrations rely heavily on informal processes to supplement the formal decisionmaking machinery, perhaps at no time more than during the transition period and immediately thereafter. Often these informal norms and procedures become entrenched, both for good and for bad. Administrations can exercise more control over the transition process if they accept the fact that informal norms and procedures, if not deliberately established early on, will emerge in any case. No wiring diagram or formal set of coordinating government structures can fully meet the needs of a complex and constantly evolving national security environment, and the existence of informal procedures is a powerful ingredient in effective government management. The goal should be to strike a balance between the informal approaches that emerge during the campaign and reflect the personal proclivities of the president and senior advisers, and the more formal mechanisms that are promulgated in the early stages of governing. Over time, a successful president will seek to incorporate many of these informal interactions into more traditional governmental structures, reserving unstructured formats and interactions for the most necessary and delicate deliberations.

12. Remember that there is not one transition, but many.

The primary focus when thinking about a transition tends to be at the White House and its associated agencies, and indeed there is considerable turnover and change that takes places in these areas of government that are of enormous consequence. However, important transitions also take place simultaneously in other key departments, particularly the Departments of Defense, State, and now Homeland Security, that require specific attention and planning. For instance, while the joint staff and services provide some critical continuity at the Pentagon during a transition period, the role of civilian oversight is important and is a clear extension of presidential authority. Particularly during a time of war, the president and his team must pay close attention to the personnel and policy issues associated with a transition at the Department of Defense.

Governing: The First Hundred Days

In many respects, simply settling in for the long haul should be a goal in and of itself when establishing a new presidency. Too often, a young administration remains in a form of campaign mode and has difficulty transitioning into a more formal, mature style of governing with established decisionmaking procedures. Settling in requires an acceptance that campaign mode is insufficient for complex governance and that some of the techniques and approaches employed during the presidential campaign are not well suited to the deliberative, careful processes required to formulate and execute government policy, particularly with respect to national security. Early successes are like a catapult for a successful presidency, while early stumbles can blunt the election mandate and even cripple a presidency in its infancy. The following are some guidelines for how to hit the ground running—and avoid common stumbles.

13. Expect and plan for confusion and disorder at the outset.

National security officials who have experienced transitions firsthand almost uniformly depict the early days of governing as well-intentioned planning running headlong into disarray and confusion. As wise military leaders always remind, even the best-conceived plans rarely survive the first contact with the enemy. Those returning to government after years away from public service are often shocked by the degree of change since they last served. Disorienting developments can include innovations in information technology and equipment, unfamiliar government procedures, entirely new agencies, and altered power relations among departments, agencies, and other groups. For instance, Donald Rumsfeld returned to service as secretary of defense after a quarter century to find the Pentagon a much changed place, with a much more influential joint staff and a weaker civilian policy directorate.

For first-time government officials, the challenge is even more daunting. It is a heady time filled with a completely new set of demands and risks. Occasionally a campaign staffer who excelled in the field will struggle in the confining bridle of government service; or someone will quite unexpectedly excel. Inevitably, the early days of a new government involve some substantial quotient of confusion.

The task of the transition is to anticipate and incorporate this ineluctable fact into planning. Prioritizing and simplifying the transition period, creating opportunities for controlled learning experiences (such as crisis simulations), and giving key officials a chance to share information and anxieties can reduce the chaos of the early days.

14. Prioritize policy objectives and be wary of "first hundred days" pressures.

It is important for a new president and the incoming team to remember that they have at least four years, and possibly eight, to govern and implement their chosen policy approaches (indeed, whether they get eight years may be crucially affected by how well they handle the first months). Everything cannot and should not be launched in the first hundred days; a rush toward early accomplishments can create distorted incentives and artificial deadlines. It is no accident that one of the wisest students of transitions, Richard Neustadt, strongly urged new presidents to ferociously resist the siren song of the hundred days.[1] To get off to a strong start, it is important to consider not only what is most important to accomplish, but also what is most achievable.

15. Defer decisions, when possible, until confident of the facts— while recognizing that there will often be gaps in information.

Many of the campaign statements made by candidates or their surrogates are based on assumptions that may or may not be correct. It is important that an incoming team not simply assume that what was thought to be true is necessarily so. A new president must be open to the possibility that the reality will prove different, or more complex, than it appeared on the campaign trail, as Kennedy discovered about the missile gap. Once a candidate becomes president, the new team gains access to a wealth of information that may well cause a change of mind.

National security decisionmaking is inherently based on imperfect information, and no amount of delay will ensure perfect knowledge to inform the decision. The challenge for a new administration is to find the fine point where key information has been collected and analyzed and where the costs of delay outweigh any benefits from further refining the information and analysis. In the early days of a new administration there is a sharp learning curve, and the value of proceeding methodically can be substantial.

16. Think carefully before reversing predecessors' policy decisions.

Since campaigns are about contrasts, there will be considerable pressure on the new president to move quickly to reverse the criticized policy of the predecessor administration. Before moving precipitously, the new president should make sure that well-developed alternatives are ready and clearly thought out. When considering alternative approaches to existing policies, even ones that are clearly not working or are no longer viable, a process of "red teaming" to evaluate the potential alternatives is especially important in the early days as officials move up the learning curve. Using such "what if" techniques can help identify and reduce uncertainties before taking decisions. A corollary of this recommendation is to make sure that the reasons for a reversal of policy are really based on the pertinent facts and not simply on untested assumptions. Also, it is vital to lay the groundwork and explain to key stakeholders (especially allies) the reasons, timing, and process for intended policy changes in advance. Consultations with allies about changes in foreign policy and national security policy are of the utmost importance and can set the tone for future diplomacy and cooperation.

17. Try to revive the principle of leaving partisanship "at the water's edge."

Choices about national security policy are inevitably driven by differing ideologies and theories, which often divide along party lines. This is not only unavoidable, but is one of the strengths of the party system. But national security is too consequential to be driven by the pursuit of partisan advantage. America has been strongest when policymakers have strived for a degree of bipartisan support. Indeed, without it, it is difficult to sustain policy for long. During the height of the cold war, Republican senator Arthur Vandenberg's support for Truman's national security policies embodied the idea that partisanship should stop "at the water's edge" and that the country should unite, when possible, behind the president on critical issues of foreign policy and national security. In the post–cold war period consensus has been difficult to come by on issues ranging from Iraq to trade policy. Yet there have also been clear examples of cooperation across the aisle on important international initiatives during this time, such as bipartisan support for NATO expansion, the war in Afghanistan, and engagement with China. Since meeting the emerging challenges of the twenty-first century will require a sustained effort over many future presidencies, this suggests the prudence of working for a degree of bipartisan support.

18. Engage Congress early and often.

Although there is considerable focus on the unique authorities of the president in the formulation and execution of national security policy, in the long run a president cannot pursue an effective foreign policy without adequate support from Congress. To some extent, this is a corollary of the need for bipartisanship, but this also entails a healthy respect for the constitutionally mandated role of Congress in foreign affairs, including the power of the purse. President George W. Bush and his lieutenants often sought to advance a theory of executive branch dominance in matters of security, foreign and domestic, but such an approach risks alienating even the most ardent members of the same party serving in the legislative branch. Searching for consensus with Congress will pay substantial dividends, yielding greater public support, an enduring basis for continued financial support for national security policies, and a degree of political protection should a policy run into trouble.

19. Prepare to interact and engage with the media, instead of expecting to control the message at all times.

In today's global media environment of round-the-clock cable news shows, aggressive blogs, and extensive commentary, it is virtually impossible to successfully "control" messages for public consumption. Although secrecy and discipline will be watchwords of any and every administration, there is often too much focus on leaks and what is perceived to be unfair coverage by the media. A disciplined approach to public affairs is essential in a well-functioning administration, but there will always be stories that anger senior officials and cause counterproductive finger-pointing and a tendency to circle the wagons and deepen secrecy. In the long run these responses both undermine public support and harm decisionmaking by excluding dissenting voices and inconvenient facts. A smart administration will develop strong and well-conceived policy approaches to global problems and work hard to get its message out, understanding that leaks and pointed criticism come with the territory.

20. Establish and be familiar with crisis management tools by day one.

Today, even more than in the past, threats to American security can arise suddenly, unpredictably, and on a large scale. Threats from natural disasters, terrorism, energy insecurity, and other sources can arrive without notice and wreak havoc during a new administration's early days. The threats are myriad, and it is virtually impossible to anticipate every one of them. Too often in the early hustle and bustle of a new administration, insufficient attention is given to preparing for "what if" scenarios involving homeland security or a sudden crisis abroad. While it is impractical to develop detailed plans for every conceivable emergency, it is paramount to at least consider certain courses of action in the event of unforeseen developments. The best way to plan for crises involving either national security or homeland security is to move quickly to become knowledgeable about existing crisis management machinery, to make necessary adaptations from the outset, and to exercise them at an early stage—even before formally taking office.

THERE IS NO magic formula that can guarantee the successful launch of a new presidency. This list of recommendations should not be seen as offering a certain path to success through a tumultuous transition, but rather as a set of guideposts for planning and maneuvering through what is an inherently complex and unpredictable process. By tackling this challenge in clear and separate stages, and by developing an approach to campaigning and governing accordingly, a new president has the best chance to succeed and prosper.

TRANSITION
VERITIES

The 2008-09 Presidential Transition

I N LATE 2000, on one of the last of his dozens of trips to the island of Okinawa as a Department of Defense representative in negotiations over the future contours of the American military presence there, Kurt Campbell realized that he just was not going to get it done. There were too many moving parts and complicated pieces to actually reach an agreement that could be successfully implemented between the United States and Japan. Although the two countries were the closest of allies, the negotiations over bases and over the legal and financial underpinnings of U.S. forward presence at times felt almost adversarial. It suddenly dawned on him that in a few months it would no longer be his responsibility, but that of his successor. Unfortunately, the timing of key financial decisions, operational decisions, and military deployments on Okinawa would come during the most difficult early days of the transition and a new administration. He hoped that whoever followed him in office understood the risks of transitions and that this delicate process of diversifying U.S. forces in the Asia Pacific region would continue uninterrupted after a short hiatus. But would it be possible to both sustain the momentum of the talks and transfer the necessary institutional knowledge to a new group of players inside the Pentagon?

For Jim Steinberg, the final months of the Clinton administration were filled with implementing the agreements that successfully ended the war in Kosovo, dealing with the challenge of the North Korean nuclear program, and continuing the effort to contain the threat posed by Iraq. But since the bombings of the U.S. embassies in Kenya and Tanzania in 1998, no issue weighed more heavily on the outgoing administration than the threat posed by al Qaeda. Although planned attacks on the United States around the millennium were thwarted by focused effort and good luck, Steinberg and his colleagues knew that the terrorists had not abandoned their intention to strike at the United States. During the weeks before the new Bush administration took office, Steinberg was asked to come to the heavily secured transition offices, just a few blocks from the White House, to meet with his recently announced successor, Steve Hadley. The two were well acquainted from years of service in alternating administrations, and the conversation was cordial. They reviewed a broad range of issues, and finally turned to the threat of terrorism. Steinberg told Hadley that if the new administration accepted only one piece of advice from the outgoing one, it should be to retain Richard Clarke as the counterterrorism czar. Although Clarke had a reputation for sometimes contentious leadership, Steinberg argued that his intimate knowledge of the threat and of U.S. plans to address it would be irreplaceable in the early days of a new administration. Hadley smiled, but remained noncommittal. Steinberg left the room wondering just what approach his successor would take toward this looming threat.

These kinds of questions invariably haunt the minds of national security officials during presidential transitions. Policy, professional, and personal uncertainties are part and parcel of the process. These uncertainties are unavoidable and are inherent in the very idea of transferring power. Foresight and careful planning can help mitigate the predictable risks, but the greater challenge is in developing strategies involving people, processes, and policies that guard effectively against the unpredictable risks. To paraphrase former secretary of defense Donald Rumsfeld, a presidential transition poses the problem of known unknowns and unknown unknowns—not to mention expected and self-instigated problems that are either blundered into or triggered unintentionally. This book has sought to identify these dangers to help the next administration prepare for the challenges to come.

As we have illustrated, there is a profoundly human dimension to transitions as individuals take on the mantle of responsibility for the nation's security. Even those with extensive government experience find themselves nearly overwhelmed by the enormous personal commitment and sacrifices required to handle the crushing workload heaped on them through the transition period and into the new term. For many, this comes hard on the heels of a punishing campaign as well. Unexpected bumps in the road, including personnel problems involving scandals or baggage, as well as adverse media attention, can distract key players in even a well-executed transition from other, more critical tasks, potentially derailing an otherwise feasible policy agenda.

We have argued here that the transition process should be seen not simply as the perilous few weeks of formal power transfer between the election and inauguration, but rather as part of a much longer process stretching many months before and after. By examining this process in its various components—the campaign, decisions around personnel, choices concerning styles of governance, and the early period in power—we have sought to identify how unique challenges during each phase can escalate in unanticipated ways to create problems of perception and governance that not only dash the best hopes of an incoming president, but actually endanger national security. It is only by carefully identifying the risks (and indeed the potential rewards) associated with each of these distinct but interrelated phases that transition managers and national security leaders in the next administration will be able to successfully navigate this harrowing yet unavoidable political ritual of American governance.

The history of the eleven presidential transitions in the post–WWII era (Roosevelt to Truman, Truman to Eisenhower, Eisenhower to Kennedy, Kennedy to Johnson, Johnson to Nixon, Nixon to Ford, Ford to Carter, Carter to Reagan, Reagan to Bush, Bush to Clinton, and Clinton to Bush) includes several different kinds of transitions, between and within parties, that arose through the constitutional calendar and also those that emerged unanticipated, though resignation, death by natural causes, or assassination. Each transition is unique, but even across these different types of transitions, many of the same uncertainties and risks prevail.

This book has sought to lay out the factors that contribute to complexity and risk during a presidential transition, ranging from the unrealistic expectations that are created by promises made during the preceding campaign to the growing range and intensity of global challenges, which are magnified by the relentless expansion and rapidity of the global news cycle. In many ways, each of these factors is simultaneously getting worse on its own and combining with other developments to complicate the transition process in both expected and unanticipated ways. The national security legacy that the next administration will inherit—from Iraq to Afghanistan to Korea to Iran, and the emerging dangers of climate change, public health, and energy insecurity—means that as much as any time in our history, the next administration truly needs to be ready to govern from day one. As the noted presidential observer and practitioner David Gergen has said before, "The national security inheritance of the next president could scarcely be more onerous."[1]

The election of 2008 is the first since 1952 in which neither the sitting president nor vice president is a contestant, which means that however the election comes out, the nation will have a president who is a newcomer to the executive branch. This very fact ensures that the transition will be a demanding challenge. And it will be further complicated by the fact that it will be the first post-9/11 transition. There is a much larger set of bureaucratic actors and critical positions that must be attended to immediately after the election to address the ongoing and urgent issues surrounding counterterrorism, involving not only the traditional national security agencies of State, Defense, and the NSC, but also the new entities, including the Department of Homeland Security and the Office of the Director of National Intelligence, which have never before experienced a transition.

The candidates have campaigned to distance themselves from many of the policies, and certainly from the perceived operational failures, of the George W. Bush administration. As such, there is little prospect for any substantial overlap in senior personnel, even with a transition inside the same political party should John McCain prevail in November. In this respect, a Bush-to-McCain transition would probably resemble in some ways the earlier Reagan-to-Bush transition, when ideological

matters and perceived personal slights combined to make for a sometimes awkward high-level handoff.

A Bush-to-Obama transition would carry with it the sort of demands
associated with the Clinton-to-Bush handoff. So deep were the antago-
nisms and so trenchant the critiques that the incoming Bush team
adopted an approach to previous policies that was dubbed "ABC"—
Anything but Clinton—by some commentators. The Obama campaign's
critique of the Bush team's policies and performance during the campaign has, in many areas, been similarly unsparing. Expectations have
been raised that an Obama administration would bring a substantial
departure from current policies on a whole range of issues, such as the
treatment of detainees, climate change, and the conduct of the wars in
Iraq and Afghanistan.

Although neither candidate brings personal experience in the executive branch, both would bring to the presidency a perspective shaped by
serving at the other end of Pennsylvania Avenue in the United States
Senate. The next president will be the first sitting senator to occupy the
presidency since 1960. Both in their Senate service and in their campaigns, the two have emphasized the need to transcend traditional partisan politics. This suggests that, irrespective of the outcome, there may
be a new opportunity to forge a different set of relationships on national
security with Congress, one of our core recommendations for getting off
to a fast and sustainable start.

While this book is filled with cautionary tales about the risks of transitions, it should in no way be read as discouraging presidential boldness
and ambition. On the contrary, our message is that by avoiding these
recurring risks and dangers, a wise chief executive will be far more likely
to succeed in achieving even dramatic change.

In truth, the historical record of U.S. postwar transitions has generally been one of good fortune—of bullets dodged and landmines cir-
cumvented. Despite the blunders and missteps, our constitutional system has shown remarkable resilience. There have been setbacks and
scandals to be sure, but no true calamities, no bolts from the blue. But
our past good fortune is not a guarantee of future success. It is critical
for an incoming team to weigh all the risks and understand the pitfalls

if it is to succeed as well as or better than its predecessors on these vital issues of national security.

By following the series of recommendations provided in the preceding chapter, we are convinced the next administration has a fighting chance to successfully negotiate the coming presidential transition and chart a brighter, more hopeful future for America and the world. In this, it is appropriate that we offer the last word to the great presidential historian and commentator Richard Neustadt. He described the transition process as "quintessentially American in both its hopes and its hazards."[2] In writing this book, our inspiration was a desire to maximize the prospects for the former and diminish the chances of the latter during the next transition of presidential power.

SCHOLARLY AND EXPERT PERSPECTIVES

The Makings of Modern History

T HERE IS ABUNDANT scholarly literature on the past practices, constitutional procedures, and policy implications of presidential transitions, and this body of writing provides an essential context and foundation for the analysis and observations found in *Difficult Transitions*. What follows is an overview of some of the critical texts and scholarly treatments of modern transitions. This overview is by no means exhaustive, but is meant to be illustrative of the work that has been done on this most American of political crossings. Here we provide a sampling of the scholarship and some context for our work on the broad subject of presidential changeovers. Indeed, it will be clear that we have sought to build and elaborate on several dimensions of the literature outlined here.

Any serious review of transition scholarship must begin with Richard Neustadt and his lucid and insightful writings on the presidency. Perhaps the most prominent scholar of modern presidential politics, Neustadt has provided a critical body of work on the modern aspects of the transition process in all of its many dimensions. Many of his observations have come to define how we think about and define a transition. For example, Neustadt outlined the notion that a transition can be seen both narrowly as the time span between election and inauguration and broadly as the time until the president and his staff have completely adjusted to the office (approximately two years).[1] The former period is often referred to as the "formal" transition period, although practically speaking the latter conceptualization is probably more accurate. Certainly this book would tend to reinforce the broader interpretation.

Neustadt identified three major hazards of transitions: ignorance, hubris, and haste. Ignorance can manifest itself in three distinct ways: a limited knowledge of Washington and its institutions, a failure to grasp the nuances of foreign policy, and a limited understanding of the nature and nuances of the executive branch. Hubris evolves from the euphoria that accompanies winning a campaign and can lead to a sense of invincibility and a willingness to disregard advice from the prior administration. Neustadt suggests that hubris is particularly detrimental in the context of a transition when the incoming staff refuses to learn from those who are leaving. New political appointees often brush off or are suspicious of career civil servants and as a result fail to take full advantage of this valuable institutional memory. Haste can arise from the excitement and prospects of going in a new direction and can give rise to ill-conceived proposals and initiatives early in a new administration.

Neustadt drew on this analysis to formulate recommendations for easing the transitional period of any new president, and they are every bit as relevant today as when he first made them: transition planning should be kept informal and anonymous; the staff should be organized as soon as possible to keep the influence of the media minimal; electing and appointing men and women with Washington experience tends to lead to more effective policymaking; and finally, the general public should lower their expectations for a new president, particularly at the outset. Neustadt argued that, during the first few years, administrations experience a steep learning curve that the public ought to take into consideration in evaluating the success of an administration.

Roger Porter, one of the nation's premier presidential scholars, later augmented Neustadt's framework.[2] He suggested that Neustadt's original work left some issues of modern transitions unaddressed, such as the role of party platforms during the interregnum. In addition, Porter argued that the transition process itself had become more important because this period had attracted more attention from the media and the public, and because recent presidents and their staffs had less

Washington experience than many of their predecessors. Moreover, Porter added a fourth hazard of transitions to Neustadt's three: a new administration's tendency to overreach, which he feared could prove detrimental to later initiatives. But despite the hazards that face a president in the beginning of his or her term, Porter stated that there are three distinct areas of opportunity available to a new administration early on: the ability to take symbolic action, to foster bipartisan politics, and to advance legislative initiatives with Congress.[3]

Much of the contemporary scholarship uses specific case studies in making its arguments. Based on their study of the Ford-Carter, Carter-Reagan, and Bush-Clinton transitions, Anthony Eksterowicz and Glenn Hastedt derived three broad lessons: "Incoming presidents who campaign against the Washington establishment and win hard-fought elections need transition help that focuses on the political and policy process"; transition planning needs to occur early; and candidates should seek funding for the transition through private contributions.[4] They also recommended that transitions occur in a two-stage process. Before the election, the incoming administration should concentrate on general management and learning about the policy process. Postelection, the administration should shift its focus to policy issues. Eksterowicz and Hastedt asserted that policy decisions and transitions from the campaign trail should be advised by experts and current members of Congress and not be left simply to campaign loyalists.

The roles of campaigning and media relations increased in importance steadily over the postwar era, and coverage of the transition itself increased manifestly over the decade of the 1990s as new media technologies led to more media scrutiny and a much greater need for administrations to deal effectively with the press. Building further on the tradition of Richard Neustadt, Charles O. Jones focused his work on the phase of the transition between campaigning and governing. Jones's work recognized the importance of the press to modern transitions and concluded with detailed recommendations. These included the importance of coordinating and integrating preelection planning and the campaign organization, the need to establish an overall campaign theme, and recognizing how press coverage of a new president will inevitably evolve during the course of a transition.[5]

Another theme in the transition literature is a distinction between "outsider" and "insider" candidates entering the White House. Using a detailed case study approach, John P. Burke analyzed the lessons of the 1980 and 1988 presidential transitions, looking for insights into how each was conducted.[6] He praised the 1980 transition of President Reagan as "the most successful of the transfers in power since the modern era of presidential transitions," and he found the 1988 transition to President George H. W. Bush instructive for its lessons on "friendly takeovers."[7]

Reagan's transition provided useful lessons on the challenges of a Washington outsider in managing this process. Reagan delegated much of the decisionmaking to those under him both during the transition itself and subsequently over the course of much of his presidency. Burke observed that Reagan used the opportunity afforded by the transition period to consider how to construct a Cabinet to fit his particular decisionmaking style and needs (not terribly successfully as it turned out). Burke also highlighted Reagan's efforts to build a good relationship with Congress from the outset. In evaluating the 1988 transition, Burke noted that George H. W. Bush, in contrast, took a much more central role in the transition process than Reagan had. Also in contrast to Reagan, Bush selected nominees whom he had previously known. Bush was also able to take advantage of the knowledge of the outgoing Reagan administration in making both policy and personnel decisions.[8]

Stephen Hess and James Pfiffner examined the evolution of presidential responsibilities and organizational capacity from Roosevelt to George W. Bush in their book *Organizing the Presidency*. They concluded that "ultimately it is the president's style . . . that will be the key to how the White House is organized." Even so, they saw the modern presidency as besieged by "prodigious growth" and increasing bureaucratization of the executive branch and as a consequence, successive presidents have made the mistake of assuming a position of "chief manager" rather than "chief political officer." They suggested a remedy to the bloating executive branch by proposing "a redefinition of the tasks of presidents" that would focus the chief executive on "a relatively small number of highly significant political decisions—among them setting national priorities . . . and devising policy to ensure the security of the country." Hess and Pfiffner call this a "minimalist theory of the presidency."[9]

Frederick Mosher, David Clinton, and Daniel Lang wrote a landmark study focused on foreign affairs and presidential transitions, building on the Miller Center's 1986–87 Commission on Presidential Transitions and Foreign Policy, co-chaired by former secretaries of state William Rogers and Cyrus Vance. Concentrating on post–World War II transitions, they described the transition challenges in the area of foreign affairs that grew and developed after Laurin Henry and Neustadt published their pioneering works in the late 1950s and early 1960s.[10] Their volume remains one of the few works to specifically address transition challenges in the international realm, and in many ways it inspired and guided our own study.

Mosher and his co-authors described the full range of transition problems that new administrations face in the international arena, from identifying, appointing, and confirming new officials, to managing the relationship between career civil servants and political appointees, to the way secrecy and compartmentalism can prevent even the best-informed appointees from smoothly assuming their new positions. They also discussed the ways in which campaign platforms can constrain and embarrass new administrations as they discover the classified reality and complex details that differ from the rhetoric of the campaign.[11] Mosher, Clinton, and Lang concluded that while managing effective transition teams has proven beyond the capabilities of most incoming administrations, success is still possible: only careful and efficient planning can mitigate the foreign affairs dangers posed by presidential transitions.[12]

Eksterowicz and Hastedt noted three problematic trends associated with foreign policy decisionmaking during transitions: presidents-elect often fail to adequately understand the issues at hand before formulating policies; new administrations sometimes fall prey to a desire to quickly distinguish themselves from the previous leadership by making commitments before establishing the proper mechanisms for doing so and paying too little attention to how policies will be perceived outside the United States. In order to avoid these dangers, Hastedt and Eksterowicz offered several recommendations to future presidents for avoiding this political quicksand. They urged candidates to familiarize themselves with the processes of foreign policymaking and suggested that attention to process may be more important than actual policy decisions in the early days of the transition. They also asserted that the president-elect should wait until after Election Day to begin establishing actual foreign policy programs and recommended convening policy summits to explore policy alternatives, involving a wide range of individuals with relevant insights and experience.[13]

John Rollins's 2008 study highlighted national security issues that may be of importance to both incoming and outgoing administrations. He noted specifically that the 2008–09 transition—the first between administrations since 9/11—could feature unique challenges for U.S. national security due to the "quantity, diversity, and breadth of security risks confronting the nation."[14] He identified three types of national security challenges that the next president will likely face. These include "current U.S. military engagements," such as Iraq and Afghanistan; "risks posed in countries and regions of concern," including Iran and North Korea; and "risks associated with contemporary issues," such as nonproliferation and homeland security.[15] Rollins also pointed out that the transfer of power from George W. Bush to the next president will be managed by several recently established or reorganized national security institutions that have never experienced a presidential transition and that are heavily staffed by political appointees who may leave office before the members of the incoming team assume office.

Rollins identified five phases of the presidential transition and provided options for dealing with the security issues associated with each phase. The phases are campaigning for the nomination, selecting the party nominees, Election Day, the period between Election Day and inauguration, and the inauguration and early days of the administration. Once into the fourth phase, the president-elect is legally permitted to apply for security clearances for transition team members who need access to classified documents. According to Rollins, some believe that phase four, the period of the "technical transition," is the most likely time for a terrorist attack. Such an attack might be undertaken in an attempt to trigger tension between the outgoing and incoming administrations with respect to presidential decisionmaking approaches and to "take advantage of perceived interagency coordination confusion" between the departure of the outgoing political appointees and the appointment and confirmation of the new ones.[16] In particular, "Some security experts are concerned that the remaining leadership in various departments and agencies, some of whom are presumably career civil servants that are serving in an acting capacity, could fall victim to receiving conflicting direction from both the outgoing and incoming national security leaders."[17]

Rollins advises a president-elect to choose individuals with good national security credentials for the transition team—experts with a background in intelligence, military affairs, and diplomacy. According to Rollins, the fourth phase gives the president and president-elect an opportunity to work together to avoid presenting a divided front to America's enemies.

Finally, Rollins noted that Congress has traditionally sought to facilitate executive branch transitions by supplying the new team with information and briefings on important issues as well as expediting security clearances for transition team members. He offered other possibilities, including undertaking public outreach efforts on national security risks, establishing joint advisory councils on transition-related risks, providing additional resources to nonfederal entities (especially first responders) with homeland security responsibilities, and holding hearings to solicit ideas on prospective national security objectives and policies.[18]

Looking ahead, Richard Armitage and Michèle A. Flournoy emphasized in a 2008 *Washington Post* article that the early months of 2009 will present a particularly difficult task for the next administration. Either Barack Obama or John McCain will "not only take charge of two wars but will also inherit daunting national security challenges: a global struggle against violent extremism; the continued proliferation of nuclear weapons to hostile states; growing challenges associated with energy security and climate change; an overstretched military under enormous strain; an economy sliding toward recession; and U.S. global standing at an all-time low." Given these conditions, it is critical, they argued, for U.S. national security that the next transition proceed smoothly. Armitage and Flournoy argued that expediting the transition process is important for two reasons. First, the next president is likely to face critical national security issues within the first few months of his administration, and second, the next incumbent needs to conduct, as rapidly as possible, "an intensive strategy development process to set clear priorities, determine how to pursue them, and decide how to manage the inevitable trade-offs."[19]

One of the most distinctive trends of presidential transitions is their increasing complexity, and therefore difficulty, over time. Writing in 1960 in a highly influential Brookings study that was avidly consumed by the incoming Kennedy administration, Laurin L. Henry had already identified three notable changes associated with the process, including less preparation time, the reduction of the "lame duck" period, and growing cooperation between outgoing and incoming administrations. The ratification of the Twentieth Amendment in 1933 had shortened the lame duck period and shifted the date of the presidential inauguration from March to January. This change helped prevent political stagnation, but it also brought new and challenging demands to the period of transition.[20] Henry also identified several transition issues that continue to be salient today. First, the incoming administration could arrive in office overly confident and distrusting of its predecessors. Second, the lack of clarity on policy issues during the early months of new leadership can create headaches for the bureaucracy. These two problems could then impede the progress of new administrations as they attempt to implement policy.

Writing several years later, Henry continued in this analytic tradition by examining the 1968–69 transition between Presidents Johnson and Nixon.[21] He noted that Nixon chose not to use the official space designated for the president-elect, but rather directed the transition from outside of Washington, D.C., from offices in New York and Florida. Nixon also seemed to lack an overriding theory of government or any notion of what he specifically wanted to do, which delayed appointments to some lower posts—an issue that has been exacerbated subsequently as the number of appointments has increased. The Johnson-Nixon transition was also marked by "an unprecedented amount of policy consultation and public display of unity on foreign policy," most certainly due to the increasing complexity of the process as the federal government continued to grow.[22] Henry concluded by arguing that the Nixon transition both followed and further developed the presidential transition process that was emerging at the time. Finally, he noted several factors in the previous three transitions that had led to a "satisfactory experience and rapid learning in the political community."[23] He believed it was significant that the turnover of power from party to party was relatively rapid, that the transitions occurred in the midst of international difficulties, and that there was a good deal of shared opinion between the presidents and their successors. As such, he felt the prospects for a favorable transition might actually be improving.

Perhaps the most worrisome trend contributing to the increasing complexity are the growing difficulties around political appointments. A November 2000 publication from the Brookings Institution's Presidential Appointee Initiative divided the task of staffing into two phases.[24] The first occurs between the election and inauguration and may spill over into the postinauguration period. That phase is often marked by ambiguity, overlap, and duplication of responsibilities, with great uncertainty about procedures for recruiting, vetting, selecting, and approving nominees. While the president-elect's aides are scouring the country for satisfactory appointees, they simultaneously field tens of thousands of unsolicited résumés from job seekers. During the pre-inauguration period, most presidents-elect try to choose the members of the Cabinet and perhaps a few other nominees for prominent positions. This is the most personalized and ad hoc phase of the personnel selection process. The president is usually deeply involved, and many of the people selected for high-level positions are well known to him.

The Brookings study goes on to describe the second phase of staffing a new administration—the post-inauguration phase—as taking on a life of its own when the president's personal involvement begins to diminish. An important reason for the change is the scope of the task. The president simply cannot commit the requisite time for the selection of thousands of people who will fill positions in the new administration. As such, effective delegation is thought to be of decisive importance. And many appointees need not only be selected, but also confirmed by the Senate. In 2000, for instance, David Sanger pointed out that the number of presidential appointees requiring Senate confirmation had grown from 196 under John F. Kennedy to 786 under Bill Clinton.[25]

Though assembling a team that meets a president's standards is difficult, getting a team in place early allows a president to take advantage of the window of opportunity that occurs at the outset of a new term. The Brookings report also studied appointees from 1984 to 1999 and found that over half (58 percent) were working inside the Beltway when nominated. It also found that over a third (35 percent) occupied another federal government position. Other appointees came from law firms (17 percent), business (18 percent), educational and research institutions (14 percent), state and local governments (8 percent), and nonprofit organizations (4 percent).[26]

Carl Brauer followed up Laurin Henry's work on the successes and failures of the presidential transitions that took place from Eisenhower through Reagan.[27] He concluded with a number of critical observations and recommendations that again are relevant to modern circumstances. Brauer reasoned that John F. Kennedy's appointment of Dean Rusk as secretary of state rather than William Fulbright confirmed a larger lesson in transitions generally: it could be valuable for the president to appoint people with whom he has had close prior relationships. He also concluded that presidents-elect must determine, before their inauguration, the tone of the relationships between the executive office and federal agencies and establish a liaison with the outgoing administration and with the bureaucracy. Although formal authority rests exclusively with the incumbent president, power rapidly begins to shift to the president-elect as agencies and foreign governments look to the incoming administration for signals about future relations. Historically, past presidents have employed the power of executive agencies to conduct diplomacy during the transition well before they actually assumed office.

Brauer observed that the first critical step for a new president in a transition period is to make personnel decisions. He took note of a rising trend among modern presidents to seek diversity in appointees, taking into consideration ethnic, racial, and regional variables. Finally, Brauer emphasized the importance of being able "to attract exceptionally able, experienced people to appointive positions and then retain them long enough for them to be effective." Rather than attempting to get appointees to commit to a minimum duration of employment, Brauer wrote that increasing retention rates would require "better pay, plus a greater sense of accomplishment and recognition for appointees."[28]

Emphasizing the importance of early planning, John P. Burke offered additional recommendations for incoming presidents-elect.[29] The variables he considered ran the gamut from the duration of a transition to staffing considerations based on the personal qualities of the president and his staff. Ultimately, he stressed the importance of planning for the transition well in advance of making decisions—especially with regard to top appointments. He advocated selecting both loyal colleagues and experienced Washington insiders. Burke placed less emphasis on the need to educate new staffers in Washington's policies and processes, but urged that the president-elect and his or her staff should work cordially with the outgoing administration.

In a later essay Burke outlined some rules for successful transitions and emphasized the importance of strong management.[30] He recommended creating distinct teams for the execution of specific tasks while keeping the broader picture in mind. For instance, while it might be wise to have separate campaign and transition staffs with clear goals and objectives, there must be trust between the teams and significant room for the flow of information. Burke noted that staff members who fill multiple roles may not be able to give full attention to their most vital tasks. Amplifying two themes addressed throughout this book, he also argued that balance between loyal and experienced staff is a crucial consideration and underscored the importance of advance planning for the transition to help ensure having an organized, cohesive staff selected early.

Unlike many articles and books on presidential transitions that focus on the incoming administration and how it prepares or fails to prepare for the move into the White House, William Howell and Kenneth Mayer examined the outgoing president's actions in the so-called lame duck period. They focused on "executive orders, proclamations, executive agreements, national security directives, memoranda, and other directives [that] presidents have at their disposal . . . to [unitarily] effectuate lasting and substantive policy changes, both foreign and domestic." This work drew attention to those times when incoming presidents could not undo the work of their predecessors "without paying a considerable political price, undermining the nation's credibility or confronting serious legal obstacles."[31] Howell and Mayer noted that, ideally, an incoming president would work with the outgoing administration to prevent undesirable discontinuities and to ensure that an accurate record of inherited executive actions is fully communicated to an incoming team.

Picking up on themes established throughout the literature, Martha Joynt Kumar explored transition prospects and pitfalls that resonate loudly today amidst the climate of increased partisanship.[32] Kumar agreed with Hastedt and Eksterowicz that, in some cases, new presidents should capitalize on their first hundred days in office to engage in policymaking, despite the inherent risks. But on the subject of staffing choices, Kumar warned that when a transition occurs between parties, the incoming administration can be unreceptive or hostile to the advice of the previous administration. Kumar also argued that "campaign momentum" can lead an overly confident incoming team to commit serious errors. Moreover, she cautioned that "a team chosen for its political expertise generally is weak in management skills." Another danger Kumar identified was that of a transition process that essentially had "no memory and no training."[33] One way to prevent a dearth of knowledge and expertise about past policies, Kumar argued, would be to select staff members who served in previous administrations to help provide institutional memory for the new team.

James Pfiffner renewed the focus on the early days of new administrations in his book *The Strategic Presidency* by including a list of suggestions for early success.[34] He wrote that there are four major steps to achieving success during a transition: getting off to a fast start, developing an effective legislative liaison operation, "courting Congress," and choosing an effective governing strategy. Pfiffner disagreed with conventional claims that new presidents can capitalize on the "honeymoon" period after the inauguration. Goodwill, he argued, was not bestowed, but earned. Instead, he argued that a new president must build momentum with early successes and set the tone for future relationships, particularly with Congress. To increase the chances of success, a president should have a legislative liaison operation that can communicate effectively with Congress during the transition period to set an agenda, work on Cabinet appointments, and meet with the president-elect himself. In addition, a president-elect must himself "court Congress" and begin the necessary political legwork to ensure later cooperation. Finally, a new administration must carefully choose which issues to pursue. Pfiffner argued that it is essential that the range and volume of issues a new president takes on be manageable and reasonable.

In 2001 Richard Neustadt again returned to the topic of the early period of governance and the first hundred days.[35] Though this period has been highlighted as particularly important since President Franklin D. Roosevelt's first term and his "Hundred Days" plan, Neustadt considered the designation antiquated. He suggested that highlighting the beginning of a presidency as its defining or most important period is not necessarily accurate or even instructive. Neustadt also rejected the notion that the beginning of a president's first term is the most opportune period for initiating new policies. He noted that during the transition period presidents have yet to fully grasp the intricacies of the position and will hence be more prone to blunder. Finding an appropriate level of policy initiative during the first hundred days while avoiding overreach is a recurring challenge confronted by every administration.

As transitions evolved in the direction of ever greater complexity, Anne Marie Shackleton explored the role of outside organizations in helping to ease presidential transitions. She concluded that although many organizations use presidential transitions to pursue an issue-oriented agenda with an incoming administration, "relatively few organizations provide transition teams with the information necessary to assume power without unduly disrupting the necessary functions of government and at the same time increasing their chances for effectively advancing the new political agenda."[36] One organization, the congressionally chartered and nonprofit National Academy of Public Administration (NAPA), attempted to provide an incoming administration with nonpartisan information about how to conduct an effective transition. NAPA noted that the George W. Bush administration received 75,000 résumés for around 3,000 positions. The study concluded that it is clearly challenging for a fledgling administration to review so many résumés and conduct interviews for such a large number of staff positions and that this process must be delegated to trusted subordinates over time.

Fortunately, as Shackleton notes, incoming presidents have significant resources at their disposal for transition planning. The Presidential Transition Act of 1963 provided for transition team salaries and authorized the General Services Administration (GSA) to provide logistical support to the incoming team. Since the enactment of the legislation, the amount spent on transition-related expenditures has increased from $900,000 to about $4 million. Shackleton pointed out that with the funding allocated to incoming presidents it may be valuable to commission organizations like NAPA, the Council for Excellence in Government, and the American Society for Public Administration to advise the transition team. She also concluded that it is important not to overlook the expertise of career civil servants, the vast majority of whom are loyal, responsive, and competent.

Stephanie Smith of the Congressional Research Service traced the development of the legislation designed to assist both outgoing and incoming presidents during the transition process, from 1963 to the most recent changes.[37] She noted that, before 1963, transitions were primarily funded by the party of the winning candidate and were facilitated by volunteers. The 1988 Presidential Transitions Effectiveness Act increased this funding and mandated stricter oversight of private donations and transition personnel. The Presidential Transition Act of 2000 also provided support for orienting staff members. Smith identified preelection planning and the need to set policy priorities as key transition issues. She also noted the significance of adequate funding. For the Clinton-Bush presidential transition, for example, $7.1 million was appropriated: $4.3 million for the incoming George W. Bush administration, $1.8 million for the departing Clinton team, and some $1 million for the GSA.[38]

The most prominent theme throughout the literature on the transition is the importance of early planning and organization in managing the process. Martha Joynt Kumar, George C. Edwards III, James P. Pfiffner, and Terry Sullivan explained the need for early planning regarding policy formulation, fact collecting, staffing, agenda setting, budgeting, and communicating with Congress, the press, and key supporters.[39] They also warned that early mistakes can have a lasting impact, a point that reinforces the values of planning, clarity, and cohesiveness. These authors stressed the importance of limiting campaign promises and prioritizing goals in order to maintain a manageable policy agenda during the transition, another important theme of this volume. Perhaps most important, the article stressed that the incoming administration must set the policy agenda lest it be set by outside organizations eager to hijack the incoming president's policy goals.

Kumar and her colleagues also reiterated that "those who have served in White House posts and know the advantages and disadvantages associated with the quality of the start of an administration, strongly believe early planning is associated with an effective first year in office."[40] In this limited timeframe, a president-elect must form a White House team, nominate Cabinet members, present an agenda to the nation, and send a multi-trillion-dollar national budget to Congress. The responsibilities are endless: dealing with hundreds of policy proposals, making staff appointments, and responding to invasive media make it difficult to "meet the freight train head on."[41] But Kumar and her coauthors suggested that a nascent administration can take advantage of the early opportunities, namely a forgiving press, an attitude of hope, and the expectation of change during a transitional period. They offer five "lessons" to presidential candidates: plan ahead for personnel decisions; avoid constraining commitments during the campaign; appoint key White House personnel as early as possible; learn from predecessors by taking advantage of resources already in place; and develop a strategic plan for policy proposals.

In an earlier work, W. David Clinton and Daniel G. Lang asserted that there are few, if any, clear guidelines for conducting a successful transition, but the strategy they offered as consistently useful is, once again, early planning and action.[42] Getting a head start on policy issues provides the president-elect with a chance to set the agenda and tone of the administration, and also to win the passage of programs once in office.

Clinton and Lang also addressed the competition for authority, intentional or otherwise, between the president-elect and the outgoing president. Although the new administration will have the final say, the outgoing administration can make last-minute commitments to try to bind its successor. With regard to foreign affairs in particular, they note the importance of clarity about who speaks for the country during the transition. Despite this inherent competition, incumbents usually volunteer information without being asked. Members of Congress can also be an invaluable resource to incoming presidents for advice on maintaining foreign policy continuity. Clinton and Lang warned, though, that this information may come with "strings attached" and that other groups may have transition teams of their own, though this is less likely if the transition is friendly. Furthermore, it is important to be as clear and open as possible with both Congress and other actors about policies and processes.

Jack Armitage responded to some of Clinton and Lang's claims with the caveat that uniform recommendations can be too general to be useful.[43] He suggested instead that assessments should consider only what was successful or unsuccessful in specific transitions. Armitage offered a more guarded perspective than most authors. For example, while agreeing that the incoming administration should be receptive to advice from the outgoing administration, Congress, or the bureaucracy, he advocated that it should also collect information independently and remain wary of unconditionally accepting the "institutional memory" and other legacies of previous administrations. Similarly, while Armitage favored earlier planning, he cautioned that this should not distract presidential candidates unduly from the tasks required to win the election campaign. He also thought that it might be beneficial to reduce the size and scope of election teams and diminish connections between the transition staff and new appointees once the administration takes office.

ULTIMATELY, THE STUDIES and recommendations in the literature on presidential transitions overwhelmingly emphasize four main points. First, transitions have steadily grown in complexity, and as we discuss in chapter 3, the dangers have increased as well. Second, since the transition process is so complex and difficult to navigate, an incoming administration should solicit advice from multiple sources: the outgoing administration, Congress, people with extensive Washington experience, and outside organizations. Third, because the challenges of the transition process are so great, especially making appointments, planning for the transition should begin as early as possible. Finally, presidents should carefully choose the types of policies they hope to pursue in the early months of the administration. Although experts disagree on the relative importance of the first hundred days, most recommend that presidents learn as much about existing policies and policymaking processes as soon as possible. Presidents should also be wary of over-reaching on their legislative goals during the early months of their administrations, even as the honeymoon period offers modest opportunities for early successes.

Despite the growing complexity of the transition process itself, the fundamental issues of campaigning, staffing, structuring, and governing have remained remarkably consistent over time. What has changed noticeably, as most analysis suggests, is that transitions have become dramatically more complex, uncertain, and fraught with security risks as the number of domestic political factors and foreign policy challenges has grown exponentially.

NOTES

Preface

1. Richard Neustadt, *Presidential Power and the Modern Presidents: The Politics of Leadership from Roosevelt to Reagan* (New York: Free Press, 1991), p. 248.

2. Clark Clifford with Richard Holbrooke, *Counsel to the President: A Memoir* (New York: Random House, 1991), p. 328.

Chapter Two

1. Harry S. Truman, *Memoirs by Harry S. Truman*, vol. 1 (Garden City, N.Y.: Doubleday, 1955), p. 5.

2. Dean Acheson, *Present at the Creation: My Years in the State Department* (New York: W. W. Norton, 1969), p. 103.

3. Theodore C. Sorensen, *Kennedy* (New York: Harper & Row, 1965), pp. 227–28.

4. Henry Kissinger, *White House Years* (Boston: Little, Brown, 1979), p. 17.

5. Bill Clinton, *My Life* (New York: Vintage Books, 2005), p. 447.

6. Ibid., p. 466.

7. Ibid., p. 467.

8. Ibid.

9. Dwight D. Eisenhower, *Mandate for Change, 1953–1956* (Garden City, N.Y.: Doubleday, 1963), p. 107.

10. George Bush and Brent Scowcroft, *A World Transformed* (New York: Knopf, 1998), p. 29.

11. Ronald Reagan, *An American Life* (New York: Simon & Schuster, 1990), pp. 228, 229.

12. Henry Kissinger, *Years of Renewal* (London: Weidenfeld & Nicolson, 1999), p. 170.

13. Kissinger, *White House Years*, pp. 12–13.

14. Ibid., p. 14.

15. Zbigniew Brzezinski, *Power and Principle: Memoirs of the National Security Adviser, 1977–1981* (New York: Farrar, Straus & Giroux, 1983), pp. 4, 12.

16. Kissinger, *White House Years*, p. 39.

17. Brzezinski, *Power and Principle*, p. 6.

18. Ibid., p. 14.

19. Ibid., p. 10.

20. Ibid., pp. 74–75.

21. Ibid., p. 78.

22. Cyrus Vance, *Hard Choices: Critical Years in America's Foreign Policy* (New York: Simon & Schuster, 1983), p. 43.

23. Brzezinski, *Power and Principle*, p. 10.

24. Ibid., p. 14.

25. Kissinger, *White House Years*, p. 48.

26. Ibid., p. 15.

27. Brzezinski, *Power and Principle*, p. 13.

28. Ibid.

29. Ibid., p. 15.

30. Bush and Scowcroft, *A World Transformed*, p. 36.

31. George P. Shultz, *Turmoil and Triumph: My Years as Secretary of State* (New York: Macmillan, 1993), p. 12.

32. Colin L. Powell, *My American Journey* (New York: Random House, 1995), p. 575.

33. Ibid.

34. Ibid., pp. 575, 576.

35. James A. Baker III, *The Politics of Diplomacy: Revolution, War and Peace 1989–1992* (New York: G. P. Putnam's Sons, 1995), p. 28.

36. Ibid., p. 36.

37. Ibid.

38. Powell, *My American Journey*, p. 253. Powell worked for John Kester, special assistant to the secretary and the deputy secretary of defense, during the Carter-Reagan transition. See p. 233.

39. Sorensen, *Kennedy*, p. 249.

40. Kissinger, *White House Years*, p. 18.

41. James A. Baker III, *"Work Hard, Study . . . And Keep out of Politics!"* (New York: G. P. Putnam's Sons, 2006), p. 334.

Chapter Three

1. Arthur M. Schlesinger, *A Thousand Days: John F. Kennedy in the White House* (Boston: Houghton Mifflin, 1965), p. 426.

2. Frederick C. Mosher, W. David Clinton, and Daniel G. Lang, *Presidential Transitions and Foreign Affairs* (Louisiana State University Press, 1987), p. 6.

3. Caspar W. Weinberger, *Fighting for Peace: Seven Critical Years in the Pentagon* (New York: Warner Books, 1990), p. 24.

4. Alvin S. Felzenberg, *The Keys to a Successful Presidency* (Washington: Heritage Foundation, 2000), chap. 1 (www.heritage.org/Research/Features/Mandate/keys_chapter1.cfm [September 20, 2008]).

5. Charles O. Jones, *Passages to the Presidency: From Campaigning to Governing* (Brookings, 1998), p. 92. Clinton announced he was going to change the Bush policy of turning back or returning Haitian refugees, after which many Haitians made preparations to head to the United States.

6. Dwight D. Eisenhower, *Waging Peace, 1956–1961: The White House Years* (Garden City, N.Y.: Doubleday, 1965), pp. 617–18.

7. Schlesinger, *A Thousand Days*, p. 258.

8. Ibid. Also see Eric K. Stern, "Probing the Plausibility of Newgroup Syndrome: Kennedy and the Bay of Pigs," in *Beyond Groupthink: Political Group Dynamics and Foreign Policy-Making*, edited by Paul 't Hart, Eric K. Stern, and Bengt Sundelius (University of Michigan Press, 1997).

9. Richard E. Neustadt, "Presidential Transitions: Are the Risks Rising?" *Miller Center Journal* I (1994): 4. These categories and some of the associated challenges are related to the three identified by Neustadt: newness, haste, and hubris.

10. Chris Demchak, "Wars of Disruption in Modern Society: Tailoring Institutions for the Emerging Information and Terrorism Age," paper presented at the annual meeting of the International Studies Association, San Francisco, 2008. For a critique of viewing terrorist attacks as a "bolt from the blue," see Charles F. Parker and Eric K. Stern, "Blindsided? September 11 and the Origins of Strategic Surprise," *Political Psychology* 23, no. 2 (2002): 601–30. However, this critique may be misguided. Even if an attack might have arguably been "preventable" from a long-term perspective, its unpredictable timing and target would make it a bolt from the blue.

11. Interestingly, terrorism expert Bruce Hoffman made almost precisely this point before the beginning of the George W. Bush administration, back in 2001. Bruce Hoffman, "Presidential Transition Team Issues: Terrorism," in *Taking Charge: A Bipartisan Report to the President-Elect on Foreign Policy and National Security,* edited by Frank Carlucci, Robert Hunter, and Zalmay Khalilzad (Santa Monica, Calif.: RAND Corporation, 2001).

12. The very question of who has authority is often unsettled in the early days of an administration, as the confusion over who was "in charge" following the attempted assassination of President Reagan in March 1981 so vividly illustrated. See David J. Rothkopf, *Running the World: The Inside Story of the National Security Council and the Architects of American Power* (New York: Public Affairs, 2005), p. 221; Alexander M. Haig Jr., *Caveat: Realism, Reagan, and Foreign Policy* (New York: Macmillan, 1984), pp. 65, 141; Laurence I. Barrett, *Gambling with History: Ronald Reagan in the White House* (Garden City, N.Y.: Doubleday, 1983), pp. 68–70; Weinberger, *Fighting for Peace*, pp. 27, 29–31; Alexander M. Haig Jr. with Charles McCarry, *Inner Circles: How America Changed the World—A Memoir* (New York: Warner Books, 1992), p. 546.

13. See Paul Blustein, *The Chastening: Inside the Crisis That Rocked the Global Financial System and Humbled the IMF* (New York: Public Affairs, 2003).

14. The George W. Bush administration faced one of the largest transition challenges of recent decades. Owing to the Florida recount controversy, it had less time to

select its national security team and pivot toward governing than past administrations. See James Mann, *Rise of the Vulcans: The History of Bush's War Cabinet* (New York: Viking Penguin, 2004), p. 261.

15. Of course, this has always been true to some degree for returning veterans after years out of office. At the beginning of the Kennedy administration, when State Department veterans George Kennan and W. Averell Harriman returned to the government, they found a department very different from the one they left: it had grown in size and acquired a new set of bureaucratic routines that frustrated Kennan and Harriman and created unforeseen difficulties in the early days of the administration. See Schlesinger, *A Thousand Days*, p. 412. The same kinds of changes had an impact on the Clinton veterans of the Carter administration.

16. Zbigniew Brzezinski, *Power and Principle: Memoirs of the National Security Adviser, 1977–1981* (New York: Farrar, Straus & Giroux, 1983), p. 13.

17. Ibid.

18. Scott McClellan, *What Happened: Inside the Bush White House and Washington's Culture of Deception* (New York: Public Affairs, 2008), pp. 62–63. Also see Norman J. Ornstein and Thomas E. Mann, eds., *The Permanent Campaign and Its Future* (Washington: AEI Press, 2000).

19. See Mosher, Clinton, and Lang, *Presidential Transitions and Foreign Affairs*, p. 67; Brzezinski, *Power and Principle*, pp. 544–46; Haig, *Caveat*, pp. 79–80.

20. Ole R. Holsti, *Public Opinion and American Foreign Policy*, 2nd ed. (University of Michigan Press, 2004); James M. Lindsay, "The New Partisanship: The Changed Politics of American Foreign Policy," *U.S. Foreign Policy Agenda 5*, no. 2 (2000); Nancy E. Roman, "Both Sides of the Aisle: A Call for Bipartisan Foreign Policy," *Council on Foreign Relations Special Report 9* (2005).

21. Ivo H. Daalder and James M. Lindsay, *America Unbound: The Bush Revolution in Foreign Policy* (Hoboken, N.J.: John Wiley, 2005), p. 37.

22. Michael Nacht, the dean of the Goldman Public Policy School at University of California–Berkeley, has written about the ABC phenomenon: "The former president and his team were reviled by the Bush leadership. Bush was determined not to adopt a single strategy or tactic that remotely resembled what Clinton had done, or said, no matter how effective." Michael Nacht, "Plotting a New Course for the U.S.," *The Age*, December 17, 2007. James Mann offers an alternative perspective, arguing that deep philosophical differences, not "reflexive anti-Clintonism," motivated the administration. Mann, *Rise of the Vulcans*, p. 279.

23. Kenneth Lieberthal, "The United States and Asia in 2001: Changing Agendas," *Asian Survey 42*, no. 1 (2002): 1.

24. Quotations and description taken from Elisabeth Bumiller, "White House Letter: Wear Tie, Be on Time, Avoid Mideast," *New York Times*, April 15, 2002.

25. Presidential Appointee Initiative, "Staffing a New Administration: A Guide to Personnel Appointments in a Presidential Transition," a project of the Brookings Institution funded by the Pew Charitable Trusts, 2000, p. 5.

26. Mosher, Clinton, and Lang, *Presidential Transitions and Foreign Affairs*, pp. 109–17.

27. Haig, *Caveat*, p. 64.

28. Mann, *Rise of the Vulcans*, pp. 109–10.

29. I. M. Destler and Ivo H. Daalder, "A New NSC for a New Administration," in *National Security Council Project Policy Brief* (Brookings, 2000).

30. Morris P. Fiorina and others, *The New American Democracy*, Alternate Fourth Edition (Boston: Pearson-Longman, 2005), p. 382; Nonpartisan Presidential Appointee Initiative, "Staffing a New Administration," p. 13.

31. Mosher, Clinton, and Lang, *Presidential Transitions and Foreign Affairs*, p. 125.

32. Paul C. Light, "The Glacial Pace of Presidential Appointments" (www.brookings.edu/opinions/2001/0404governance_light.aspx [September 10, 2008]).

Chapter Four

1. Henry Kissinger, *White House Years* (Boston: Little, Brown, 1979), p. 16.

2. Frederick C. Mosher, W. David Clinton, and Daniel G. Lang, *Presidential Transitions and Foreign Affairs* (Louisiana State University Press, 1987), p. 88.

3. Ibid., p. 89.

4. Ibid., pp. 89–90.

5. Ibid., p. 8.

6. Zbigniew Brzezinski, *Power and Principle: Memoirs of the National Security Adviser, 1977–1981* (New York: Farrar, Straus & Giroux, New York, 1983), pp. 135–36.

7. This phrase comes from a transition veteran quoted in Charles O. Jones, *Passages to the Presidency: From Campaigning to Governing* (Brookings, 1998), p. 54.

8. Zbigniew Brzezinski has stated that "a presidential campaign distorts foreign policy. It tends to primitivize foreign policy, reducing it to simple black-and-white issues." Quoted in Alvin S. Felzenberg, *The Keys to a Successful Presidency* (Washington: Heritage Foundation, 2000), chap. 5 (www.heritage.org/Research/Features/Mandate/keys.cfm [September 20, 2008]).

9. Mosher, Clinton, and Lang, *Presidential Transitions and Foreign Affairs*, p. 224.

10. While Eisenhower's tactics were viewed by their proponents as "psychological warfare" as much as anything else, in reality they angered American allies, and many scholars think they achieved very little substantively. In practice, the idea of rollback was relatively quickly jettisoned by the Eisenhower administration after conducting what came to be known as the "Solarium" policy review.

11. Stanley Hoffman, *Gulliver's Troubles, or the Setting of American Foreign Policy* (New York: McGraw-Hill for the Council on Foreign Relations, 1968), pp. 232–33.

12. This phrase was made famous by Ronald Reagan in his Farewell Address to the Nation, January 11, 1989 (www.reaganlibrary.com/reagan/speeches/farewell.asp [September 10, 2008]).

13. Martin J. Medhurst, "Text and Context in the 1952 Presidential Campaign: Eisenhower's 'I Shall Go to Korea' Speech," *Presidential Studies Quarterly* 30, no. 3 (2000): 464.

14. Dwight D. Eisenhower, *Mandate for Change, 1953–1956* (Garden City, N.Y.: Doubleday, 1963), p. 72.

15. Laurin L. Henry, *Presidential Transitions* (Brookings, 1960), pp. 460 and 63–65.

16. The refusal to specify details was deliberate: "Nixon did not follow the advice and decided to keep things murky, throughout the 1968 campaign. He never did spell out a detailed policy to fulfill his pledge to end the war. Indeed, Nixon's election found him uncertain on detailed planning of any kind for foreign policy, including the war in Southeast Asia." Rowland Evans Jr. and Robert D. Novak, *Nixon in the White House: The Frustration of Power* (New York: Random House, 1971), p. 77.

17. Kissinger, *White House Years*, p. 256.

18. Ibid., pp. 227–28.

19. Christopher A. Preble, "Who Ever Believed in the 'Missile Gap'? John F. Kennedy and the Politics of National Security," *Presidential Studies Quarterly* 33, no. 4 (2003): 803–04.

20. James C. Dick, "The Strategic Arms Race, 1957–61: Who Opened a Missile Gap?" *Journal of Politics* 34, no. 4 (1972): 1077; S. Nelson Drew, "Expecting the Approach of Danger: The 'Missile Gap' as a Study of Executive-Congressional Competition in Building Consensus on National Security Issues," *Presidential Studies Quarterly* 19, no. 2 (1989): 321, 325.

21. Drew, "Expecting the Approach of Danger," p. 331.

22. Continuing the tradition begun by Truman, Eisenhower also had top officials brief each of the candidates in the 1960 general election. While Dulles apparently did not directly answer Kennedy's queries about a missile gap, General Wheeler reportedly told him the gap did not exist. See Preble, "Who Ever Believed in the 'Missile Gap'?" pp. 814–15.

23. Ibid., p. 816; Gregg Herken, *Counsels of War* (New York: Alfred A Knopf, 1985), p. 140.

24. Preble, "Who Ever Believed in the 'Missile Gap'?" pp. 818–19.

25. Arthur M. Schlesinger, *A Thousand Days: John F. Kennedy in the White House* (Boston: Houghton Mifflin, 1965), pp. 499–500.

26. Preble, "Who Ever Believed in the 'Missile Gap'?" pp. 821–22.

27. Christopher Tudda, "'Reenacting the Story of Tantalus': Eisenhower, Dulles, and the Failed Rhetoric of Liberation," *Journal of Cold War Studies* 7, no. 4 (2005): 8–10.

28. Craig A. Rimmerman, "Promise Unfulfilled: Clinton's Failure to Overturn the Military Ban on Lesbians and Gays," in *Gay Rights, Military Wrongs: Political Perspectives on Lesbians and Gays in the Military*, edited by Craig A. Rimmerman (New York: Garland, 1996), p. 113.

29. Elizabeth Drew, *On the Edge: The Clinton Presidency* (New York: Simon & Schuster, 1994), pp. 42–43.

30. Clyde Wilcox and Robin M. Wolpert, "President Clinton, Public Opinion, and Gays in the Military," in *Gay Rights, Military Wrong*, edited by Rimmerman, p. 128; Drew, *On the Edge*, p. 43.

31. Drew, *On the Edge*, p. 42.

32. William T. Corbett, "Clinton Wrong on Gay Ban," *USA Today*, January 27, 1993, p. 10A.

33. Drew, *On the Edge*, pp. 43–44; Colin L. Powell, *My American Journey* (New York: Random House, 1995), p. 564.

34. Rimmerman, "Promise Unfulfilled," p. 116.

35. Quoted in Drew, *On the Edge,* p. 47.

36. Ibid., pp. 250–51.

37. Patricia H. Conley, *Presidential Mandates: How Elections Shape the National Agenda* (University Of Chicago Press, 2001), p. 43.

38. Hoffman, *Gulliver's Troubles,* pp. 231–32.

Chapter Five

1. Charles Jones points out that those involved in the Clinton and Carter transitions, for example, focused on creating "a leadership structure to reassure voters that they had made the right choice." He added that this seemed more imperative for these two presidents-elect since their margins of victory were narrow, and they had been governors of "relatively small states" with no "Washington experience." See Charles O. Jones, *Passages to the Presidency: From Campaigning to Governing* (Brookings, 1998), pp. 62–63.

2. Henry Kissinger, *White House Years* (Boston: Little, Brown, 1979), p.16; James A. Baker III. *The Politics of Diplomacy: Revolution, War and Peace, 1989–1992* (New York: G. P. Putnam's Sons, 1995), p. 17; Dwight D. Eisenhower, *Mandate for Change 1953–1956* (Garden City, N.Y.: Doubleday, 1963), p. 86.

3. For a detailed review of the timing of these appointments, see Jones, *Passages to the Presidency,* pp. 93–98.

4. W. H. Lawrence, "Kennedy Names 3," *New York Times,* December 13, 1960; W. H. Lawrence, "Ford Head Named to Defense Post," *New York Times,* December 14, 1960; Wallace Carroll, "Bundy of Harvard to Be Security Aide—Post for Finletter Seen," *New York Times,* December 30, 1960.

5. Charles Mohr, "Vance Is Selected by Carter to Run State Department," *New York Times,* December 4 1976; "Carter Pays Some of His Debts," *Economist,* December 25 1976; James T. Wooten, "Carter Names Three to Posts in Cabinet; One a Black Woman; Mrs. Harris Will Run H.U.D.," *New York Times,* December 22, 1976.

6. Alison Mitchell, "Bush Names Powell to Head State Department, Signaling Stability in Foreign Policy," *New York Times,* December 17, 2000; Richard A. Oppel Jr. and Frank Bruni, "Bush Fills Security Post and 2 Jobs for Advisors," *New York Times,* December 18, 2000; Eric Schmitt, "Defense Secretary Chosen; Held Same Post under Ford," *New York Times,* December 29, 2000; Zbigniew Brzezinski, *Power and Principle: Memoirs of the National Security Adviser, 1977–1981* (New York: Farrar, Straus & Giroux, 1983), p.12.

7. For example, in the Department of State alone, there are approximately thirty-four positions at the deputy, under secretary, and assistant secretary levels. See U.S. Department of State, "Department Organization Chart" (www.state.gov/r/pa/ei/rls/dos/99494.htm [September 20, 2008]). In the Office of the Secretary of Defense, there are more than three dozen. See Director of Administration & Management, Office of the Secretary of Defense, "DoD Organizational and Functions Guidebook" (www.defenselink.mil/odam/omp/pubs/GuideBook/ToC.htm [September 20, 2008]). And in the National Security Council there are more than two dozen positions at the deputy or senior director level. See Alan G. Whittaker, Frederick C. Smith, and Elizabeth McKune, "The National Security Policy Process: The National Security Council

and Interagency System" (Washington: Industrial College of the Armed Forces, National Defense University, 2007).

8. Since Nixon, all of the Cabinet-level national security appointees have been confirmed within twenty-four hours of the inauguration. See Jones, *Passages to the Presidency*, p. 97. George W. Bush's secretaries of defense and state were also confirmed within a day of the inauguration. See Alison Mitchell, "Senate Confirms 7 Cabinet Members at Once," *New York Times*, January 21, 2001. George H. W. Bush's initial nomination for secretary of defense, John Tower, was rejected by the Senate in 1989. See Michael Oreskes, "Senate Rejects Tower, 53-47; First Cabinet Veto since '59; Bush Confers on New Choice," *New York Times*, March 10, 1989.

9. Former deputy secretary of state Richard Armitage and former deputy assistant secretary of defense for strategy Michèle Flournoy called for "an expedited clearance and confirmation process for the top 40 to 50 members of the new president's national security team," which would require the president-elect to submit nominations for these positions by December 1 and commitments for speedy vetting by the Office of Personnel Management, the FBI, and the Senate. See Richard Armitage and Michèle A. Flournoy, "No Time for 'Nobody Home,'" *Washington Post*, Monday, June 9, 2008. The American Enterprise Institute (AEI) organized a 1999–2000 project titled "Transition to Governing." The Heritage Foundation has done some valuable work on the judicial confirmation process; and Paul Light at Brookings and Virginia Thomas at Heritage have made helpful contributions as part of the "Presidential Appointee Initiative."

10. Jones, *Passages to the Presidency*, pp. 73–76, 79.

11. Ibid., pp. 78–80.

12. James Mann, *Rise of the Vulcans: The History of Bush's War Cabinet* (New York: Viking Penguin, 2004), p. 255.

13. See, for instance, Condoleezza Rice, "Campaign 2000: Promoting the National Interest," *Foreign Affairs* 79, no. 1 (2000): 45–62; Robert B. Zoellick, "Campaign 2000: A Republican Foreign Policy," *Foreign Affairs* 79, no. 1 (2000): 63.

14. Frederick C. Mosher, W. David Clinton, and Daniel G. Lang, *Presidential Transitions and Foreign Affairs* (Baton Rouge: Louisiana State University Press, 1987), p. 64. Candidates do learn from past mistakes. As Edwin Meese pointed out regarding the Reagan team, "We had learned from the experience of other candidates . . . planning to govern before being elected would smack of smugness and have a negative effect on the electorate . . . Reagan, particularly . . . always worried about being a latter-day Thomas Dewey." See Jones, *Passages to the Presidency*, p. 66.

15. Jones, *Passages to the Presidency*, p. 58.

16. Pendleton James describes how he managed the personnel selection process for Ronald Reagan. He drew up lists of three to seven names for the key Cabinet positions based on capability, philosophical orientation, and relationship with Reagan. He took this list to the president-elect and his close aides the day after the election: "Everybody in that room had been focusing all their time on getting the man elected. They were not thinking about anything else except votes, fund-raising, ballots, Electoral College. Now, all of a sudden, 'Gee, now we've got to put together a team.' So by doing just the staff work, now we had the names. We passed it around, and then for the first time the President-elect started focusing . . . and the process went on." Quoted in Alvin S. Felzenberg, *The Keys to a Successful Presidency* (Washington: Heritage Foundation 2000), chap. 3 (www.heritage.org/Research/Features/Mandate/keys.cfm [September 10, 2008]).

17. In practice, of course, there are no bright lines between the categories. For example, we classify Colin Powell and Donald Rumsfeld as all-stars even though they also played modest roles as campaign advisers to Governor Bush. Similarly, U.S. Representative Les Aspin, who became Clinton's first secretary of defense, fits the model of a worthy, although he was clearly also recognized as a defense policy expert by virtue of his long service on the House Armed Services Committee.

18. On the appointment of Nixon's secretaries of state and defense, see Robert B. Semple Jr., "Nixon Presents the New Cabinet, Pledges to Seek Peace and Unity," *New York Times,* December 12, 1968. On Kissinger's appointment, see R. W. Apple Jr., "Kissinger Named a Key Nixon Aide in Defense Policy," *New York Times,* December 3, 1968. Clinton announced his national security team in one go. See Gwen Ifill, "Focusing Overseas: Clinton Draws on Carter Years in Filling Most of Security Posts," *New York Times,* December 23, 1992.

19. On the Carter appointments, see Mohr, "Vance Is Selected by Carter to Run State Department"; Wooten, "Carter Names Three to Posts in Cabinet." On the Reagan appointments, see Steven R. Weisman, "Reagan Designates Eight to Fill Posts at Cabinet Level," *New York Times,* December 12, 1980; Steven R. Weisman, "Reagan Names Haig to State Dept. Post," *New York Times,* December 24, 1980.

20. Stephen Hess, *Organizing the Presidency* (Brookings, 1988), p. 44.

21. Robert H. Ferrell, *Harry S. Truman* (Washington: CQ Press, 2003), p. 230.

22. Byrnes had been elected to the House of Representatives seven times and in 1930 was elected to the Senate. In June 1941, Roosevelt appointed Byrnes to the Supreme Court. Finding his work there boring, however, Byrnes resigned sixteen months later to become director of economic stabilization during World War II. His work during this effort was so successful that Roosevelt concurrently appointed Byrnes to take charge of industrial mobilization. Byrnes had also been Truman's rival for the vice presidency in 1944. Ibid.

23. Byrnes's notes were the only verbatim record of the meeting between Roosevelt, Prime Minister Winston Churchill, and Premier Joseph Stalin. Truman erroneously believed that Byrnes had important information about Yalta. Ibid.

24. Historian Robert Messer notes that during and after the Potsdam Conference, "Byrnes operated essentially on his own with the broadest possible mandate from the President and apart from the bureaucracy in Washington." See Robert Messer, *The End of an Alliance: James F. Byrnes, Roosevelt, Truman, and the Origins of the Cold War* (University of North Carolina Press, 1982). Unfortunately, this approach, tainted by the personal animosity between the men, soon began to backfire. In the winter of 1945, Byrnes was tasked with attending the Foreign Ministers Conference in Moscow. Averell Harriman, then the U.S. ambassador to the Soviet Union, later recalled offering to help Byrnes draft the customary report of the meeting to send to Truman. Byrnes replied, "I'm not going to send any daily reports. I don't trust the White House. It leaks. And I don't want any of this coming out in the papers until I get home." When Truman found out about Byrnes's failure to report on the Moscow Conference, he was furious. Truman, always concerned about defending presidential prerogatives, recalled in his memoirs, "I read him the riot act. A Secretary of State should never have the illusion that he is President of the United States." See Cabell B. H. Phillips, *The Truman Presidency: The History of a Triumphant Succession* (New York: Macmillan, 1966), pp. 148, 147.

25. Truman was more successful with later appointments to key national security posts. In the assessment of one historian, "Truman made few of the mistakes in his second- and third-wave cabinet appointments that he had made in the first. Experience had taught him much. He now had a higher sophistication in equating a man's qualifications with the job at hand." Ibid., p. 157.

26. According to Stephen Hess, Eisenhower's limited involvement was "partly an application of his theory of delegation; partly an expression of his distaste for the process of patronage; and partly a reflection of his limited circle of acquaintances outside the military, coupled with his strong belief in not appointing military people to civilian jobs if equally capable civilians were available." See Hess, *Organizing the Presidency*, p. 60.

27. Although they did not have a close personal relationship at the time of Dulles's appointment as secretary of state, Eisenhower truly respected Dulles's diplomatic abilities, from his participation in the American delegation to the Versailles Peace Treaty to his work on the Japanese Peace Treaty. Eisenhower once told his chief of staff, Sherman Adams, that "Foster has been in training for this job all his life" and later revealed to his speechwriter, Emmet Hughes, "There's only one man I know who has seen more of the world and talked with more people and knows more than he [Dulles] does—and that's me." See Robert Divine, *Eisenhower and the Cold War* (New York: Oxford University Press, 1997), p. 21. But some believe that the most important consideration behind the Dulles appointment was the desire to appeal to the conservative wing of the Republican Party after Eisenhower's defeat of Taft. See Divine, *Eisenhower and the Cold War*, p. 20.

28. Eisenhower was uncomfortable with what he perceived as the large number of military officials who had used connections on Capitol Hill to gain presidential appointments. He wanted something different: "We have tried two investment bankers [James Forrestal and Robert Lovett], a politician [Louis Johnson] and a military man [George Marshall]," he [Eisenhower] told Henry Cabot Lodge. "Maybe we should try an industrialist." And he knew just the man—Kaufman T. Keller, president of Chrysler. When he put this idea to Clay, however, Clay said, "If you are going into the business world, why not get the head of the biggest business we have?" Eisenhower accepted Clay's logic, and the Defense appointment was offered to Charles E. Wilson, president of General Motors. See Geoffrey Perret, *Eisenhower* (Avon, Mass.: Adams Media, 1999), p. 423.

29. David J. Rothkopf, *Running the World: The Inside Story of the National Security Council and the Architects of American Power* (New York: Public Affairs, 2005), pp. 65–74.

30. Kennedy of course was not the only president to continue a CIA director in office. Richard Helms was initially appointed by Johnson and carried over through Nixon's first term; Ford kept William Colby on; William Webster served as CIA director under both Reagan and George H. W. Bush; and George Tenet served both Clinton and George W. Bush. Both Helms and Webster were considered "apolitical" appointments. Among the non-holdover appointments to the CIA were Allen Dulles for Eisenhower; Ted Sorensen/Stansfield Turner for Carter; William Casey for Reagan; and James Woolsey for Clinton. See Central Intelligence Agency, "Directors of Central Intelligence" (www.cia.gov/library/center-for-the-study-of-intelligence/csi-publications/

books-and-monographs/directors-and-deputy-directors-of-central-intelligence/directors-of-central-intelligence.html [September 19, 2008]).

31. According to former Treasury and national security official William Wechsler, it is perhaps ironic that Kennedy failed to get a second benefit from carrying over Dillon; Dillon had been briefed on the Bay of Pigs operation but was not included in the Kennedy administration's policy discussions on Cuba. Whether Dillon might have offered insights that could have warned the new president of the approaching disaster is, of course, a matter of speculation.

32. Theodore C. Sorensen, *Kennedy* (New York: Harper & Row, 1965), pp. 251–52.

33. Ibid., p. 252; Michael O'Brien, *John F. Kennedy: A Biography* (New York: St. Martin's, 2005), p. 504.

34. O'Brien, *John F. Kennedy*, p. 539.

35. Sorensen, *Kennedy*, p. 631.

36. When asked by Richard Nixon why he had kept so many of Kennedy's appointees, according to Lady Bird Johnson, President Johnson responded, "Well, there are several reasons. One, respect for President Kennedy. He had trusted me, and I tried to put myself in his shoes. How would I have felt if, as soon as I was gone, he had disposed of all my people? I wanted to be loyal to him. Two, I didn't know for a good while whether I had an excellent man or an incompetent. And three, I didn't always have all the troops I needed." See Irwin Unger and Debi Unger, *LBJ: A Life* (New York: John Wiley, 1999), p. 318.

37. Henry Kissinger, *Diplomacy* (New York: Simon & Schuster, 1994), p. 657.

38. Of the holdovers, arguably only Rostow became part of Johnson inner circle. See Merle Miller, *Lyndon: An Oral History* (New York: Putnam, 1982).

39. Patricia Dennis Witherspoon, *Within These Walls: A Study of Communication between Presidents and Their Senior Staffs* (New York: Praeger, 1991), pp. 113, 160.

40. "Trying to Be One of the Boys," *Time*, October 4, 1976.

41. "I was an eager student, and took full advantage of what Brzezinski had to offer. . . . We got to know each other well." Carter quoted in Carl M. Brauer, *Presidential Transitions: Eisenhower through Reagan* (Oxford University Press, 1986), p. 206.

42. Lawrence Van Gelder, "Charles H. Kirbo, 79, Is Dead; Was Carter's Closest Adviser," *New York Times*, September 4, 1996.

43. Wendell Rawls Jr., "Sorensen Withdraws, Bowing to Resistance to CIA Nomination; Carter Is Regretful," *New York Times*, January 18, 1977; Hedrick Smith, "Assertion of Will by Congress; Republicans Were against Sorensen Ideologically and Democrats Feared Bitter and Divisive Fight," *New York Times*, January 18, 1977; Charles Mohr, "Adm. Turner Picked by Carter to Head Intelligence Agency . . . No Sign Officer Will Meet Kind of Opposition Sorensen Did," *New York Times*, February 8, 1977.

44. Hess, *Organizing the Presidency*, pp. 148, 65–66.

45. Colin Campbell and S. J. Rockman, *The Bush Presidency: First Appraisals* (London: Chatham House, 1991), p. 99.

46. John Robert Greene, *The Presidency of George Bush* (University Press of Kansas, 2000), p. 45.

47. George Bush and Brent Scowcroft, *A World Transformed* (New York: Knopf, 1998), p. 18.

48. Greene, *The Presidency of George Bush,* p. 45.

49. David Mervin, *George Bush and the Guardianship Presidency* (New York: St. Martin's, 1996), p. 161.

50. Ibid., p. 164.

51. Michael Wines, "The 1992 Campaign: The Republicans; Baker Is Reported to Take New Post Guiding Campaign," *New York Times,* July 22, 1992.

52. Many have criticized his administration as characterized by an overabundance of congeniality and like-minded thinking or groupthink. See, for instance, Steve A. Yetiv, "Groupthink and the Gulf Crisis," *British Journal of Political Science* 33 (July 2003): 419–42; Campbell and Rockman, *The Bush Presidency.*

53. Warren Christopher was regarded as a skilled political tactician and consummate professional. He had previous experience in the State Department, having served in the Carter administration as deputy secretary of state from 1977 until 1981. Christopher worked for Clinton in 1992 by heading the search team for vice president. When Clinton got elected, Christopher served as chief of the transition team. By that time, Christopher had already been mentioned as a possible secretary of state. See David Halberstam, *War in a Time of Peace: Bush, Clinton, and the Generals* (New York: Scribner, 2001), pp. 169–75. Also see Leslie H. Gelb, "Foreign Affairs: Who Gets What Jobs," *New York Times,* November 5, 1992.

54. Because of his lack of military experience, Clinton felt he needed to appoint a respected defense expert as defense secretary. Aspin's background included working as a systems analyst in the Pentagon under Secretary of Defense Robert McNamara. More important, he served in Congress for two decades, becoming chairman of the House Armed Services Committee. Aspin also had strong ties to the centrist wing of the party, having angered more liberal Democrats through his support of the Reagan administration's MX/Midgetman compromise, a position he shared with then senator Al Gore. Aspin solidified his friendship with Clinton when he became his chief adviser on military policy in the 1992 presidential campaign. See Leslie H. Gelb, "Foreign Affairs; Inside Bill's Head," *New York Times,* December 10, 1992.

55. Woolsey had been secretary of the navy to President Carter and chief of staff to Senator Henry M. (Scoop) Jackson, and had served as an arms control negotiator in the Reagan administration. Woolsey's was a politically strategic appointment, because Woolsey was not ideologically aligned with Clinton. In fact, Clinton barely even knew him. David Halberstam wrote that Woolsey's appointment was due to Clinton's efforts to achieve political diversity. See Halberstam, *War in a Time of Peace,* pp. 191–93.

56. Lake had been a Foreign Service officer, had worked under Henry Kissinger, was director of the State Department Policy Staff during the Carter administration, and during the Reagan and Bush years was a professor at Amherst College.

57. During the campaign, Clinton had promised "an administration that looks like America." See Chris Black, "Clinton: America Needs 'Mother's Love,'" *Boston Globe,* May 11, 1992.

58. Aspin departed in December 1993, Woolsey in January 1995. During Woolsey's two-year tenure, he never once had a one-on-one meeting with Clinton and only

managed to have two semi-private meetings. Woolsey said, "It wasn't that I had a bad relationship with the president. It just didn't exist." Quoted in Kathryn Jean Lopez, "Clinton's Loss? How the Previous Administration Fumbled on Bin Laden: A Q&A with Richard Miniter," *National Review Online* (2003) (www.nationalreview.com/interrogatory/interrogatory091103b.asp [September 20, 2008]). Woolsey's favorite joke became, "Remember the guy who in 1994 crashed his plane onto the White House lawn? That was me trying to get an appointment to see President Clinton." See Paula Kaufman, "Woolsey Wary of More Attacks," *Insight on the News,* June 3, 2002.

59. Mann, *Rise of the Vulcans,* p. 273.

60. Ibid., p. 274.

61. Ibid., p. 270. Ironically, the younger Bush ousted a key Bush 43 adviser, Brent Scowcroft, from his role as head of the president's Foreign Intelligence Board.

62. Rumsfeld's problems were compounded by his poor relations with members of the congressional national security committees. See Jane Perlez, "Bush Team's Counsel Is Divided on Foreign Policy; Bush Team's 2 Faces, at Pentagon and State," *New York Times,* March 27, 2001; "The Bush Merry-Go-Round," *New York Times,* December 8, 2001; James Dao, "In Protest, Republican Senators Hold Up Defense Confirmations," *New York Times,* May 10, 2001; James Dao, "As Defense Secretary Calls for Base Closings, Congress Circles the Wagons," *New York Times,* June 29, 2001; Philip Gold, "Savaging Donald Rumsfeld; Secretary Needs the President's Support," *Washington Times,* August 28, 2001; Stan Crock, "Why the Hawks Are Carpet-Bombing Rumsfeld," *Buisness Week,* August 6, 2001.

63. Although they shared many views, Scowcroft and Baker did on occasion differ during the Bush administration. See Mervin, *George Bush and the Guardianship Presidency,* p. 182.

64. For details about the teams, see John P. Burke, *Presidential Transitions: From Politics to Practice* (Boulder, Colo.: Lynne Rienner, 2000), pp. 291–93.

Chapter Six

1. See, for example, David J. Rothkopf, *Running the World: The Inside Story of the National Security Council and the Architects of American Power* (New York: Public Affairs, 2005); William W. Neumann, *Managing National Security Policy: The President and the Process* (University of Pittsburgh Press, 2003); Amy B. Zegart, *Flawed by Design: The Evolution of the CIA, JCS, and NSC* (Stanford University Press, 1999).

2. Robert H. Ferrell, *Harry S. Truman* (Washington: CQ Press, 2003), p. 230.

3. Richard Tanner Johnson, *Managing the White House: An Intimate Study of the Presidency* (New York: Harper & Row, 1974), p. 40.

4. Stephen Hess, *Organizing the Presidency* (Brookings, 1988), p. 44.

5. Cecil V. Crabb and Kevin V. Mulcahy, "Presidential Management of National Security Making, 1947–1987," in *The Managerial Presidency,* edited by James Pfiffner (Pacific Grove, Calif.: Brooks/Cole, 1991), p. 254.

6. Stanley L. Falk, "The National Security Council under Truman, Eisenhower, and Kennedy," *Political Science Quarterly* 79, no. 3 (1964): 418.

7. Rothkopf, *Running the World*, p. 65. Cutler was also instrumental in creating the Operations Coordinating Board, which was charged with ensuring that policy decisions were implemented.

8. His openness to competing ideas can be seen most clearly in the Solarium Project (discussed in chapter 4), an effort in which Eisenhower commissioned three teams of advisers to develop alternative strategies for national security. See Richard Armitage and Michèle A. Flournoy, "No Time for 'Nobody Home,'" *Washington Post*, June 9, 2008.

9. See Bureau of Public Affairs, Office of the Historian, "History of the National Security Council, 1947–1948," United States Department of State (www.fas.org/irp/offdocs/NSChistory.htm [September 20, 2008]).

10. "President Eisenhower considered the Cabinet to be in the nature of a corporate Board of Directors. Decisions would be made by the Cabinet and he would carry them out. This is contrary to every basic concept of the Presidency and should be junked. Cabinet meetings were attended by 30 to 40 persons, and as a result were sterile and time consuming." Clark Clifford, *Counsel to the President: A Memoir* (New York: Random House, 1991). Kennedy, perhaps in part because of his personal desire to have greater control over the decisionmaking process, took this advice to heart. "Cabinet meetings are simply useless," Kennedy said. "Why should the Postmaster General sit there and listen to a discussion of the problems of Laos?" Quoted in James P. Pfiffner, "White House Staff versus the Cabinet: Centripetal and Centrifugal Roles," *Presidential Studies Quarterly* 16 (Fall 1986: 666–90.

11. Rothkopf, *Running the World*, p. 85.

12. Johnson, *Managing the White House*, p.124.

13. Rothkopf, *Running the World*, pp. 90–91.

14. Theodore C. Sorensen, *Kennedy* (New York: Harper & Row, 1965), pp. 284–85.

15. Crabb and Mulcahy, "Presidential Management of National Security Making," pp. 256–57.

16. Hess, *Organizing the Presidency*, pp. 100–01. David M. Barrett, "Doing 'Tuesday Lunch' at Lyndon Johnson's White House: New Archival Evidence on Vietnam Decisionmaking," *PS: Political Science and Politics* 24, no. 4 (1991): 676–79.

17. Henry Kissinger, *White House Years* (Boston: Little, Brown, 1979), pp. 38–48.

18. Rothkopf, *Running the World*, pp. 114–17.

19. James P. Pfiffner, "Can the President Manage the Government? Should He?" in *The Managerial Presidency*, edited by Pfiffner, p. 9.

20. National Security Decision Memorandum 3, signed on January 18, 1969, one day before Nixon formally took office. See Frederick C. Mosher, W. David Clinton, and Daniel G. Lang, *Presidential Transitions and Foreign Affairs* (Louisiana State University Press, 1987), p. 184.

21. The Institute for Defense Analysis had prepared a study critical of the informal decisionmaking processes of Kennedy and Johnson, which may have influenced Nixon's thinking on this issue. Ibid.

22. Rothkopf, *Running the World*, pp. 153–54.

23. Charles O. Jones, *Passages to the Presidency: From Campaigning to Governing* (Brookings, 1998), p. 94.

24. Carl M. Brauer, *Presidential Transitions: Eisenhower through Reagan* (Oxford University Press, 1986), pp. 206–10.

25. Rothkopf, *Running the World,* pp. 167–68.

26. John P. Burke, *Presidential Transitions: From Politics to Practice* (Boulder, Colo.: Lynne Rienner, 2000), p. 171.

27. A National Security Planning Group, which has been called "a kind of NSC-plus," was created in Reagan's first year in office to oversee crisis management, but it was chaired by the vice president, not the national security adviser. Rothkopf, *Running the World,* p. 218.

28. Burke, *Presidential Transitions,* p. 172.

29. Many of the decisions were made by the so-called National Security Planning Group, which consisted of Haig, Weinberger, Casey, Vice President Bush, Meese, Baker, and Deaver, with Allen as the note taker. For a lively account of the "erratic" process, see Les Gelb, "Foreign Policy System Criticized by U.S. Aides," *New York Times,* October 19, 1981. See also Burke, *Presidential Transitions,* pp. 172–73. Alexander Haig commented on Reagan's White House: "To me the White House was as mysterious as a ghost ship; you heard the creak of the rigging and the groan of the timbers and sometimes even glimpsed the crew on the deck. But which of the crew had the helm? . . . It was impossible to know for sure." Alexander M. Haig Jr., *Caveat: Realism, Reagan, and Foreign Policy* (New York: Macmillan, 1984), p. 85.

30. See Baker's account quoted in Burke, *Presidential Transitions,* pp. 176–77.

31. Scowcroft took it upon himself to reform the National Security Council. According to Richard Haass, a principal aide to Scowcroft, the National Security Council had lost sight of its original purpose during the Reagan administration. Haass said it "was both too weak and too strong. It was too weak to do what it was supposed to do and too strong at what it wasn't supposed to do." See David Mervin, *George Bush and the Guardianship Presidency* (New York: St. Martin's, 1996), pp. 162–63. Most notably, during the Iran-Contra scandal, the National Security Council staff had gone beyond their intended function and taken on operational roles. Scowcroft began this reform of the National Security Council by reducing the staff and redefining its role. "The president runs the government. He has expert advice from the state and defense, and it is my job to ensure the integration of that advice, to fill in where there are holes, and hopefully to help provide a strategic concept which covers the whole field of national security." Scowcroft carried out this reform. Then he left the daily management of the National Security Council staff largely to his deputy, Robert M. Gates, focusing on his other responsibility of serving as the president's chief personal counselor on foreign policy and national security. See Mervin, *George Bush and the Guardianship Presidency,* p. 163. For another description see Burke, *Presidential Transitions,* pp. 260–65. The structure was formalized through NSD-1. See Rothkopf, *Running the World,* p. 266.

32. Burke, *Presidential Transitions,* p. 261.

33. Colin Campbell and S. J. Rockman, *The Bush Presidency: First Appraisals* (London: Chatham House, 1991); Steve A. Yetiv, "Groupthink and the Gulf Crisis," *British Journal of Political Science* 33 (July 2003).

34. Burke, *Presidential Transitions,* p. 263.

35. Rothkopf gives credit to Anthony Lake and Sandy Berger for resisting the tendency for incoming administrations to overhaul the NSC structure and for realizing that the existing system "made sense"—an acknowledgement that "institutionalized the processes of the council." Rothkopf, *Running the World*, p. 313.

36. Perhaps to give some sense of a new beginning, the formal names for some of the procedures were changed.

37. For a brief biography of Jane Wales, see "Biography of Jane Wales" (http://clinton1.nara.gov/White_House/EOP/OSTP/Security/html/Wales_Bio.html). David Sandalow held the positions of associate director for global environment at CEQ and senior director for environmental affairs at the NSC. See Al Kamen, "In the Deep," *Washington Post*, February 16, 1996. On Clarke, see Rothkopf, *Running the World*, p. 383.

38. Rothkopf, pp. 402–03.

39. Although Vice President Gore played an important advisory role to President Clinton on foreign policy issues and was supported by a substantial group of experts on the vice president's staff, Gore's advisers operated almost exclusively through the NSC channels.

40. Brzezinski noted: "Every President shortly after the assumption of office issues an order structuring his decision-making system, in fact, very deliberately—frankly, out of political and personal ego—renaming the key steps for the documents that are going to be issued in the President's name, the names of committees, and so forth." Quoted in Alvin S. Felzenberg, *The Keys to a Successful Presidency*, (2000), chap. 5 (www.heritage.org/Research/Features/Mandate/keys_chapter5.cfm [September 10, 2008]).

41. The Project on National Security Reform is one manifestation of this interest. See www.pnsr.org/ [September 20, 2008]).

42. See, for instance, James R. Locher III, "The Most Important Thing: Legislative Reform of the National Security System," *Military Review* (May–June 2008): 4–12.

Chapter Seven

1. Paul C. Light, *The President's Agenda: Domestic Policy Choice from Kennedy to Clinton* (Johns Hopkins University Press, 1999), p. 10.

2. Frederick C. Mosher, W. David Clinton, and Daniel G. Lang, *Presidential Transitions and Foreign Affairs* (Louisiana State University Press, 1987), pp. 110–11.

3. Lincoln P. Bloomfield, "What's Wrong with Transitions?" *Foreign Policy 55* (1984): 29–30.

4. In April 2001, a U.S. Navy reconnaissance plane collided with a Chinese fighter jet, resulting in the death of the Chinese pilot and an emergency landing by the U.S. aircraft on a Chinese island.

5. See Robin Toner and Michael Oreskes, "Tower Vote: Party Power, Deftly Shown," *New York Times*, March 12, 1989; Michael Oreskes, "4 More Democrats to Oppose Tower; Dole Expects Loss," *New York Times*, March 9, 1989.

6. Michael Oreskes, "Senate Rejects Tower 53–47; First Cabinet Veto since '59; Bush Confers on New Choice," *New York Times*, March 10, 1989.

7. For the impact on the social scene, see "Welcome to the House of Fun," *Independent,* January 19, 1995; Karen DeWitt, "Party Politics (but Where's the Party?)," *New York Times,* December 31, 1995. On Clinton's attitude toward the press corps, see Carl Johnston, "Clinton's 'Change' Starts with Door Slammed on Press," Dow Jones Newswires, January 21, 1993. On his chief of staff pick, see Ann Devroy, "Clinton Picks Brown for Commerce Post; Friend, 'Outsider' McLarty to Be Chief of Staff," *Washington Post,* December 13, 1992.

8. John P. Burke, *Presidential Transitions: From Politics to Practice* (Boulder, Colo.: Lynne Rienner, 2000), p. 110.

9. Baker outlined this philosophy in his memoir. James A. Baker III, *"Work Hard, Study . . . And Keep Out of Politics!"* (New York: G. P. Putnam's Sons, 2006), p. 212.

10. James Dao, "In Protest, Republican Senators Hold Up Defense Confirmations," *New York Times,* May 10, 2001.

11. The approach to getting legislation through Congress was described as "Present Capitol Hill with a fully formed policy, rush it through the House with near-perfect Republican unity, and then pick off a couple of Democrats in the closely divided Senate." See Dana Milbank, "Bush Legislative Approach Failed in Faith Bill Battle; White House Is Faulted for Not Building a Consensus in Congress," *Washington Post,* April 23, 2003. There were some exceptions to the strategy, primarily in domestic policy, such as the No Child Left Behind bill, which was supported by Senator Edward Kennedy, among other Democrats.

12. Glenn P. Hastedt and Anthony J. Eksterowicz, "Perils of Presidential Transition," *Seton Hall Journal of Diplomacy and International Relations* (Winter/Spring 2001): 72–74.

13. See Mosher, Clinton, and Lang, *Presidential Transitions and Foreign Affairs,* p. 231; Burke, *Presidential Transitions,* p. 175.

14. Hastedt and Eksterowicz, "Perils of Presidential Transition," p. 73.

15. In March 2002, Bush's press secretary Ari Fleischer stated, "Actually, I think if you go back to when the violence began, you can make the case that in an attempt to shoot the moon and get nothing, more violence resulted . . . as a result of an attempt to push the parties beyond where they were willing to go, that it led to expectations that were raised to such a high level that it turned into violence." See Elisabeth Bumiller, "Bush Aide Attacks Clinton on Mideast, Then Retracts Remark," *New York Times,* March 1, 2002.

16. Mosher, Clinton, and Lang, *Presidential Transitions and Foreign Affairs,* pp. 191–92.

17. "H.AMDT.974 to H.R. 7355: Amendment Offered by Representative Boland," December 8, 1982. A year later another amendment sponsored by Boland prohibited "covert assistance for military operations in Nicaragua." See "H.Amdt.461 to H.R. 2968: Amendment offered by Representative Boland," October 20, 1983.

18. On Iran-Contra, candidate Bush said he had been kept out of the loop on the matter and didn't know that it was an arms-for-hostages deal. Joel Brinkley, "Bush's Role in Iran Affair: Questions and Answers," *New York Times,* January 29, 1988. Bush blamed Congress, not President Reagan, for the result of Central America policy, stating "the policy in Central America, regrettably, has failed, because the Congress

has been unwilling to support those who have been fighting for freedom." See "Transcript of the Second Debate between Bush and Dukakis," *New York Times,* October 14, 1988.

19. Before his confirmation, Baker spoke to members of Congress. See Robert D. Hershey Jr., "Bush Said to Plan No Early Contra Aid Move," *New York Times,* December 21, 1988. He continued his meetings on the question after his confirmation. See Robert Pear, "Baker Plea for Interim Contra Aid Evokes the Skepticism of Congress," *New York Times,* March 4, 1989; Bernard Weinraub, "Bush and Congress Sign Policy Accord on Aid to Contras," *New York Times,* March 25, 1989.

20. Burke, *Presidential Transitions,* p. 206.

21. Mosher, Clinton, and Lang, *Presidential Transitions and Foreign Affairs,* pp. 248–49.

22. See Bernard Gwertzman, "U.S. And Iran Sign Accord on Hostages: 52 Americans Could Be Set Free Today," *New York Times,* January 19, 1981; Bernard Gwertzman, "New Administration Says It Will Honor Accord on Hostages," *New York Times,* January 23, 1981.

23. Burke, *Presidential Transitions,* p. 191.

24. Mosher, Clinton, and Lang, *Presidential Transitions and Foreign Affairs,* pp. 68–69.

25. The Democrat interviewed stated, "Generally speaking, the outgoing people want to help the incoming folks." The Republican said, "It's been my experience that the outgoing team . . . wants very much to help. . . . But it's usually not appreciated." See Charles O. Jones, *Passages to the Presidency: From Campaigning to Governing* (Brookings, 1998), p. 131.

26. Mosher, Clinton, and Lang, *Presidential Transitions and Foreign Affairs,* p. 69. Cheney is quoted in Martha Joynt Kumar, George C. Edwards III, and James P. Pfiffner, "The Contemporary Presidency: Meeting the Freight Train Head On: Planning for the Transition to Power," *Presidential Studies Quarterly* 30, no. 4 (2000): 765.

27. Dwight D. Eisenhower, *Mandate for Change, 1953–1956* (Garden City, N.Y.: Doubleday, 1963), pp. 135–36.

28. Ibid., 136.

29. Ibid.

30. Henry Kissinger, *White House Years* (Boston: Little, Brown, 1979), p. 633; Mosher, Clinton, and Lang, *Presidential Transitions and Foreign Affairs,* p. 80.

31. For more on this issue, see Mosher, Clinton, and Lang, *Presidential Transitions and Foreign Affairs,* pp. 75–77. Also, Jones quotes former Carter adviser Stuart Eizenstat as saying, "Even more troubling is the absence of documents at the White House from the outgoing Administration, to which reference could be made on important decisions . . . the offices [the President] and his new team enter are empty of past memos and files on major events—records which had been there the day before. . . . A structure such as this makes it virtually impossible from the onset to instill institutional memory and to make transitions effective." See Jones, *Passages to the Presidency,* pp. 12–13.

32. At Vladivostok in 1974, the United States and the USSR had come to agreement on the basic SALT II framework, but the SALT II negotiations had not been completed by the time President Ford left office.

33. A. Eksterowicz and G. Hastedt, "Modern Presidential Transitions: Problems, Pitfalls, and Lessons for Success," *Presidential Studies Quarterly* 28, no. 2 (1998).

34. "Presidential Review Memorandum/NSC-10: Comprehensive Net Assessment and Military Force Posture Review" (White House, 1977).

35. David J. Rothkopf, *Running the World: The Inside Story of the National Security Council and the Architects of American Power* (New York: Public Affairs, 2005), pp. 181–82.

36. Burke, *Presidential Transitions*, p. 265.

37. To some extent, this falls into the category of repudiating the previous administration, since candidate Carter sought to distinguish his approach from the value-neutral "realism" of the Ford-Kissinger administration.

38. Mosher, Clinton, and Lang, *Presidential Transitions and Foreign Affairs*, p. 217.

39. Donald D. Haider, "Presidential Transitions: Critical, if Not Decisive," *Public Administration Review* 41, no. 2 (1981): 208.

40. Hugh Heclo noted, "The outgoing President's budget has become a pernicious influence. It creates the wrong structure of incentives for both old and new Presidents. For the old President, it encourages the striking of a budgetary posture without responsibility for execution. For the new, it becomes a target against which one has to bid." Quoted in Mosher, Clinton, and Lang, *Presidential Transitions and Foreign Affairs*, p. 100.

41. Howell Raines, "Reagan Calls Arms Race Essential to Avoid a 'Surrender' or 'Defeat,'" *New York Times*, August 19, 1980; Leonard Silk, "The Candidates' Debating Points," *New York Times*, September 17, 1980.

42. Leslie H. Gelb, "Conflict in Reagan's Favorite Goals," *New York Times*, August 23, 1981.

43. Eisenhower, *Mandate for Change*, pp. 135–36.

44. Bill Clinton, *My Life* (New York: Vintage Books, 2005), p. 481.

45. Ibid., p. 514.

46. Ibid.

47. Kennedy wanted to focus on economic expansion by encouraging exports and foreign investment in the United States rather than spending cuts. See Mosher, Clinton, and Lang, *Presidential Transitions and Foreign Affairs*, pp. 160–67.

48. David Halberstam, *War in a Time of Peace: Bush, Clinton, and the Generals* (New York: Scribner, 2001), pp. 267–73, 78–82.

49. Anthony J. Eksterowicz and Glenn P. Hastedt, "The George W. Bush Presidential Transition: The Disconnect between Politics and Policy," *White House Studies* 5, no. 1 (Winter 2005): 88.

50. Burke, *Presidential Transitions*, p. 260.

51. Charles Jones quotes James Fallows, who left the Carter administration in its early days, as saying, "Carter believes fifty things, but no one thing. He holds explicit, thorough positions on every issue under the sun, but he has no large view of the relations between them, no line indicating which goals . . . will take precedence over which . . . when the goals conflict. . . . Carter thinks in lists, not arguments; as long as the items are there, their order does not matter, nor does the hierarchy among them." See Jones, *Passages to the Presidency*, p. 72.

52. Zbigniew Brzezinski, *Power and Principle: Memoirs of the National Security Adviser, 1977–1981* (New York: Farrar, Straus & Giroux, 1983), p. 57. Also see Carl M. Brauer, *Presidential Transitions: Eisenhower through Reagan* (New York: Oxford University Press, 1986), p. 207.

53. Burke, *Presidential Transitions,* p. 295.

54. Ibid., p. 110.

55. Ibid., p. 34.

56. See Jones, *Passages to the Presidency,* pp. 128–29.

57. Clark Clifford, *Counsel to the President: A Memoir* (New York: Random House, 1991), p. 328.

Chapter Eight

1. Richard E. Neustadt, "The Presidential 'One Hundred Days': An Overview," in *Triumphs and Tragedies of the Modern Presidency: Seventy-Six Case Studies in Presidential Leadership,* edited by David Abshire (Westport, Conn.: Praeger, 2001).

Chapter Nine

1. David Gergen, in conversation with author Kurt Campbell, November 2004.

2. Campbell taught with Neustadt for three years at Harvard (along with Ernie May). Neustadt would say this in his lecture on transitions.

Appendix

1. Richard Neustadt, *Presidential Power and the Modern Presidents: The Politics of Leadership from Roosevelt to Reagan* (New York: Free Press, 1991).

2. R. Porter, "Of Hazards and Opportunities: Transitions and the Modern Presidency," Presidential Power Revisited Conference, Woodrow Wilson Center, Washington, 1996.

3. Ibid.

4. A. Eksterowicz and G. Hastedt, "Modern Presidential Transitions: Problems, Pitfalls, and Lessons for Success," *Presidential Studies Quarterly* 28, no. 2 (1998): 225.

5. Charles O. Jones, *Passages to the Presidency: From Campaigning to Governing* (Brookings, 1998), pp. vii–viii, 184–88.

6. John P. Burke, "A Tale of Two Transitions: 1980 and 1988," *Congress and the Presidency* 28, no. 1 (2001). See also John P. Burke, *Presidential Transitions: From Politics to Practice* (Boulder, Colo.: Lynne Rienner, 2000), pp. 377–414.

7. Burke, "A Tale of Two Transitions," p. 1.

8. Ibid., p. 14.

9. Stephen Hess with James P. Pfiffner, *Organizing the Presidency,* 3rd ed. (Brookings, 2002), pp. 188, 5–6, 204.

10. Frederick C. Mosher, W. David Clinton, and Daniel G. Lang, *Presidential Transitions and Foreign Affairs* (Louisiana State University Press, 1987), p. xiii.

11. Ibid., p. 250.

12. Ibid., p. 255.

13. Eksterowicz and Hastedt, "Modern Presidential Transitions," p. 317.

14. John Rollins, "CRS Report for Congress: 2008–2009 Presidential Transition: National Security Considerations and Options" (Washington: Congressional Research Service, 2008), pp. 4–5.

15. Ibid., p. 5.

16. Ibid., p. 23

17. Ibid., pp. 23–24.

18. Ibid., pp. 4, 34–36.

19. Richard Armitage and Michèle A. Flournoy, "No Time for 'Nobody Home,'" *Washington Post*, June 9, 2008.

20. Laurin L. Henry, "Transferring the Presidency: Variations, Trends, and Patterns," *Public Administration Review* 20, no. 4 (1960): 187–95.

21. Laurin Henry, "Presidential Transitions: The 1968–69 Experience in Perspective," *Public Administration Review* 29, no. 5 (1969): 471–82.

22. Ibid., p. 476.

23. Ibid., p. 481.

24. Presidential Appointee Initiative, "Staffing a New Administration: A Guide to Personnel Appointments in a Presidential Transition," a project of the Brookings Institution funded by the Pew Charitable Trusts, 2000.

25. David E. Sanger, "Transition: The Changing of the (786) Guards," *New York Times*, December 3, 2000.

26. Presidential Appointee Initiative, "Staffing a New Administration," p. 14.

27. Carl M. Brauer, *Presidential Transitions: Eisenhower through Reagan* (Oxford University Press, 1986); Carl M. Brauer, "Lost in Transition," *Atlantic Monthly*, November 1988.

28. Brauer, "Lost in Transition," p. 76.

29. John P. Burke, "Lessons from Past Presidential Transitions: Organizations, Management, and Decision Making," *Presidential Studies Quarterly* 31, no. 1 (2001): 5–24.

30. John P. Burke, "Lessons from Past Presidential Transitions: Organization, Management, and Decision Making," in *The White House World: Transitions, Organizations, and Office Operations*, edited by Martha Joynt Kumar and Terry Sullivan (Texas A&M University Press, 2003), pp. 25–44.

31. W. G. Howell and K. R. Mayer, "The Last One Hundred Days," *Presidential Studies Quarterly* 35, no. 3 (2005): 533, 543.

32. Martha Joynt Kumar, "Opportunities and Hazards: The White House Interview Program" (White House 2001 Project, 1998).

33. Ibid., pp. 9, 10.

34. James. P. Pfiffner, *The Strategic Presidency: Hitting the Ground Running* (University Press of Kansas, 1996).

35. Richard E. Neustadt, "The Presidential 'One Hundred Days': An Overview," in *Triumphs and Tradegies of the Modern Presidency: Seventy-Six Case Studies in Presidential Leadership*, edited by David Abshire (Westport, Conn.: Praeger, 2001), pp. 47–52.

36. Anne Marie Shackleton, "The Grand Gurus of Transition (National Academy of

Public Administration Examines Transition Process)," *Public Manager* 29, no. 3 (2000): 21–23.

37. Stephanie Smith, "CRS Report for Congress: Presidential Transitions" (Washington: Congressional Research Service, 2007).

38. Ibid., pp. 9–10.

39. Martha Joynt Kumar and others, "Meeting the Freight Train Head On: Planning for the Transition to Power," in *The White House World: Transition, Organization, and Office Operations,* edited by Kumar and Sullivan, pp. 5–24; Martha Joynt Kumar, George C. Edwards III, and James P. Pfiffner, "The Contemporary Presidency: Meeting the Freight Train Head On: Planning for the Transition to Power," *Presidential Studies Quarterly* 30, no. 4 (2000): 754–69.

40. Kumar and others, "Meeting the Freight Train Head On," p. 23; Kumar, Edwards, and Pfiffner, "The Contemporary Presidency," p. 768.

41. Kumar and others, "Meeting the Freight Train Head On."

42. W. David Clinton and Daniel G. Lang, "What Makes a Successful Transition? The Case of Foreign Affairs," in *What Makes a Successful Transition?* edited by W. David Clinton and Daniel G. Lang (Lanham, Md.: University Press of America, 1993), pp. 1–38.

43. Jack Armitage, "Presidents, Candidates, and Career Officials," in *What Makes a Successful Transition?* edited by Clinton and Lang, pp. 39–44.

BIBLIOGRAPHY

Acheson, Dean. *Present at the Creation: My Years in the State Department.* New York: W. W. Norton, 1969.

Armitage, Jack. "Presidents, Candidates, and Career Officials." In *What Makes a Successful Transition?* edited by W. David Clinton and Daniel G. Lang, pp. 39–44. Lanham, Md.: University Press of America, 1993.

Baker, James A. III. *The Politics of Diplomacy: Revolution, War and Peace 1989–1992.* New York: G. P. Putnam's Sons, 1995.

———. *"Work Hard, Study . . . and Keep out of Politics!"* New York: G. P. Putnam's Sons, 2006.

Barrett, David M. "Doing 'Tuesday Lunch' at Lyndon Johnson's White House: New Archival Evidence on Vietnam Decisionmaking." *PS: Political Science and Politics* 24, no. 4 (1991): 676–79.

Barrett, Laurence I. *Gambling with History: Ronald Reagan in the White House.* Garden City, N.Y.: Doubleday, 1983.

Bloomfield, Lincoln P. "What's Wrong with Transitions?" *Foreign Policy* 55 (1984): 23–39.

Blustein, Paul. *The Chastening: Inside the Crisis That Rocked the Global Financial System and Humbled the IMF.* New York: Public Affairs, 2003.

Brauer, Carl M. *Presidential Transitions: Eisenhower through Reagan.* Oxford University Press, 1986.

Brzezinski, Zbigniew. *Power and Principle: Memoirs of the National Security Adviser, 1977–1981.* New York: Farrar, Straus, & Giroux, 1983.

Burke, John P. "Lessons from Past Presidential Transitions: Organization, Management, and Decision Making." In *The White House World: Transitions, Organizations, and Office Operations,* edited by Martha Joynt Kumar and Terry Sullivan, pp. 25–44. Texas A&M University Press, 2003.

———. "Lessons from Past Presidential Transitions: Organizations, Management, and Decision Making." *Presidential Studies Quarterly* 31, no. 1 (2001): 5–24.

———. *Presidential Transitions: From Politics to Practice.* Boulder, Colo.: Lynne Rienner, 2000.

———. "A Tale of Two Transitions: 1980 and 1988." *Congress & the Presidency* 28, no. 1 (2001): 1–18.

Bush, George, and Brent Scowcroft. *A World Transformed.* New York: Knopf, 1998.

Campbell, Colin, and S. J. Rockman. *The Bush Presidency: First Appraisals.* London: Chatham House, 1991.

Clifford, Clark, *Counsel to the President: A Memoir.* New York: Random House, 1991.

Clinton, Bill. *My Life.* First Vintage Books Edition. New York: Vintage Books, 2005.

Clinton, W. David, and Daniel G. Lang. "What Makes a Successful Transition? The Case of Foreign Affairs." In *What Makes a Successful Transition?* edited by W. David Clinton and Daniel G. Lang, pp. 1–38. Lanham, Md.: University Press of America, 1993.

Conley, Patricia H. *Presidential Mandates: How Elections Shape the National Agenda.* University of Chicago Press, 2001.

Crabb, Cecil V., and Kevin V. Mulcahy. "Presidential Management of National Security Making, 1947–1987." In *The Managerial Presidency,* edited by James Pfiffner. Pacific Grove, Calif.: Brooks/Cole, 1991.

Daalder, Ivo H., and James M. Lindsay. *America Unbound: The Bush Revolution in Foreign Policy.* Hoboken, N.J.: John Wiley, 2005.

Demchak, Chris. "Wars of Disruption in Modern Society: Tailoring Institutions for the Emerging Information and Terrorism Age." Paper presented at the annual meeting of the International Studies Association. San Francisco, 2008.

Destler, I. M., and Ivo H. Daalder. "A New NSC for a New Administration." In *National Security Council Project Policy Brief.* Brookings, 2000 (www.brookings.edu/papers/2000/11governance_daalder.aspx).

Dick, James C. "The Strategic Arms Race, 1957–61: Who Opened a Missile Gap?" *Journal of Politics* 34, no. 4 (1972): 1062–1110.

Divine, Robert. *Eisenhower and the Cold War.* Oxford University Press, 1997.

Drew, Elizabeth. *On the Edge: the Clinton Presidency.* New York: Simon & Schuster, 1994.

Drew, S. Nelson. "Expecting the Approach of Danger: The "Missile Gap" as a Study of Executive-Congressional Competition in Building Consensus on National Security Issues." *Presidential Studies Quarterly* 19, no. 2 (1989): 317–35.

Eisenhower, Dwight D. *Mandate for Change, 1953–1956.* Garden City, N.Y.: Doubleday, 1963.

———. *Waging Peace, 1956–1961: The White House Years.* Garden City, N.Y.: Doubleday, 1965.

Eksterowicz, Anthony J., and Glenn P. Hastedt. "The George W. Bush Presidential Transition: The Disconnect between Politics and Policy." *White House Studies* 5, no. 1 (Winter 2005): 88.

———. "Modern Presidential Transitions: Problems, Pitfalls, and Lessons for Success." *Presidential Studies Quarterly* 28, no. 2 (1998).

Evans Jr., Rowland, and Robert D. Novak. *Nixon in the White House: The Frustration of Power.* New York: Random House, 1971.

Falk, Stanley L. "The National Security Council under Truman, Eisenhower, and Kennedy." *Political Science Quarterly* 79, no. 3 (1964): 403–34.

Felzenberg, Alvin S. "The Keys to a Successful Presidency." Washington: Heritage Foundation, 2000 (www.heritage.org/Research/Features/Mandate/keys.cfm).

Ferrell, Robert H. *Harry S. Truman.* Washington: CQ Press, 2003.

Fiorina, Morris P., Paul E. Peterson, Bertram Johnson, and D. Stephen Voss. *The New American Democracy,* Alternate Fourth Edition. Boston: Pearson-Longman, 2005.

Greene, John Robert. *The Presidency of George Bush.* University Press of Kansas, 2000.

Haider, Donald D. "Presidential Transitions: Critical, if not Decisive." *Public Administration Review* 41, no. 2 (1981): 207–11.

Haig, Alexander M., Jr. *Caveat: Realism, Reagan, and Foreign Policy.* New York: Macmillan, 1984.

Haig, Alexander M., Jr., and Charles McCarry. *Inner Circles: How America Changed the World—A Memoir.* New York: Warner Books, 1992.

Halberstam, David. *War in a Time of Peace: Bush, Clinton, and the Generals.* New York: Scribner, 2001.

Hastedt, Glenn P., and Anthony J. Eksterowicz. "Perils of Presidential Transition." *Seton Hall Journal of Diplomacy and International Relations* (Winter/Spring 2001): 67–85.

Henry, Laurin L. *Presidential Transitions.* Brookings, 1960.

———. "Presidential Transitions: The 1968–69 Experience in Perspective." *Public Administration Review* 29, no. 5 (1969): 471–82.

———. "Transferring the Presidency: Variations, Trends, and Patterns." *Public Administration Review* 20, no. 4 (1960): 187–95.

Herken, Gregg. *Counsels of War.* New York: Alfred A Knopf, 1985.

Hess, Stephen. *Organizing the Presidency.* Brookings, 1988.

Hess, Stephen, with James P. Pfiffner. *Organizing the Presidency.* 3rd ed. Brookings, 2002.

Hoffman, Bruce. "Presidential Transition Team Issues: Terrorism." In *Taking Charge: A Bipartisan Report to the President-Elect on Foreign Policy and National Security,* edited by Frank Carlucci, Robert Hunter, and Zalmay Khalilzad, pp. 191–200. Santa Monica, Calif.: RAND Corporation, 2001.

Hoffman, Stanley. *Gulliver's Troubles, or the Setting of American Foreign Policy.* New York: McGraw-Hill for the Council on Foreign Relations, 1968.

Holsti, Ole R. *Public Opinion and American Foreign Policy.* 2nd ed. University of Michigan Press, 2004.

Howell, W. G., and K. R. Mayer. "The Last One Hundred Days." *Presidential Studies Quarterly* 35, no. 3 (2005): 533–53.

Johnson, Richard Tanner. *Managing the White House: An Intimate Study of the Presidency.* New York: Harper & Row, 1974.

Jones, Charles O. *Passages to the Presidency: From Campaigning to Governing.* Brookings, 1998.

Kissinger, Henry. *Diplomacy.* New York: Simon & Schuster, 1994.

———. *White House Years.* Boston: Little, Brown, 1979.

———. *Years of Renewal.* London: Weidenfeld & Nicolson, 1999.

Kumar, Martha Joint. "Opportunities and Hazards: The White House Interview Program." White House 2001 Project, 1998.

Kumar, Martha Joynt, George C. Edwards III, and James P. Pfiffner. "The Contemporary Presidency: Meeting the Freight Train Head On: Planning for the Transition to Power." *Presidential Studies Quarterly* 30, no. 4 (2000): 754–69.

Kumar, Martha Joynt, George C. Edwards III, James P. Pfiffner, and Terry Sullivan. "Meeting the Freight Train Head On: Planning for the Transition to Power." In *The White House World: Transition, Organization, and Office Operations,* edited by Martha Joynt Kumar and Terry Sullivan, pp. 5–24. Texas A&M University Press, 2003.

Lieberthal, Kenneth. "The United States and Asia in 2001: Changing Agendas." *Asian Survey* 42, no. 1 (2002): 1–13.

Light, Paul C. "The Glacial Pace of Presidential Appointments." Washington: Brookings, April 4, 2001 (www.brookings.edu/opinions/2001/0404governance_light.aspx).

———. *The President's Agenda: Domestic Policy Choice from Kennedy to Clinton.* Johns Hopkins University Press, 1999.

Lindsay, James M. "The New Partisanship: The Changed Politics of American Foreign Policy." *U.S. Foreign Policy Agenda* 5, no. 2 (2000) (http://usinfo.state.gov/journals/itps/0900/ijpe/pj52lind.htm).

Locher, James R., III. "The Most Important Thing: Legislative Reform of the National Security System." *Military Review* (May–June 2008): 4–12.

Mann, James. *Rise of the Vulcans: The History of Bush's War Cabinet.* New York: Viking Penguin, 2004.

McClellan, Scott. *What Happened: Inside the Bush White House and Washington's Culture of Deception.* New York: Public Affairs, 2008.

Medhurst, Martin J. "Text and Context in the 1952 Presidential Campaign: Eisenhower's 'I Shall Go to Korea' Speech." *Presidential Studies Quarterly* 30, no. 3 (2000): 464–84.

Mervin, David. *George Bush and the Guardianship Presidency.* New York: St. Martin's, 1996.

Messer, Robert. *The End of an Alliance: James F. Byrnes, Roosevelt, Truman, and the Origins of the Cold War.* University of North Carolina Press, 1982.

Miller, Merle. *Lyndon: An Oral History.* New York: Putnam, 1982.

Mosher, Frederick C., W. David Clinton, and Daniel G. Lang. *Presidential Transitions and Foreign Affairs.* Louisiana State University Press, 1987.

Neumann, William W. *Managing National Security Policy: The President and the Process.* University of Pittsburgh Press, 2003.

Neustadt, Richard E. "The Presidential 'One Hundred Days': An Overview." In *Triumphs and Tragedies of the Modern Presidency: Seventy-Six Case Studies in Presidential Leadership,* edited by David Abshire. Westport, Conn.: Praeger, 2001.

———. *Presidential Power and the Modern Presidents: The Politics of Leadership from Roosevelt to Reagan.* New York: Free Press, 1991.

———. "Presidential Transitions: Are the Risks Rising?" *Miller Center Journal* 1 (1994): 1–12.

O'Brien, Michael. *John F. Kennedy: A Biography.* New York: St. Martin's, 2005.

Ornstein, Norman J., and Thomas E. Mann, eds. *The Permanent Campaign and Its Future.* Washington: AEI Press, 2000.

Parker, Charles F., and Eric K. Stern. "Blindsided? September 11 and the Origins of Strategic Surprise." *Political Psychology* 23, no. 2 (2002): 601–30.

Perret, Geoffrey. *Eisenhower.* Avon, Mass.: Adams Media, 1999.

Pfiffner, James P. "Can the President Manage the Government? Should He?" In *The Managerial Presidency,* edited by James Pfiffner. Pacific Grove, Calif.: Brooks/Cole, 1991.

———. *The Strategic Presidency: Hitting the Ground Running.* University Press of Kansas, 1996.

———. "White House Staff versus the Cabinet: Centripetal and Centrifugal Roles." *Presidential Studies Quarterly* 16, no. 4 (Fall 1986): 666–90.

Phillips, Cabell B. H. *The Truman Presidency: The History of a Triumphant Succession.* New York: Macmillan, 1966.

Porter, R. "Of Hazards and Opportunities: Transitions and the Modern Presidency." Paper presented at the conference "Presidential Power Revisited," Woodrow Wilson Center, Washington, 1996.

Powell, Colin L. *My American Journey.* New York: Random House, 1995.

Preble, Christopher A. "Who Ever Believed in the 'Missile Gap'? John F. Kennedy and the Politics of National Security." *Presidential Studies Quarterly* 33, no. 4 (2003): 801–26.

Presidential Appointee Initiative. "Staffing a New Administration: A Guide to Personnel Appointments in a Presidential Transition." A project of the Brookings Institution funded by the Pew Charitable Trusts, 2000.

Reagan, Ronald. *An American Life.* New York: Simon & Schuster, 1990.

Rice, Condoleezza. "Campaign 2000: Promoting the National Interest." *Foreign Affairs* 79, no. 1 (2000): 45–62.

Roman, Nancy E. "Both Sides of the Aisle: A Call for Bipartisan Foreign Policy." *Council on Foreign Relations Special Report* 9 (2005) (www.cfr.org/content/publications/attachments/Bipartisan_CSR.pdf).

Rimmerman, Craig A. "Promise Unfulfilled: Clinton's Failure to Overturn the Military Ban on Lesbians and Gays." In *Gay Rights, Military Wrongs: Political Perspectives on Lesbians and Gays in the Military,* edited by Craig A. Rimmerman, pp. 111–26. New York: Garland, 1996.

Rollins, John. "CRS Report for Congress: 2008–2009 Presidential Transition: National Security Considerations and Options." Washington: Congressional Research Service, 2008.

Rothkopf, David J. *Running the World: The Inside Story of the National Security Council and the Architects of American Power.* New York: Public Affairs, 2005.

Schlesinger, Arthur M. *A Thousand Days: John F. Kennedy in the White House.* Boston: Houghton Mifflin, 1965.

Shackleton, Anne Marie. "The Grand Gurus of Transition. National Academy of Public Administration Examines Transition Process." *Public Manager* 29, no. 3 (2000): 21–23.

Shultz, George P. *Turmoil and Triumph: My Years as Secretary of State.* New York: Macmillan, 1993.

Smith, Stephanie. "CRS Report for Congress: Presidential Transitions." Washington: Congressional Research Service, 2007.

Sorensen, Theodore C. *Kennedy.* New York: Harper & Row, 1965.

Stern, Eric K. "Probing the Plausibility of Newgroup Syndrome: Kennedy and the Bay of Pigs." In *Beyond Groupthink: Political Group Dynamics and Foreign Policy-Making,* edited by Paul 't Hart, Eric K. Stern, and Bengt Sundelius, pp. 153–89. University of Michigan Press, 1997.

Truman, Harry S. *Memoirs by Harry S. Truman.* Vol. 1. Garden City, N.Y.: Doubleday, 1955.

Tudda, Christopher. "Reenacting the Story of Tantalus: Eisenhower, Dulles, and the Failed Rhetoric of Liberation." *Journal of Cold War Studies* 7, no. 4 (2005): 3–35.

Unger, Irwin, and Debi Unger. *LBJ: A Life.* New York: John Wiley, 1999.

Vance, Cyrus. *Hard Choices: Critical Years in America's Foreign Policy.* New York: Simon & Schuster, 1983.

Weinberger, Caspar W. *Fighting for Peace: Seven Critical Years in the Pentagon.* New York: Warner Books, 1990.

Whittaker, Alan G., Frederick C. Smith, and Elizabeth McKune. "The National Security Policy Process: The National Security Council and Interagency System." Washington: Industrial College of the Armed Forces, National Defense University, 2007.

Wilcox, Clyde, and Robin M. Wolpert. "President Clinton, Public Opinion, and Gays in the Military." In *Gay Rights, Military Wrongs: Political Perspectives on Lesbians and Gays in the Military,* edited by Craig A. Rimmerman, pp. 127–46. New York: Garland, 1996.

Witherspoon, Patricia Dennis. *Within These Walls: A Study of Communication between Presidents and Their Senior Staffs.* New York: Praeger, 1991.

Worley, D. Robert. 2008. "The National Security Council: Recommendations for the New President." In *Presidential Transitions Series.* Washington: IBM Center for Business and Government, 2008.

Yetiv, Steve A. "Groupthink and the Gulf Crisis." *British Journal of Political Science* 33 (July 2003): 419–42.

Zegart, Amy B. *Flawed by Design: The Evolution of the CIA, JCS, and NSC.* Stanford University Press, 1999.

Zoellick, Robert B. "Campaign 2000: A Republican Foreign Policy." *Foreign Affairs* 79, no. 1 (2000): 63.

INDEX